TROUBADOUR POEMS

FROM THE SOUTH OF FRANCE

For Catherine and Will

Troubadour Poems
From the South of France

translated by

William D. Paden
Frances Freeman Paden

D. S. BREWER

First published 2007
D. S. Brewer, Cambridge
Paperback edition 2014

ISBN 978–1–84384–129–6 hardback
ISBN 978–1–84384–408–2 paperback

D. S. Brewer is an imprint of Boydell & Brewer Ltd
PO Box 9, Woodbridge, Suffolk IP12 3DF, UK
and of Boydell & Brewer Inc,
668 Mt Hope Avenue, Rochester, NY 14620–2731, USA
website: www.boydellandbrewer.com

The Northwestern University Research Grants Committee
has provided partial support for the publication of this book.
We gratefully acknowledge this assistance.

A CIP catalogue record for this book is available
from the British Library

This publication is printed on acid-free paper

Typeset in Adobe Caslon Pro by Word and Page, Chester, UK

CONTENTS

ILLUSTRATIONS

The authors and publishers are grateful to copyright holders for permission to reproduce the materials in which they hold copyright. Every effort has been made to trace the copyright holders; apologies are offered for any omission, and the publishers will be pleased to add any necessary acknowledgement in subsequent editions.

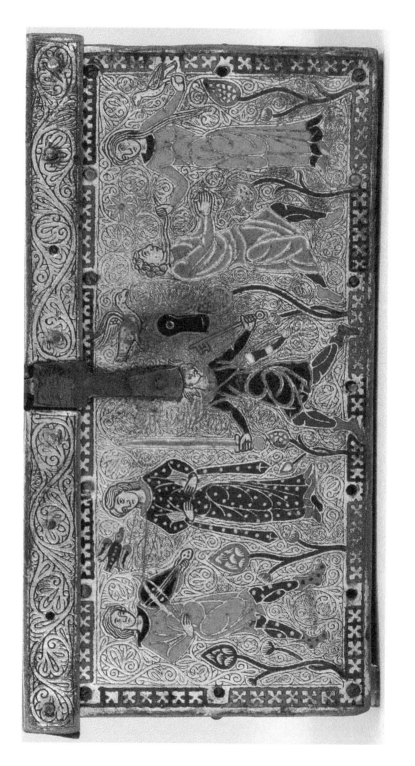

Frontispiece. Detail from enameled casket, Limoges, *circa* 1180; dimensions 21.1 x 15.6 x 11 cm. London, British Library, M&ME 1859.1–10.1. (Reproduced with permission of the British Library)

PREFACE

O N the twelfth-century Limoges casket that we have used as our frontispiece, the enameled figures enact a narrative in which a bird, by moving across space, suggests the passage of time.[1] On the left, a man gazes at a woman whose dress contains the night sky. She returns his glance, and they dance together as he fiddles. In the sky above, a night bird seems to watch them. It passes across the horizon and reappears on the right, perched on the hand of the same woman, who is now dressed in the green of springtime. Her lover half kneels before her, enthralled by the object of his desire. The dawn witnesses their engagement. Below the hasp, the watchman's feet move toward the dancing couple, but his eyes turn toward the lovers at dawn. Holding both a sword and a key, he protects the treasure, their intimacy.

The casket provides an exquisite visual representation of the *alba* or dawn poem, and, by extension, of the love sung throughout troubadour poetry composed in medieval Occitania, the land we know today as the South of France. For the troubadours and their listeners, sexuality is the worldly expression of the sacred. The pleasure of desire brings happiness, and the sexual narrative holds the promise of continuity. The yearning and fulfillment that lovers experience make sense of the world—its seasons, its wars, its anguish. On the casket the bird's flight is circular; at the end of the story it is poised for flight, signaling that the narrative may begin again. The poets, too, sing of continuity and the kinship between people and nature. So it is that in an early poem, a lover yearns to be a goshawk (Poem 4); in another the poet implies a kinship with his falcon (Poem 22). When Peire Vidal sings of inhaling a breeze from afar, he suggests the communion he feels with both the distant land (Provence) and his lady (Poem 59).[2]

In this book, intended primarily for the reader who does not know Occitan, we present English translations that we hope will communicate not only what the troubadours said but some of the excitement in how they said it. We have approached each poem as a performance, as an artifact within a context; we have considered its language, its place in history, its prosodic structure, and its treatment by scribes and editors. Our goal has been to offer the reader translations that are both accurate and evocative of the poems' medieval present.

---

[1]   The technique of time-lapse representation seen here in the treatment of the hawk is frequent in medieval imagery. See, for example, the departure of Saint Alexis in the twelfth-century Saint Albans Psalter, where one picture represents him saying goodbye to his wife, leaving her, and sailing away: Otto Pächt, C. R. Dodwell, and Francis Wormald, *The St. Albans Psalter (Albani Psalter)* (London: The Warburg Institute, 1960), plate 35. Later the Books of Hours employed "depiction of successive episodes in a story within a single miniature": John Harthan, *The Book of Hours* (New York: Crowell, 1977), p. 21.

[2]   See also Poem 18, in which a sparrowhawk soars toward the lady. For other resemblances to the casket, see Poem 57, where a lover kneels before his lady and offers obeisance; Poems 32 and 95, for the lover as prisoner of his lady; and Poems 19, 20, and 35 for the bird as messenger bearing the poet's love.

From the beginning, we knew that we wanted to render verse translations, but that trying to imitate the rhyme patterns of the original would be a distraction. Occitan is a language far richer in rhymes than English. We decided to be true to stanzaic patterns and, as much as possible, to line lengths, but to suggest the patterning of the original prosody rather than adhere to systematic rhyme-schemes that would have obliged us to adopt forced rhymes. We have avoided archaic diction because our goal is to regain the poems' presence.

As our collaboration evolved, we felt we were in close dialogue with the original poems and wanted to replicate that experience for the reader as much as possible. To that end, we provide a substantial selection of poems for the English-speaking reader rather than a smaller sampling of poems with facing translations. In order to help our readers gain a sense of the original, we offer a general introduction that addresses the historical context of the poems and includes notes on the music, the language, and the performance situation. We also provide notes on each of the poems, illustrations from manuscripts, sources of texts in the original language, and a bibliography.

We have collaborated in the deepest sense; rather than dividing the labor, we have worked closely together on all aspects of the book. As we approached each poem, we both read it in its original language and drafted an English translation. As a seasoned expert in medieval lyric poetry, William Paden produced renderings informed by extensive scholarship. It is his knowledge that gives this volume its range and its depth. Frances Freeman Paden, who is relatively new to Occitan studies, brought her experience as a writer and student of English poetry to the translation process. Her knowledge of gender and performance made us aware of nuances we might otherwise have missed. As we passed the translations back and forth, striving to bring the poems closer and closer to the meaning and spirit of the originals, we consulted a range of scholarly works. In doing so, we felt engaged in a collaboration not only with the troubadours and trobairitz, but with scribes, editors, and scholars who have been working on the poems over the past eight or nine hundred years. This book is deeply indebted to all of them.

We are also indebted to many colleagues, students, and friends who have supported this project as it has evolved. We are especially grateful to Richard Barber, who graciously invited us to produce this volume; to Ruth Harvey, who suggested he do so; and to Caroline Palmer, the editorial director at Boydell and Brewer, who saw the project through the press. Northwestern University, especially the Weinberg College of Arts and Sciences; Andrew Wachtel, Dean of the Graduate School; and Robert Gundlach, Director of the Writing Program, supported this project with a research leave for Fran Paden and a subvention from the University Research Grants Committee. Janice Spencer and Matthew Taylor, of the Multimedia Learning Center, provided invaluable help with the illustrations. For their prompt response in providing illustrations we thank the British Library, the Bibliothèque communautaire et interuniversitaire (Clermont-Ferrand), the Morgan Library (New York), the Bibliothèque nationale de France, and Luc de Goustine, President of the Association Carrefour Ventadour. Wendy Pfeffer gave us a careful reading of the Introduction; we appreciate her valuable suggestions. For their generous hospitality and warm support for our research in France and Italy, we thank Christine and Luc Amiech. Finally, we are grateful to our children, who have continually stimulated our imaginations. It is to them that we dedicate this book.

ABBREVIATIONS

Bec, *Burlesque* = Pierre Bec, *Burlesque et obscénité chez les troubadours: pour une approche du contre-texte médiéval* (Paris: Stock, 1984).

Bec, *Chants d'amour* = Pierre Bec, *Chants d'amour des femmes-troubadours* (Paris: Stock, 1995).

Bec, *Lyrique française* = Pierre Bec, *La lyrique française au moyen âge (XIIᵉ–XIIIᵉ siècles)*, 2 vols. (Paris: Picard, 1977–8).

Boutière, *Biographies* = J. Boutière and A.-H. Schutz with I.-M. Cluzel, *Biographies des troubadours: textes provençaux des XIIIᵉ et XIVᵉ siècles.* 2nd ed. (Paris: Nizet, 1973).

Bruckner, *Songs* = Matilda Tomaryn Bruckner, Laurie Shepard, and Sarah White, *Songs of the Women Troubadours* (New York: Garland Publishing, 1995).

Carmi, *Penguin Book of Hebrew Verse* = T. Carmi, *The Penguin Book of Hebrew Verse* (New York: Viking Press, 1981).

Dante, *De Vulgari Eloquentia* = Dante Alighieri, *De Vulgari Eloquentia*, ed. and trans. Steven Botterill (Cambridge: Cambridge University Press, 1996).

Hill and Bergin, *Anthology* = R. T. Hill and T. G. Bergin, *Anthology of the Provençal Troubadours*, 2nd ed., with the collaboration of Susan Olson, William D. Paden, Jr., and Nathaniel Smith, 2 vols. (New Haven: Yale University Press, 1973).

Meyer, *Derniers troubadours* = Paul Meyer, *Les derniers troubadours de la Provence* (Paris, 1871; reprint Geneva: Slatkine, 1973).

Noulet and Chabaneau, *Deux manuscrits* = J.-B. Noulet and Camille Chabaneau, *Deux manuscrits provençaux du XIVᵉ siècle* (Paris: Leclerc, 1888).

Paden, "Before the Troubadours" = William D. Paden, "Before the Troubadours: The Archaic Occitan Texts and the Shape of Literary History," in *"De sens rassis": Essays in Honor of Rupert T. Pickens*, ed. Keith Busby, Bernard Guidot, Logan E. Whalen (Amsterdam: Rodopi, 2005), pp. 509–28.

Paden, *Introduction to Old Occitan* = William D. Paden, *An Introduction to Old Occitan* (New York: The Modern Language Association of America, 1998).

Paden, *Medieval Pastourelle* = William D. Paden, *The Medieval Pastourelle*, 2 vols. (New York: Garland Publishing, 1987).

Paden, "Petrarch, Poet of Provence" = William D. Paden, "Petrarch as a Poet of Provence," *Annali d'italianistica* 22 (2004): 19–44.

Paden, "Troubadours and Jews" = William D. Paden, "Troubadours and Jews," in *Études de langue et de littérature médiévales offertes à Peter T. Ricketts*, ed. Dominique Billy and Ann Buckley (Turnhout: Brepols, 2005), pp. 471–84.

Paden, *Voice* = William D. Paden, ed., *The Voice of the Trobairitz: Perspectives on the Women Troubadours* (Philadelphia: University of Pennsylvania Press, 1989).

Petrarch's Lyric Poems, ed. Durling = *Petrarch's Lyric Poems*, ed. Robert M. Durling (Cambridge, MA: Harvard University Press, 1976).

Rieger, *Trobairitz* = Angelica Rieger, *Trobairitz: Der Beitrag der Frau in der altokzi-tanischen höfischen Lyrik, Edition des Gesamtkorpus*, Beihefte zur Zeitschrift für romanische Philologie 233 (Tübingen: Niemeyer, 1991).

Riquer, *Trovadores* = Martín de Riquer, *Los trovadores: historia literaria y textos*, 3 vols. (Barcelona: Planeta, 1975).

Rosenberg, *Songs of the Troubadours* = Samuel N. Rosenberg, Margaret Switten, and Gérard Le Vot, *Songs of the Troubadours and Trouvères: An Anthology of Poems and Melodies* (New York: Garland Publishing, 1998).

Wilson, *Women in the Middle Ages* = Katharina M. Wilson and Nadia Margolis, *Women in the Middle Ages: An Encyclopedia*, 2 vols. (Westport: Greenwood Press, 2004).

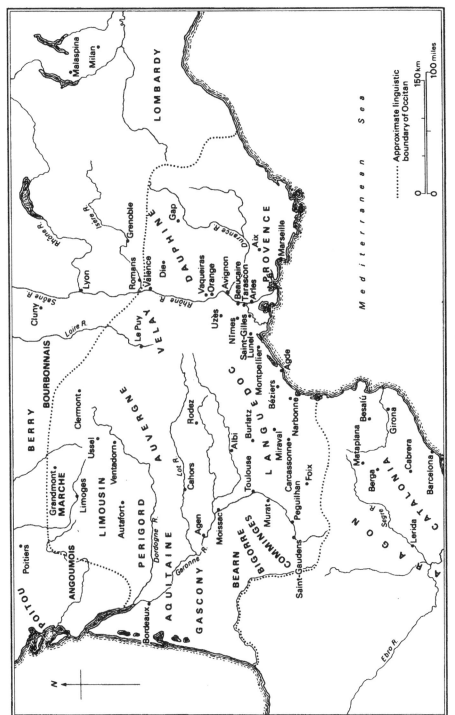

Map of Occitania and adjacent regions.

xiii

Introduction

In the twelfth and thirteenth centuries, and continuing into the fourteenth, the region that we know as the South of France was home to the troubadours, poets whose lyrics were heard from the Pyrenees to the Alps. These poets did not speak French but Occitan, the vernacular language of the region. The word "troubadour" represents Occitan *trobador*, from the verb *trobar*, meaning "to find," "to invent," or "to compose"; hence, a troubadour is "one who finds, invents, or composes." Women troubadours are called by the infrequent feminine form of the word, *trobairitz*. Although we know about twenty trobairitz by name, relatively few of their works survive. We have about fifty poems that we attribute to trobairitz, including several anonymous poems that appear to have been written by women. This number compares with about 2,500 poems composed by 360 men and women combined.[1]

Some troubadours kept a number of *joglars* in their service. The word *joglar* corresponds to *jongleur* in French and English, "an itinerant minstrel, who sang and composed ballads, told stories and otherwise entertained people" (*Oxford English Dictionary*, 2nd ed.). Troubadours who employed *joglars*, such as Bertran de Born, would send one of them off to perform a new composition before the addressee. The distinction between troubadour and *joglar* was not hard and fast: both composed and both performed, but the troubadour tended to be primarily the composer, and the *joglar* the performer.

In the beginning, troubadour poems were transmitted as songs from one musical performance to the next. The poems gained increasing prestige over time, and by the mid-thirteenth century, if not earlier, scribes began to write them down. In the manuscripts that have survived, the poems present themselves to us directly, enveloped in an aura of prestige that implies high esteem for their art. The original environment of the poems, however—their social, political, literary, and musical context—is more difficult to grasp. These poets and singers lived in a world very different from our own.

Rather than living in modern nation-states with sharply defined borders, the troubadours inhabited spheres of influence that constantly shifted and changed.[2] Though most of them lived in the land we call France today, they did not consider themselves French. When the troubadours spoke of *Fransa* (France), they meant

---

[1] This statement is based on the listing by Alfred Pillet and Henry Carstens, *Bibliographie der Troubadours* (Halle: Niemeyer, 1933), brought up to date by Peter T. Ricketts, *Concordance de l'occitan médiéval: COM 2, Les troubadours, les textes narratifs en vers* (Turnhout: Brepols, 2005). It does not take account of the many "lost troubadours," those for whom we have no poems but some other trace of their existence. On the lost troubadours see Kathryn Klingebiel, "Lost Literature of the Troubadours: A Proposed Catalogue," *Tenso* 13.1 (1997): 1–23.

[2] Ronnie Ellenblum, "Were There Borders and Borderlines in the Middle Ages? The Example of the Latin Kingdom of Jerusalem," in *Medieval Frontiers: Concepts and Practices*, ed. David Abulafia and Nora Berend (Aldershot: Ashgate, 2002), pp. 105–19.

1

either the large expanse that had once been ruled by the Franks, reaching from the Pyrenees to the Rhine, or, more commonly, the smaller area that was actually controlled by the kings of France in the twelfth and thirteenth centuries. At times, the royal domain was almost as small as the Ile de France, the region surrounding Paris.[3] The kings of France struggled to expand their territory at the expense of local lords. Most troubadours were not vassals of the king, or if they were, that relation was more nominal than real. Instead, many of the troubadour poets served dukes or counts, while others, such as Guilhem IX, duke of Aquitaine and count of Poitou, were powerful noblemen.

Guilhem IX was the earliest troubadour whose works survive. Though the king of France was his titular overlord, Guilhem was largely independent. His granddaughter, Eleanor of Aquitaine, married Louis VII, who was then king of France. After that marriage failed, she wed Henry Plantagenet, originally of Anjou. In 1154, when Henry became king of England as Henry II, he brought Aquitaine under English rule for three hundred years. While this situation continued in the Southwest, the land east of the Rhône was controlled for generations by the kings of Aragon in eastern Spain. Once they acquired the title of count of Provence, these kings traveled frequently between Barcelona and Aix-en-Provence. Although his own language was Catalan, Alfonso II, king of Aragon, count of Barcelona, and count of Provence, composed songs in Occitan in order to appeal to his vassals in Provence. For similar reasons, Guilhem IX had composed the earliest troubadour songs in Occitan instead of Poitevin French, the language we assume was his mother tongue.

Land hunger strongly motivated these peripatetic lords. They went to war for land, both close to home and abroad. It was their hunger for land, combined with piety and intolerance toward Islam, that sent them off on the Crusades (1095–1272). These armed pilgrimages to recapture Jerusalem from the Muslims appear in a number of troubadour songs.[4] Serving their lords in Occitania, many troubadours regarded the French with antipathy, especially because of the French role in the Albigensian Crusade (1209–49), a religious war organized by Pope Innocent III against believers who were centered in the town of Albi, a town that lies in the hills east of Bordeaux. The Albigensians claimed to be Christians, but their radical theology, including their belief in two gods (one good, one evil), made the Church regard them as heretics. The Pope offered the lands of the heretics to anyone who would fight against them for the Church. French nobles led by Simon de Montfort joined forces with the Church to attack the Albigensians, against the resistance of local lords and the king of Aragon. The troubadour Peire Cardenal, an orthodox Catholic himself, was sharply critical of clerical abuses and the French (see Poems 80 and 81).

The Albigensian Crusade set in motion a complex series of events that resulted in the passage of the county of Toulouse to the king of France in 1271. But fighting for land continued across the rest of Occitania for hundreds of years. Below Toulouse, where the Pyrenees approach the Mediterranean, Perpignan belonged to Aragon until 1276, then to the Kingdom of Majorca until 1346; the city became

---

[3]   See Angus MacKay and David Ditchburn, eds., *Atlas of Medieval Europe* (London: Routledge, 1997), p. 70.

[4]   See Marcabru, Poem 14; for reservations about the idea of crusade, compare Marcabru, Poem 15, and Gaucelm Faidit, Poem 55.

part of France in 1659. Most of the Southeast, the area we know today as Provence, was acquired by France in the 1480s. But the city of Avignon belonged to the pope until 1791, while Nice and its surrounding area were acquired from Sardinia as late as 1860.

People living in the South of France during the time of the troubadours spoke Occitan, not French, as their native language. Occitan descended from Latin and was a sister language of Italian, Spanish, and French; it is what we call today a Romance language, a term and concept that developed in the nineteenth century.[5] French, on the other hand, was the language of the North; it was spoken from Paris to London from the time of the Norman Conquest in 1066 until the end of the Middle Ages.

At the time of the troubadours, the Occitan language did not have a generally recognized name. Guilhem IX, the first troubadour, called it *Romans* in contrast to the Latin of the Church; it was his vernacular, his spoken, local speech.[6] Eventually, Occitan came to be called *Provençal* by Italians who traced their own poetic origins to Provence, the land that lay east of the Rhône; it was called *Lemosí* by the Catalans, who looked to the troubadours from the western area around Limoges. For a long time, speakers of English, continuing the Italian tradition, called the language Provençal. As a name for the language, Provençal achieved wide currency when Frédéric Mistral, the poet from Provence, won the Nobel Prize in 1904. However, this term inevitably misrepresents the language that was spoken not only in Provence, the region east of the Rhône, but with dialectal variations across the entire South of France. During the twentieth century, the language of the troubadours has come increasingly to be called Occitan. Based on the word *oc*, which means "yes" in this language, the term better represents the people who speak it while affirming its importance as a living language.

Speakers of Occitan have felt pressure to shift to French ever since the Albigensian Crusade. In the nineteenth century Mistral and his fellow poets, in a movement called the *Félibrige*, strove to restore their language to the prestige it had enjoyed in the days of the troubadours, although they knew that it was severely threatened. A determined movement to revive the language goes on in the South of France today, even though it has not been learned as a mother tongue since the 1930s. As the European Union continues to develop, the fate of languages such as Occitan, Catalan, and Gaelic remains a lively issue.

If we wish to imagine the performance of troubadour art in its own time, we must remember that many of the poets wrote songs, both the words and the melody. One in ten of these poems comes to us with a notation of its melody in the manuscripts. The notations provide the pitch of each syllable but not the length of the note, so we are left to guess at the rhythm that was employed. It seems most likely that the songs were set to a declamatory rhythm, that is, a rhythm suitable for declaiming the verbal text.[7] Out of 2,500 extant poems, only one song in medieval Occitan is accompanied by a musical transcription that extends over all the stanzas.[8] The other poems that include musical notations have them only for the

5   William D. Paden, *An Introduction to Old Occitan* (New York: The Modern Language Association of America, 1998), p. 5.
6   See Guilhem IX of Aquitaine, Poem 8, stanza 6.
7   Hendrik van der Werf, *The Chansons of the Troubadours and Trouvères: A Study of the Melodies and Their Relation to the Poems* (Utrecht: Oosthoek, 1972), pp. 35–45.
8   Anonymous, Poem 3.

first stanza. Scholars believe that subsequent stanzas followed the same essential melody with variations in musical detail, variations that were appropriate to the evolving verbal text.

Some scholars assume that all troubadour poems were written to be sung. Since writing down melodies required the services of a specialized scribe, many poems may have been performed as songs that were not accompanied by melodies in the manuscripts. Still, to imagine that all troubadour poems were sung is to overlook the historical development of reading. Since the art form of the troubadours began as song and evolved toward writing, it seems likely that the performance of the poems may also have moved toward reading aloud, or even silent reading.[9]

To today's nonspecialist listener, the melodies that survive resemble Gregorian chant. The tunes are sinuous, with frequent rises and falls and occasional leaps within a range that is usually no wider than an octave. The musical style is syllabic; that is, it has one note for each syllable in the verbal text until the end of a line, which is frequently ornamented with a melisma, a group of several notes sung to one syllable. The combination of the sinuous line with ornamental melismas can be haunting, as it is in Jaufré Rudel's "Love from afar" (Poem 10), or vivacious, as it is in Raimbaut de Vaqueiras's "When May Day comes" (Poem 64).[10] It is most likely that troubadour music evolved from the liturgy that troubadours heard at Mass, but the possibility of influence from Arabic music cannot be excluded.[11]

The troubadours exemplify vivid secular individualism as well as recurrent religious impulses. It goes without saying that in their own time they were not perceived as medieval. The notion of a Middle Age derives from the idea of a Renaissance, which may be defined as a rebirth of the values of Classical Antiquity in Italy in the thirteenth to sixteenth centuries. For Jacob Burckhardt, the Swiss historian whose vision of the *Civilization of the Renaissance in Italy* (1860) remains influential, the Italian Renaissance rediscovered the values of secular individualism from Antiquity, in contrast to an intervening dark time of religious community.[12] But this view, which incorporates the way some Renaissance figures saw themselves, has been challenged on several grounds.[13] Just as it is not true that the civilization of the Renaissance abandoned religious values, it is also not true that the earlier

[9] See Paul Saenger, *Space between Words: The Origins of Silent Reading* (Stanford: Stanford University Press, 1997).

[10] Many recordings have been made of troubadour songs. Musical performances on compact disks accompany Rosenberg, *Songs of the Troubadours*, and Paden, *Introduction to Old Occitan*. For reference to the musical scores and performances of some of the poems translated in this book, see Music.

[11] The Occitan names of instruments such as the lute, the rebec (a fiddle), and the tambour (a drum) come from Arabic etyma. See Peter T. Ricketts, "L'influence de la culture arabe sur le lexique de l'ancien occitan, en particulier dans le domaine musical," *L'espace lyrique méditerranéen au Moyen Age: nouvelles approches* (Toulouse: Presses Universitaires du Mirail, 2006), pp. 291–301.

[12] Jacob Burckhardt, *Die Cultur der Renaissance in Italien: Ein Versuch* (Basel: Schweighauser, 1860); translated by S. G. C. Middlemore as *The Civilization of the Renaissance in Italy* (London: Penguin, 1990).

[13] See Colin Morris, *The Discovery of the Individual, 1050–1200* (New York: Harper & Row, 1972); Caroline Walker Bynum, *Jesus as Mother: Studies in the Spirituality of the High Middle Ages* (Berkeley: University of California Press, 1982); John Jeffries Martin, *Myths of Renaissance Individualism* (New York: Palgrave Macmillan, 2004). "The study of Renaissance notions of identity has often been based on a baffling indifference to what came before": Martin, p. 11.

period was devoted entirely to religious community, as in the monastery. Rather than a historical progression from religious community to secular individualism, it seems more reasonable to think that religious community and secular individualism represent varieties of experience and that both were available from the twelfth century to the sixteenth, as well as earlier and later.

The troubadours anticipated the spirit and the poetry of such figures as Dante and Petrarch, both of whom publicly acknowledged their inheritance with admiration and gratitude.[14] For this reason Italian culture to this day regards the troubadours as the source of its poetic tradition. Given this perspective, the Burckhardtian master narrative, so widely entrenched in our general culture, may be regarded as an artifact that is out of date. It depends for its existence on an implicit nineteenth-century sense that the Renaissance continues into the present, and with it a revolt against preceding religious tradition.

A more contemporary view of the past enables us to dispense with the prejudice against the Middle Ages and opens our minds to the richness and diversity of medieval culture, particularly to troubadour poetry. The poems range from pious hymns to the Virgin to heartfelt celebration of the joys of warfare, but the most prominent theme in the troubadour corpus is sexual desire. A man exclaims that God Himself wants no woman nobler than his mistress; a woman cajoles her reluctant lover by saying that if he lets her die of unsatisfied desire, he will "commit a sin and go to torment," and leave her to be "more desired at the Judgment."[15] In the eyes of these lovers, the ways of God are subordinate to the force of erotic love. The poetry of the troubadours and trobairitz compels us to recognize that members of fashionable society felt free, when they chose, to ignore the strictures of the Church regarding sexuality.[16]

For more than two centuries, the troubadour poems spoke of desire that was usually but not always heterosexual. In general, male poets describe male desire for a woman, and women poets describe a woman's desire for a man, but there are also poems in which a troubadour imagines a woman's desire and a trobairitz imagines the desire of a man.[17] The expression of desire ranges from frank sex talk in the first troubadour, Guilhem IX of Aquitaine, to humble beseeching for the lady's intimate favor in Bernart de Ventadorn, and from the self-confident projection of the Comtessa de Dia to the long-suffering misery of Castelloza. The beloved, in the eyes of the lover, possesses *pretz* or "merit," *valor* or "worth," *cortesia* or "courtesy," and above all *jovén* or "youth, youthfulness."[18] Occasionally, the singer identifies his or her beloved as married,[19] but we do not have good reason to imagine adulterous desire as the norm. If anything, the norm is a man's love for a lady who is young

[14] For examples of continuity from the troubadours see Dante, Poem 119, and Petrarch, Poems 125 and 126.

[15] Jaufré Rudel, Poem 11, stanza 3; Castelloza, Poem 74, stanza 6. For further impertinence see the Monk of Montaudon, Poem 66, and Peire Cardenal, Poem 82.

[16] "It was a world in which a normative religious discourse taught that sexuality was something sinful and evil, and yet where large segments of the society chose to ignore that teaching": Ruth Mazo Karras, *Sexuality in Medieval Europe: Doing unto Others* (New York: Routledge, 2005), p. 21.

[17] Male poets depict female desire, for example, in Marcabru, Poem 13, and perhaps in Raimon Jordan, Poem 49. The trobairitz Castelloza imagines her lover's desire distrustfully. Bietris de Romans may have depicted male, if not lesbian, desire in Poem 117.

[18] On *jovén* in women and men, contrasted with age, see Bertran de Born, Poem 43.

[19] Jaufré Rudel, Poem 9, stanza 3; Castelloza, Poem 72, stanza 5.

and whom we may imagine as unmarried, but the subject of marriage arises in few poems. Frequently mentioned obstacles to love include the *gilós*, the "jealous" or "zealous" one, either singular or plural, which may refer to the lady's husband (if she has one) or, in the case of an unmarried woman, to anyone—father, brother, or relatives, both male and female—who resists her will to love. The *lauzengiers* are the advisers, flatterers or gossips who work against the loving couple.

The converse of sexual desire is the misogyny that is characteristic of Marcabru, and the misandry found in late songs about unhappily married women or girls.[20] Nuances of same-sex desire surface in Giraut de Bornelh's *alba*, in which the watchman focuses on the male lover; in the homophobia invoked by Guilhem de Berguedà; in a leper's nostalgia for his male lover; in an ambiguous pronoun that complicates an anonymous bawdy poem; and in a song by Bietris de Romans in which the female speaker expresses love for a woman.[21] Filial love underlies the lamentations on the death of a leader like Richard Lionheart (Poem 56) or Saint Louis (Poem 108). Love for a mother figure appears in Peire Vidal's yearning for his lady in Provence or for Provence in his lady (Poem 59). Jaufré Rudel's love for his faraway lady comes very close to desire for desire itself (Poem 10). Other troubadours, from early to late, sang of their desire for poetry, which, since they sang as poets, becomes a kind of self-love.[22] Love of God or the Virgin becomes a stronger theme in troubadour lyric of the thirteenth century than it had been in the twelfth.[23]

During the time that it flourished, troubadour poetry evolved, driven by the rising status of the vernacular language. From the fall of Rome to the advent of the Renaissance, the sociolinguistic situation in Europe changed profoundly. At first the prestige language throughout Western Europe was Latin, and the popular language in each place was the local vernacular, spoken but rarely recorded. Gradually, the vernaculars were elevated, first from speech into writing and then into further functions of high language. The transition culminated when the vernaculars became competitive with Latin. In the fourteenth century it was still natural for Dante and Petrarch to regard Latin as superior, even for the purpose of describing the vernacular in Dante's *De Vulgari Eloquentia*; but by the sixteenth century the vernacular had become the norm for Montaigne, Cervantes, and Shakespeare, with his "small Latin."[24] Even though Montaigne said his mother tongue was Latin,[25] he chose to write in French.

The rise of the vernacular over the course of a millennium is mirrored by the development over centuries of medieval Occitan. The language was first written in the tenth century. Early, fragile bits of poetry include a charm, perhaps related to midwifery (Poem 1), a vernacular refrain in a Latin religious allegory (Poem 2), an eleventh-century hymn to the Virgin (Poem 3), and an early expression of hetero-

---

[20] Marcabru, Poem 12; Cerverí de Girona, Poem 106.
[21] Giraut de Bornelh, Poem 37; Guilhem de Berguedà, Poem 34, stanzas 3 and 4; the anonymous leper, Poem 122; the ambiguity, Poem 116; Bietris de Romans, Poem 117.
[22] Raimbaut d'Aurenga, Poem 25; Arnaut Daniel, Poem 51; Raimon de Cornet, Poem 124; Petrarch, Poem 125.
[23] Alais, Iselda, and Carenza, Poem 69; Falquet de Romans, Poem 77; Peire Cardenal, Poem 84; Arnaut Vidal, Poem 120.
[24] Ben Jonson, "To the memory of my beloved, the author Mr. William Shakespeare, and what he hath left us" (1623).
[25] "De l'institution des enfans" (*Essais* I.xxvi).

sexual desire (Poem 4). These very short compositions have been preserved in the margins of manuscripts dedicated to weightier subjects that are treated in Latin.[26] Full-blown Occitan lyric began in the twelfth century with the first known troubadour, Guilhem IX of Aquitaine, and those who followed him. At first this lyric had no established subtypes, or genres; the early songs that describe themselves at all are simply called *vers*, or "songs." During the twelfth century, when poets began to write increasingly about sexual desire, *vers* with this theme came to be called *cansós*. As the genres proliferated, the *cansó* gradually came to contrast with other themes, such as those found in the *sirventés* or satire, etymologically a "servant-like" song. Forms such as the *pastorela*, a song about a shepherdess, and the *planh*, a "plaint" or "funeral lament," appeared first as experiments. Later, through imitation, they became institutionalized as genres. The *cobla*, or isolated stanza, came into use late in the twelfth century, and dance songs such as the *balada* arrived in the thirteenth.

As genres evolved, other ways to monumentalize the poems also developed. In the early thirteenth century, prose commentaries on the poets and their songs came into fashion; scholars distinguish between the *vida*, or "life," a brief, usually fictionalized biography of the poet, and the *razo*, or "reason" for a particular composition.[27] In 1254 the first dated, extant troubadour manuscript was transcribed.[28] Most of the *chansonniers*, or songbooks, were compiled in the late thirteenth or fourteenth century, and one as late as the nineteenth. About ninety-five manuscripts containing troubadour poetry survive today; more than half of them were written in Italy, others in northern France or Spain, about twenty in the South of France. Only four of them provide notation of melodies. The imposing presence of the manuscripts speaks eloquently of the prestige that the troubadours came to enjoy toward the end of the period when they flourished, not only at home but in regions remote from their own.

In the early fourteenth century a literary society, the *Sobregaya companhia del Gay Saber*, or the "Exceedingly Merry Company of the Merry Wisdom," was founded at Toulouse to preserve the best of the troubadour tradition. Its board of governors, the *Mantenedors*, or "Maintainers," authorized a clerk, Guilhem Molinier, to draw up a massive poetic treatise called the *Leys d'amors*, or "Laws of Love," in which "love" was understood to mean love poetry. Guilhem Molinier defined more than twenty distinct genres of lyric poetry, providing judges with criteria for awarding prizes in each category. The elevation of troubadour poetry, and with it the Occitan language, might have seemed to be complete. But from today's perspective, the multiplying of categories can be seen to signal a phenomenon on shaky ground; the

[26] Compare Figure 1, showing Poem 1 in the margin of a breviary, with Figure 2, a page from a troubadour songbook.
[27] We include three *vidas* (86, 87, 88) and one *razo* (76) to illustrate the monumentalization of the troubadours, and we draw upon *vidas* in our introductions to individual troubadours. For more on the *vidas* and *razos*, see Margarita Egan, trans., *The Vidas of the Troubadours* (New York: Garland Publishing, 1984), and Elizabeth Wilson Poe, *From Poetry to Prose in Old Provençal: The Emergence of the* Vidas, *the* Razos, *and the* Razos de trobar (Birmingham, AL: Summa, 1984). The standard edition is J. Boutière and A.-H. Schutz, with I.-M. Cluzel, *Biographies des troubadours: textes provençaux des XIIIᵉ et XIVᵉ siècles*, 2nd ed. (Paris: Nizet, 1973).
[28] Called D (Modena, Biblioteca Nazionale Estense, Estero 45, formerly Alpha R.4.4), this large manuscript has been partially published in facsimile: see *Il canzoniere provenzale estense*, 2 vols. (Modena: STEM-Mucchi, 1979–82).

Occitan language and its literature were already under siege. France was emerging as a nation, and Occitan, in comparison to French, was becoming a regional language. This threat motivated the effort to make permanent and fixed what had been, for several hundred years, a poetic art in constant evolution.

The poems that have survived show us that the production of troubadour poetry waxed and waned through the years. In the generation of Guilhem IX and Marcabru, troubadour poetry was sparse, but the volume of poems grew considerably in the later twelfth century with poets such as Raimbaut d'Aurenga. The production of poems reached a peak in the years around 1200, only to fall as the thirteenth century advanced, and to fall again as that century drew toward its close. In other words, the production first rose sharply, then declined more slowly. Underlying the rise and fall was, we believe, the emergence of vernacular language followed by the decline of Occitan when it began to compete with French on its own terrain.

The interweaving of linguistic, literary, and musical traditions richly complicated the milieu in which the troubadours composed. We have already noted the Latin tradition, robust in liturgical culture, from which troubadour music seems to have arisen, and the possible influence of Arabic music from Spain. The recurring theme of the breeze that brings the fragrance of the lady's perfume to the lover may have been inspired by Arabic poetry.[29] When the earl of Orkney, an archipelago off the north coast of Scotland, passed through Narbonne on a pilgrimage to Jerusalem, he flirted with the viscountess of the city and, in a skaldic stanza in Old Norse, praised her intelligence and beauty (Poem 22). A polyglot troubadour, Raimbaut de Vaqueiras, composed a song in which he used Occitan in the first stanza and followed it with stanzas in Italian, French, Gascon (a language spoken from Bordeaux to the Pyrenees) and Galician-Portuguese (Poem 61).[30] In the thirteenth century, poets who were native to Catalonia employed Occitan for lyric compositions (Poems 78 and 94).

Some poems that survive from medieval Occitania were composed in Hebrew. Jews had been present throughout the South of France since before the fall of Rome, despite hostile traditions such as the ritual lapidation, or stoning, of Jewish houses in Béziers and the colaphization, or slap, of a Jew in Toulouse—a slap that could be fatal. In Provence Jews enjoyed the protection of the pope. There in the thirteenth century, Jewish poets wrote, usually in Hebrew (Poems 111, 114, 115, 121), but in one poem a Jewish poet speaks Occitan in a dialogue with the troubadour Guiraut Riquier (Poem 105).

By the thirteenth century a steady cultural flow had begun between the lands that are now Italy and the South of France. Sordello fled from his enemies in Verona to Provence, where he became the troubadour known in Occitan as Sordel (Poem 90). A trobairitz named Guilhelma de Rosers left Provence for Genoa, where she engaged in an Occitan *tensó* with a local judge (Poem 92). Guido Cavalcanti, Dante's friend and one of the founders of the *dolce stil nuovo*, or "sweet new style," visited Toulouse and wrote in Italian of his love for a lady he met there (Poems 109 and 110). Dante composed Occitan verses for the shade of Arnaut Daniel,

---

29   See Poems 29, 59, 62, and 112. On contacts with Arabic culture by the first troubadour, Guilhem IX, see notes to Poems 5 and 6 (stanza 2).

30   Multilingual compositions were also written by Bonifaci Calvo in three languages (Occitan, French, and Galician-Portuguese), and by Cerverí de Girona in six (Galician-Portuguese, Castilian, Occitan, French, Gascon, and Italian). See Bonifaci Calvo in Riquer, *Trovadores*, no. 296; vol. 3, p. 1422, and Cerverí in Riquer, *Trovadores*, no. 330; vol. 3, p. 1571.

whom the pilgrim encountered in Purgatory (Poem 119). In the fourteenth century Petrarch, who was educated as a boy in Provence and lived half his adult life there, wrote poems in Provence and in Italy that mark the passage of the poetic tradition from Occitan into Italian (Poems 125 and 126). Through Dante and Petrarch, the troubadour tradition flowed into modern poetry.

Troubadour poetry has a recognizable set of formal conventions. Most of the poems are based on the stanza, which, in Occitan, turns on a strict rhyme scheme that recurs identically throughout the song. The specific rhyme sounds employed in the unchanging pattern may vary in a controlled way. Supplementing the rhyme scheme is a second structural feature: the syllabic pattern, which also recurs identically throughout the song. A frequent stanzaic form, for example, has the rhyme scheme *abbacddc*, with each line containing eight syllables. The same rhyme scheme may also involve lines of a different number of syllables; in fact, the lines in a stanza often have different lengths, arranged in a pattern that recurs throughout the composition. Many songs end with a shorter final stanza, called the *tornada*, which reproduces the rhymes and syllabic pattern of the corresponding lines in the preceding full stanza.

In our translations we have indicated the relative length of Occitan lines along the left margin. When the line length does not vary, the left margin is straight, as we may see in the first stanza of a song by Guilhem IX of Aquitaine (Poem 5), one of the earliest in the repertoire:

> Ab la dolchor del temps novel
> Foillo li bosc, e li aucel
> Chanton, chascus en lor lati,
> Segon lo vers del novel chan;
> Adonc esta ben c'om s'aisi
> D'acho don hom a plus talan.

> With the sweet beauty of the new season
> The woods leaf out, and the birds
> Sing, each one in its language
> To the measure of a new song;
> Then it is well for a man to enjoy
> What he most desires.

The stanza is made up of six lines. The rhyme scheme in Occitan is *aabcbc*, with the rhymes *-el, -el, -i, -an, -i, -an*. All the rhymes are masculine; that is, they end on a stressed vowel. The rhymes are the same for the following stanza but then change for each subsequent pair of stanzas; this pattern is called *coblas doblas*, or "double stanzas." All the lines have eight syllables. The translation follows the original closely for meaning but does not reproduce the rhyme scheme or the syllable count. Since the lines in Occitan all have the same number of syllables, the left margin has no indentations. We do the same with the left margin in English.

Somewhat more elaborate in design is the first stanza of an *alba*, or dawn song, attributed without certainty to Gaucelm Faidit (Poem 54):

> Us cavaliers si jazia
> Ab la re que plus volia.
> Soven baizan li dizia,

9

"Doussa res, ieu que farai?
Que.l jorns ve et la nueytz vai,
   Ay!
Qu'ieu aug que li gaita cria,
'Via! Sus! Qu'ieu vey lo jorn
  Venir apres l'alba.'"

Once a knight was lying
With the woman he loved best.
He kissed her many times and said,
"Sweetheart, what should I do?
The day comes and the night goes,
   Oh,
I hear the watchman crying,
'Away! Up! For I see day
  Coming after dawn.'"

This stanza is nine lines long, including the substantial refrain comprising the last four lines. The Occitan rhyme scheme is *aaabbbacd*, with the rhymes *-ía, -ía, -ía, -ái, -ái, -ái, -ía, jorn, alba*. The rhyme sounds do not change from stanza to stanza, a structure called *coblas unissonans*, or "one-sounding stanzas." Most of the lines are seven syllables long, either feminine—that is, with an unstressed and uncounted (eighth) last syllable, as in lines one to three and seven—or masculine, as in lines four, five, and eight. Two lines differ in length. Line six is the monosyllabic introduction of the refrain, and line nine has five syllables and a feminine ending. Most editors indent the shorter lines in Occitan as above. Our English version does not replicate the rhyme scheme or the syllable count; however, we indent the last line once and the monosyllabic line twice, so that the left margin of the translation calls attention to the syllabic design of the stanza in Occitan.

 An elaborately structured stanza begins this song by Arnaut Daniel (Poem 50):

L'aura amara	1
Fa.ls bruoills brancutz	2
Clarzir	3
Que.l doussa espeissa ab fuoills,	4
E.ls letz	5
Becs	6
Dels auzels ramencs	7
Ten balps e muts,	8
Pars	9
E non-pars;	10
Per qu'eu m'esfortz	11
De far e dir	12
Plazers	13
A mains, per liei	14
Que m'a virat bas d'aut,	15
Don tem morir	16
Si.ls afans no m'asoma.	17

The bitter breeze	1
Makes the branchy bushes	2
Brighten	3
(The gentle one thickens them with leaves),	4
And cheery	5
Beaks	6
Of the birds among branches	7
Keeps stammering or mute,	8
Paired	9
Or not paired;	10
And so I strive	11
To speak and make	12
Pleasures	13
For people, for the sake of her	14
Who has turned me upside down,	15
Making me fear I'll die	16
Unless she ends my agony.	17

This extraordinary stanza of seventeen lines contains lines of six syllables, five, four, three, two, and one. The rhyme scheme is *abcdefgbhhicjklcm*. The first line has three syllables plus the uncounted feminine ending: *l'aura amara* (with elision of the final *-a* of *aura* before the beginning *a-* of *amara*). The second line has four syllables, and so on. One may combine the rhyme scheme with the syllable count in a rather forbidding formula as follows: *a3 b4 c2 d6 e2 f1 g5 b4 h1 h3 i4 c4 j2 k4 l6 c4 m6*. The first and last rhymes are feminine. To prove that this fantastic elaboration is not a delusion, one has only to read further, observing that the poem repeats exactly this rhyme scheme, preserving the rhyme sounds (*coblas unissonans*) and the precise syllabic structure, through six full stanzas and a tornada.[31] This stanza typifies the intricate style of *trobar clus*, or "closed composition," for which Arnaut Daniel is famous.

For more examples of Occitan language see Poem 119, Dante's encounter with Arnaut Daniel in *Purgatorio*, and Figures 1 and 2.

Since these poems were written for performance, we suggest that readers try to pronounce a few lines of verse in order to hear the sound of the language. The pronunciation of vowels in Old Occitan follows the "Continental" manner, as in Italian, Spanish, or French, including the French sound of *u* as in *tu*, "you" (the familiar form). The diphthongs *ié* and *uó* are stressed on the second element. Triphthongs are stressed on the central element, as in *iéi* (like English "Yay!"), *uóu* (like English "Woe"), and so on. Most consonants are pronounced as they are in English. The consonants *c* and *g* could be either hard or soft: hard in *cantar*, "to sing," and *gai*, "merry"; soft in *cen*, "hundred," and *gelos*, "jealous, zealous." The graphies *lh*, *nh* represent sounds like those in English *million*, *canyon*; thus *melhor*, "better," and *senhor*, "sir" (pronounced like Spanish *señor*). The *r* is tapped when single and trilled when double, as in Spanish. In general, words ending in a consonant are stressed on the final syllable (*cantár, gelós, melhór, senhôr*), while those ending in a

---

[31]   It is possible to combine the short lines of this poem into longer ones, arriving at the scheme *a8 b8 c8 d8 e10 f10 g10*, which looks more reasonable but obscures the systematic recurrence of the rhymes in the short lines. Evidently, Arnaut did not care to seem reasonable. See Riquer, *Trovadores*, no. 115; vol. 2, p. 624.

vowel are stressed on the preceding syllable (*cánta*, "he sings"; *dómna*, "lady"). We indicate the position of stress with an acute accent, even though accent marks are not normally used in Occitan.[32]

As translators, we pass the poems along to our readers, hoping to show that the world the troubadours inhabited was dynamic and present. With its share of persecution, intolerance, violence, and cruelty, it was not an ideal world, but neither was it lacking in powerful ideals. The troubadours and trobairitz cultivated a youthful spirit, a requisite quality for their engagement in arms and their expression of desire. Their songs resound with vigor and passion. Their words can open a world.

---

[32] For more on pronunciation of the language see Paden, *Introduction to Old Occitan*, pp. 10–14. The compact disk that accompanies that book illustrates pronunciation in normal speech and in musical performance.

Before the Troubadours
950–1100

THE earliest traces of written Occitan go back to the tenth and eleventh centuries. They include legal documents written in a blend of Latin and Occitan, or *latin farci* ("stuffed Latin"), that is, Latin interspersed with vernacular elements. Typically, Latin is employed for the more impersonal passages and Occitan for passages in which the speaker engages himself more directly.

The oldest literary texts date from the same period. Their language is often difficult to determine precisely, in part because their transmission was unreliable. We have selected a tenth-century charm from folk medicine and, from the eleventh century, a bilingual dawn song with an Occitan refrain, a hymn to the Virgin, and a lyrical stanza. The stanza seems to have been written shortly before Guilhem IX of Aquitaine began to sing his songs. It differs from the other early texts in that it turns from ritualized incantation to expression of amorous desire. Like the dawn song, it seems to have been sung, since the transcription includes neumes, or musical lines; but in neither case did the scribe insert the notes. These four Occitan texts are anonymous and very short. Their transmission, compared to that of troubadour poems, was very frail. The charm and the amorous stanza were unknown until they were discovered in the margins of manuscripts in the 1980s.[1]

---

[1] See Paden, "Before the Troubadours."

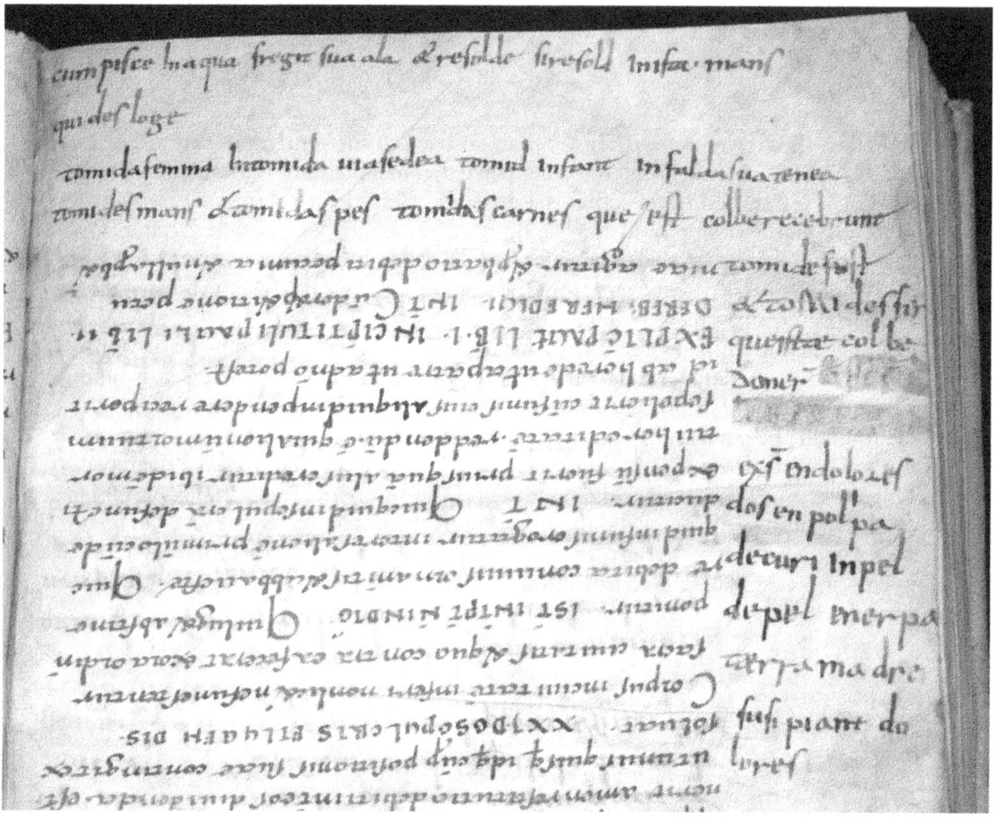

Figure 1. Manuscript of Poem 1 (Clermont-Ferrand, Bibliothèque communautaire et interuniversitaire, ms. 201, folio 89 verso) (Reproduced by permission of the Bibliothèque communautaire et interuniversitaire de Clermont-Ferrand)

The unique text of Poem 1 is preserved as a marginal insertion, upside-down, in a treatise on law from the ninth or tenth century. Our Poem 1 begins on the third line down. The text reads:

tomida femina in tomida uia sedea tomid infant in falda sua tenea
tomides mans & tomidas pes tomidas carnes que est colbe recebrunt

> tomide fust
> & tomides fer
> que istae colbe
> doner — [erasure]
> [erasure]
> exs — en dolores
> dos en polpa
> de curi in pel
> de pel en erpa
> taerra madre
> susipiant do
> lores

The poem may be edited as follows:

> Tomida femina
> in tomida via sedea;
> tomid infant
> in falda sua tenea;   4
> tomides mans
> et tomidas pes,
> tomidas carnes
> que est colbe recebrunt;   8
> tomide fust
> et tomides fer
> que istæ colbe doner*unt*.
> Exs*unt* en dolores   12
> d'os en polpa
> [de polpa en curi]
> de curi in pel
> de pel en erpa.   16
> Terra madre susipiat dolores.

Line 14, lacking in the manuscript, is conjectured on the basis of the pattern of the following lines.

15

Anonymous

Tomida femina / A swollen woman

Written down in the second half of the tenth century (see Figure 1), this charm has been interpreted as a cure for an edema, or swelling. The patient may be the "swollen woman" alone; if so, her "swollen child" is invoked for the purpose of sympathetic magic, as is the "swollen road." Alternatively, both the mother and the child may be patients, or only the child. The practitioner seeks to gain control over the swelling by invoking it in the patient, expanding it to the road and then to the wood and iron, presumably referring to a knife. With a blow of the knife, perhaps striking it against the swelling, the practitioner disperses the pain. The charm employs what we call today physical therapy and a talking cure.

It seems more likely that the charm concerns a pregnant woman with the "swollen child" in her womb, said to be in her lap by metonymy. In this reading the practitioner is a midwife, the wood and iron her birthing instruments. The purpose of the charm is to help the woman endure childbirth by dispersing her pain. This reading places an image of birth at the beginning of Occitan poetry.

> A swollen woman
> Sat in a swollen road;
> A swollen child
> She held in her lap;
> Swollen hands
> And swollen feet,
> Swollen flesh
> That will take this blow;
> Swollen wood
> And swollen iron
> That will give this blow.
> The pain goes out
> From bone to flesh,
> From flesh to skin,
> From skin to hair,
> From hair to grass;
> Let mother earth receive the pain.

2

Anonymous

Phebi claro nondum orto iubare / By the bright glow of Phoebus, ready to rise

The bilingual dawn song, now dated in the eleventh century, consists of three stanzas in Latin with a refrain in the vernacular. Many scholars have considered it a proto-*alba*, an antecedent of the songs describing the separation of lovers at dawn that were written later in Occitan, and that have parallels in poetry written around the world.[1] We interpret the refrain as a description of dawn that suggests a Christian allegory of the resurrection. It may also anticipate the erotic *albas* to come. The poem hovers between religious and amorous reference.

1   By the bright glow of Phoebus, ready to rise,
    The first light falls over the earth.
    The watchman calls to the sleepers, "Arise!"
        The dawn glimmers, the seas swell; the sun
        Rises, watchful, to destroy dark night.

2   Behold the evil ruses of enemies, spread
    To carry away the careless and slow
    Who fail to hear the herald's cries.
        The dawn glimmers, the seas swell; the sun
        Rises, watchful, to destroy dark night.

3   Polaris pulls away from Arcturus;
    The stars of heaven hide their rays;
    The Great Bear moves toward the East.
        The dawn glimmers, the seas swell; the sun
        Rises, watchful, to destroy dark night.

---

[1]   See Poems 37, 54, 63, 77, 112, 113. On the global diffusion of such songs see Arthur T. Hatto, ed., *Eos: An Enquiry into the Theme of Lovers' Meetings and Partings at Dawn in Poetry* (The Hague: Mouton, 1965). For discussion of the interpretation of this poem see Paden, "Before the Troubadours."

3

Anonymous

O Maria, Deu maire / O Mary, mother of God

In the eleventh century the abbey of Saint Martial in Limoges was a flourishing center of monastic culture. Sacred songs in the liturgy combined Latin with the vernacular as the monks sought to communicate more meaningfully to the faithful. These songs may have played a role in the later development of the art of the troubadours, which continues their characteristic musical style.

Among the monastic songs from Saint Martial, this is the only one written entirely in Occitan. It is also the only Old Occitan song transmitted with a musical transcription extending over all its stanzas. The transcription varies from stanza to stanza in regard to incidental details, but it represents the same essential melody throughout. The songs of the troubadours, with their melodies transcribed for only one stanza, probably varied in a similar way in their melodic detail from one stanza to another. This song bears a close melodic resemblance to a Latin hymn to the Virgin beginning *Ave maris stella / Hail, star of the sea* that is at least as old as the ninth century.[1] It also resembles the *alba*, or dawn-song, by Giraut de Bornelh (Poem 37).

1   O Mary, mother of God,
       God is both your father and son;
       Lady, to your glorious son
       Pray for us.

2   And for all people
       Pray to his father, too.
       If he does not help us,
       We shall turn to weeping.

3   Eve obeyed a serpent,
       A resplendent angel;[2]
       Through her felicitous fall
       God became man.

4   Since he was of woman born,
       God saved women;
       And he was born a man
       To save men.

5   Since Eve, wife of Adam,
       Obeyed the devil Satan,
       She put us in such torment
       That we hunger and thirst.

6   Eve committed folly
       When she ate the fruit
       That God forbade her;
       As did Adam, who obeyed her.

[1]   See Frederick Brittain, *The Penguin Book of Latin Verse* (Baltimore: Penguin, 1962), p. 129.
[2]   The hymn depicts the serpent as Lucifer (the "Light-Bringer") in disguise.

7   If he had not obeyed her
     And eaten of the fruit,
     Those who love our Lord
     Would never die.

8   So many souls
     Would be going to salvation,
     Those who now are lost
     Never would have lived.[3]

9   Adam ate the fruit
     By which we all were lost;
     By disobeying God
     He brought us all to shame.

10   Because of him, God died
     Most wrongly on the cross
     But on the third day rose
     Just as Mary said;[4]

11   Saying she spoke with God,
     Mary told the apostles,
     "We shall see him live again
     On the mount of Galilee."

12   By killing death, his life
     Gave us paradise;
     May God also in truth
     Grant us his glory!

---

[3]   That is, God would not have allowed such an excess of lost souls.
[4]   Mary Magdalen, whom Jesus sent to the disciples to tell them that he would ascend (John 20:18).

4

Anonymous

Las, qu'i non sun sparvir, astur / Oh, to be a sparrow-hawk, a goshawk!

This stanza of secular desire was discovered in the margin of a British Library manuscript, where a German scribe wrote it at some time in the eleventh century, perhaps near the end of the century. It was first published in 1984. The lover imagines himself as a hunting hawk, a male symbol that would recur in troubadours, such as Bernart Marti (Poem 18), and in one of the founding texts of Middle High German lyric by Der von Kürenberc, perhaps in the mid-twelfth century.[1] The motif became widespread in later folklore.[2] The lover's pain, *dulur*, recalls the pain, *dolores*, in the earlier charm (Poem 1), but contrasts with that text by the softness of the beloved's lips and the sweetness of a kiss. The opposition of the lover's grief and imagined joy anticipates the emotional polarity of *joi* and *dolor*, "joy" and "grief," that will characterize the songs of the troubadours, for example, Guilhem IX, Poem 5.

> Oh, to be a sparrow-hawk, a goshawk![3]
>   I'd fly to my love,
>   Touch her, embrace her,
>   Kiss her lips so soft,
> Sweeten and soothe our pain.

---

[1]   *Ich zôch mir einen falken / I trained a falcon*: see Leonard Forster, *The Penguin Book of German Verse* (Harmondsworth: Penguin, 1957), p. 8.

[2]   For the folkloric motif see Pierre Bec, "Prétroubadouresque ou paratroubadouresque? Un antécédent médiéval d'un motif de chanson folklorique *Si j'étais une hirondelle . . .*," *Cahiers de civilisation médiévale* 47 (2004): 153–62. In the third line Bec proposes to read *la sinti[r]*, "to touch her"; the manuscript reads *la sintil*, which others have interpreted as normal Occitan *la gentil*, "the worthy one."

[3]   The sparrow-hawk was valued most highly when it resembled the larger, more beautiful, and stronger goshawk.

Spring

1100–1150

THE earliest known troubadours include some who were notable figures in their time, either because of their social standing or their poetic genius or both. The first, Guilhem IX, duke of Aquitaine and count of Poitou, was the lord of about one-third of what we call France. His successor, Jaufré Rudel, was called "prince" of Blaye, a town at the mouth of the Garonne river near Bordeaux. In contrast, Jaufré's contemporary Marcabru was of uncertain origin; according to his *vida* he was a foundling from Gascony, the region lying along the Atlantic coast between Bordeaux and the Pyrenees. Cercamon, Bernart Martí, and Peire d'Alvernhe were all influenced by Marcabru. Cercamon was Marcabru's contemporary and may have been a fellow Gascon; we know little about Bernart Martí; Peire d'Alvernhe was perhaps the son of a burgher. Except for Peire d'Alvernhe, these early troubadours came from the western part of the Occitan region.

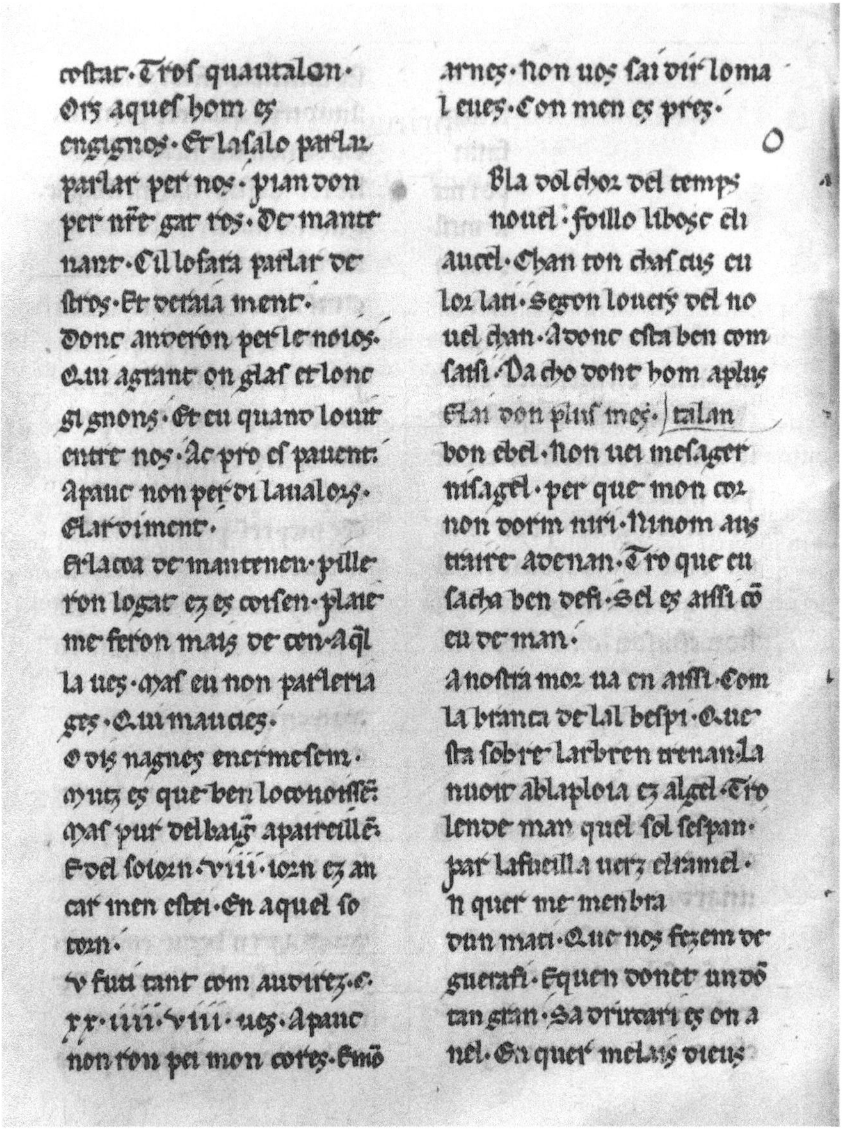

Figure 2. Manuscript of Poem 5 (New York, Pierpont Morgan Library, ms. M 819, folio 225 verso). (Reproduced by permission of the Morgan Library)

Poem 5, by Guilhem IX of Aquitaine, is preserved twice in the only troubadour manuscript now located in the Western hemisphere, manuscript N. This manuscript was composed in the late thirteenth century (ca. 1285–1300) in Italy, probably in Padua; its earliest known owners were the dukes of Mantua. The text of Poem 5 shown here (in the right column, starting three lines down) lacks the initial letter of the stanza, perhaps because it was intended to be ornamented by a different scribe. The manuscript reads:

Bla dolchor del temps
nouel . foillo libosc eli
aucel. Chanton chascus en
lor lati. segon louers del no
uel chan. Adonc esta ben com
saisi: Dacho dont hom aplus
Ela don plus mes. /_ talan

The scribe uses a period, or point, to signal the end of each verse line. The first stanza may be edited as follows:

Ab la dolchor del temps nouel
Foillo li bosc e li aucel
Chanton chascus en lor lati
Segon lo vers del novel chan;
Adonc esta ben c'om s'aisi
D'acho dont hom a plus talan.

Guilhem IX of Aquitaine

Guilhem,[1] the ninth of his name to be duke of Aquitaine and seventh to be count of Poitou, lived his turbulent life from 1071 to 1126. At the age of fourteen he inherited the lordship of fiefs in southwestern France that were more extensive than those controlled by the king of France, his nominal overlord. In the aftermath of what we call the First Crusade, he took the cross and, in 1101, led an army to Turkey. The army was annihilated, but Guilhem escaped and completed a pilgrimage to Jerusalem before returning to his lands. Like many lords, he lived in frequent conflict with his neighbors, his vassals, and the Church. He was excommunicated twice. In 1120 he joined a more successful crusade against the Moors in Spain. It was at this time that he may have received a precious vase, now in the Louvre, that was a gift from the Muslim king of Saragossa.[2] Guilhem married twice but was flagrantly unfaithful. He was the father of Guilhem X of Aquitaine, whose death at Compostela would be sung by Marcabru and Cercamon (Poems 14 and 16), and the grandfather of Eleanor of Aquitaine. Eleanor married Louis VII of France and then Henry Plantagenet, who became Henry II of England.

"Count of Poitou" was a more meaningful title than "duke of Aquitaine." The troubadour manuscripts attribute eleven poems to the *Coms de Peitieus*, or count of Poitou, whom we identify on reasonable grounds as Guilhem IX.[3] If this identification is correct, Guilhem is the first troubadour whose name we know and whose works we have. The area where Occitan was spoken included Aquitaine but probably did not extend as far north as Poitou. It appears that Guilhem adopted the Occitan language for his poetry out of a desire to emphasize his solidarity with his vassals to the south.[4]

---

[1] Stressed *Guilhém*, with *-lh-* pronounced like the *-lli-* in *million*. In English the name corresponds to William.

[2] George T. Beech, "The Eleanor of Aquitaine Vase, William IX of Aquitaine, and Muslim Spain," *Gesta* 32 (1993): 3–10.

[3] George T. Beech, "L'attribution des poèmes du Comte de Poitiers à Guillaume IX d'Aquitaine," *Cahiers de civilisation médiévale* 31 (1988): 3–16.

[4] Although scholars do not know the specific dates of any of Guilhem's songs, it has become customary to publish them in an order proceeding from youthful indiscretion to relative maturity. Believing such an order to be groundless, particularly in view of Guilhem's noteworthy indiscretions in his mature years, we prefer an order that mixes his shifting moods.

5

Guilhem IX of Aquitaine

Ab la dolchor del temps novel / With the sweet beauty of the new season

For one manuscript version of this song, see Figure 2.

1   With the sweet beauty of the new season
The woods leaf out, and the birds
Sing, each one in its language
To the measure of a new song;
Then it is well for a man to enjoy
What he most desires.

2   From the source of my greatest delight
No messenger comes and no message.
My heart neither sleeps nor laughs,
Nor dare I go forward
Until I know for certain
She will keep her promise.

3   Our love goes now
Like the limb of a hawthorn tree
That stands upon its trunk
At night, through frost and rain
Until morning, when the sun spreads
Through its green leaves and branches.

4   I still remember the day
When we made an end to war,
And she gave to me so great a gift,
Her loving and her ring.
God let me live until again
I put my hands beneath her cloak.

5   I do not care what people say
Who would part me from my neighbor,
For I know how words turn
Into rumors that travel abroad.
People who hunger boast about love,
But we have the bread and the knife!

6

Guilhem IX of Aquitaine

En Alvernhe, part Lemozi / In Auvergne, beyond the Limousin

1. In Auvergne, beyond the Limousin,[1]
   I traveled alone as a pilgrim.
   I found the wives of Sir Garin
       And Sir Bernart;
   They spoke to me frankly
       By Saint Leonart.[2]

2. Now hear what I told them:
   I never talked of bricks or bats,
   But only spoke like so:
       "Tarrababart,
   marrababelio riben
   saramahart."[3]

3. Lady Agnes said to Erma,
   "We've found what we've been seeking!
   Let's take him in without delay,
       For he's a babbler,
   And never will he breathe a word
       About our secret."

4. One of them took me under her cloak,
   And I liked that just fine;
   They walked me to their cozy hearth
       And lit the fire.
   I warmed myself with great delight
       By their hot coals.

5. To eat they gave me capons,
   And I dined till I was full.
   The bread was warm, the wine was good,
       Vigorous and strong;
   There were no kitchen-boys,
       Just us three.

6. "Girl, this fellow is full of tricks,
   The babble is only an act.
   Go and get the big, red cat
       On the double—
   He will make him tell the truth
       If he's lying."

---

[1] The region around Limoges, presumably seen from Guilhem's town of Poitiers.

[2] Stressed *Leonárt*; Saint Leonard, patron saint of prisoners.

[3] This passage, which may represent humorous pseudo-Arabic, has been much discussed, but not conclusively. For a plausible claim that Guilhem IX may have known Arabic himself, see George T. Beech, "Troubadour Contact with Muslim Spain and Knowledge of Arabic: New Evidence Concerning William IX of Aquitaine," *Romania* 113 (1992–5): 14–42.

7 I saw that tomcat coming in;
His fur was thick, his whiskers fierce.
I wanted him to go away,
  He scared me so.
I almost lost my appetite,
  My burning lust.

8 But no, we drank and ate and then
I took off all my clothes;
They got that mean old cat and put
  Him against my back,
And flayed me from my head
  Down to my heel.

9 Lady Erma grabbed the cat
And yanked him by the tail.
He scratched me more than a hundred times
  All at once;
He scorched me, but even so,
  I did not budge.

10 I would not move no matter what
Till I had banged them both
Aplenty; we began the night
  The way I liked,
And so I chose to suffer pain
  And heavy hurt.

11 I tell you, I fucked them
A hundred eighty-eight times!
I nearly broke
  My equipment
And ached in agony,
  It hurt so bad.

12 Monet, go in the morning,
With my song in your purse
Straight to the wives of Sir Garin
  And Sir Bernart,
And tell them, for love of me,
  Go kill the cat!

7

Guilhem IX of Aquitaine

Farai un vers de dreit nien / I'll make a song about nothing at all

This poem, called a *vers* or "song" in the text itself (stanzas 1 and 7), is identified in one manuscript as a *devinalh*, or "riddle." At the end Guilhem opens his puzzling composition to the performer's art and the reader's interpretation.

1   I'll make a song about nothing at all:
Not about me or others,
Not about love or being young
    Or anything else,
For it was composed while I was asleep
    On a horse.

2   I don't know the hour when I was born;
I am not cheerful, I am not sad,
I'm not from there, I'm not from here,
    And there is nothing I can do
Because one night I was bewitched
    High on a hill.

3   I don't know when I fall asleep
Or when I awake, if no one tells.
My heart has almost split in two
    From aching;
Still it matters not a mouse,
    By Saint Martial![1]

4   I am sick and I fear to die,
But all I know is what I hear;
I'll get a doctor that I like,
    But I don't know which one;
He'll be good if I am cured,
    But not if I get worse.

5   I've got a girl, I know not who.
I never saw her, by my faith;
She does not please or anger me,
    Nor do I care;
I have never had Normans or French
    In my house.

6   I never saw her, but I love her well;
She's done me neither right nor wrong.
When I don't see her I do fine,
    And I don't give a cock;
I know another sweeter and cuter,
    A better prize.

---

[1]   The patron of the Limousin, in whose abbey at Limoges monastic songs such as Poem 3 were transcribed.

7   I've made this song, about whom I don't know;
    I will send it along to somebody
    Who will send it by way of somebody else
        Over toward Anjou,
    And from his writing case, he can send me
        The key.

8

Guilhem IX of Aquitaine

Pos de chantar m'es pres talenz / Since I want to make a song

In this song Guilhem contemplates a departure from his lands and lordship. It suggests pilgrimage, armed pilgrimage (crusade), monastic retreat, and death.

1 Since I want to make a song,
  I'll sing about what makes me sad.
  No more will I pay mind to men
  In Poitou or the Limousin.

2 I take myself to exile now
  In peril and great fear;
  My son, in war, must stay behind,
  To fight our neighbors here.

3 To leave the lordship of Poitiers
  Is hard for me to do;
  I now must place my land and son
  In care of his cousin, Folcón.

4 If Folcón of Angers doesn't help
  Nor the king who grants my fief,[1]
  Warriors will come to hurt my son,
  Evil Gascons and Angevins.

5 Unless he is smart and stays alert
  When I have gone away,
  They'll turn him around and upside down,
  For the boy is weak and still so young.

6 I beg for mercy from my friend;[2]
  If I wronged him, may he forgive,
  And I pray to Jesus on the throne
  In Occitan and his own Latin.[3]

7 I've been a man of joy and pride
  But now it's time to turn aside;
  I give myself away to him
  Who brings to sinners lasting peace.

8 I've been bright and full of cheer
  But the Lord permits no more.
  The load is more than I can bear,
  For I am drawing near the end.

---

[1] Louis VI of France ("the Fat"), Guilhem's nominal overlord and the father of Louis VII, who would marry Guilhem's granddaughter, Eleanor of Aquitaine.

[2] Presumably Folcon d'Angers.

[3] In *romans*, the vernacular of this poem (that is, Occitan), and in the Latin of the Church.

9   I've said goodbye to all I love,
My horsemanship and fame;
I now embrace the will of God,
And pray he keeps me close to him.

10   I call my friends, come one, come all,
Grant me honor at my death,
For I have known the joy of play
In my home and far away.

11   Thus I surrender joy and play
And furs: the sable, vair,[4] and gray.

---

[4]   Fur made by sewing together the pelts of squirrels; their dark backs and white bellies produced a pattern of variegated colors.

9

Jaufré Rudel, Prince of Blaye

Pro ai del chan essenhadors / I have many singing-masters

Jaufré Rudel was styled "prince," or lord, of the castle of Blaye, on the Gironde river north of Bordeaux, at the border between the territories where Occitan and French were spoken. The lords of Blaye were vassals of the counts of Angoulême and Poitiers. Jaufré appears in a legal document written after 1125; in 1148 Marcabru addressed a song to him "overseas" (*outramar*), that is, undoubtedly, in the Holy Land on the Second Crusade. In the thirteenth century Jaufré's life became the subject of a celebrated but unreliable *vida* (see Selection 86).

1   I have many singing-masters
     All around me, and mistresses:
     Meadows and orchards, trees and flowers,
     Warbling of birds and cries and songs
     In the sweet, soft season,
     For I live in a bubble of joy,
     And no delight can make me rejoice
     As much as the presence of valiant love.

2   Let the shepherds have their pipes
     And the children have their play,
     And let me have the kind of love
     That pleases her and pleases me.
     I know she's every bit as good
     To her lover, even when the path is hard;
     Still I often feel despair
     That she's not mine, my heart's desire.

3   Far away are the castle and the keep
     Where she lies with her husband,
     And if I do not soon advance,
     Obeying the counsel of my teachers—
     No other counsel does much good,
     Because my love's so pure at heart—
     I'll have nothing else to do but die,
     If I don't find joy soon.

4   I say in the land where her joy was born
     Her neighbors must all be lords;
     It's a point of honor to me
     To believe that even the peasants there
     Must be loyal and true;
     The love that I hold in my heart
     Makes me happy and gives me good will,
     And I know that she knows this well.

5   My heart is so completely there
     It has no tip or root elsewhere,
     And when I sleep beneath my sheet
     My spirit goes to where she lies;
     My love for her does me harm,
     Since I love so much, and she doesn't care;

32

Soon I will see if by suffering
I can find the way to rejoicing.

6   My longing hurries away to her
Through night and by the light of day,
Going in hope of finding help;
At last it returns, and at last it speaks:
"Friend," she says, "jealous brutes
Have stirred up such a bother
That it will be hard for you and me
To find peace and have our pleasure."

7   My grief is growing worse and worse
Because I cannot see her alone;
I do not sigh so deeply
Or weep so long that only one kiss
Would not make my heart well and strong.
This love is good; it has great power
To bring me a cure for this disease
Without a learned doctor's care.

10

Jaufré Rudel

Lanqan li jorn son lonc en mai / When days grow long in May

For many readers this is among the greatest of troubadour songs because it represents the
mystery of the desire they sang.

1   When days grow long in May
I rejoice in songs of birds from afar,
For now that I have traveled far
I think of a love from far away.
So bent and bowed with desire I go
That neither song nor hawthorn flower
Pleases me more than winter's snow.

2   No love will ever make me glad
Unless I rejoice in this love from afar;
I know no lady as fair or good
Anywhere, near or far.
She is so true, so pure
That over there, in Saracen lands,
I'd gladly be captured for her.

3   Sad but rejoicing, I'd take my leave
If I could see this love from afar;
But I do not know when we'll meet,
For our lands lie far apart.
The passes and roads are so abundant
That I cannot see what lies ahead,
But let all be as it pleases God.

4   Surely joy will come to me, come from far
When for love of God, I seek my lodging there.
And if it pleases her, I shall reside
Close by her though I come from afar.
Then we shall speak truly, one to another,
When I come so near, a faraway lover,
That her gracious words will bring me joy.

5   Indeed I'll know the lord is true
Who lets me see this love from afar,
But for every blessing that comes my way
I feel two blows, she's so far away.
I wish I could go as a pilgrim
And see my staff and cloak
Reflected in her lovely eyes!

6   May God, who made what comes or goes
And created this love from afar,
Give me power, for I have the desire
Soon to see this love from afar
Truly, in places so pleasant

That chamber and garden
Will always seem a palace to me.

7   He speaks the truth who says I yearn
     And lust for love from afar,
     For no other joy so pleases me
     As the pleasure of love from afar.
     But the woman I want despises me,
     Since my godfather doomed me
     To love but never to be loved.

8   But the woman I want despises me;
     A curse on the godfather
     Who doomed me never to be loved!

11

Jaufré Rudel

Qan lo rius de la fontana /
When the brook that flows from the spring

This *vers* begins as a love song, with the spring setting that was fast becoming traditional; toward the end it turns to take up the motif of Crusade.

1   When the brook that flows from the spring
     Clears, as it does every year,
     And a flower blooms on the sweetbriar,
     And a nightingale on a branch
     Turns, modulates, smoothes
     And embellishes his sweet song,
     It is right for me to change mine, too.

2   O love from a distant land,
     For you my body aches,
     And I can find no medicine
     Unless I heed your call,
     Seductive with sweet love
     In an orchard or behind a curtain
     With a desired companion.

3   But since I never get a chance
     It's no wonder I'm on fire,
     For a nobler woman has never been,
     Christian, Jew or Saracen,
     Nor does God desire one;
     He is surely fed on manna[1]
     Who gets any of her love!

4   My body always longs
     For the creature I love best,
     But I fear my will betrays me
     If my yearning makes her leave;
     My pain is sharper than a thorn,
     But joy makes it heal,
     So let no one feel sad for me.

---

[1]   Compare the motif of manna in Marcabru's *pastorela* (Poem 13).

5   Without a parchment roll
     I send the song we sing
     In the tongue of plain Romance[2]
     By Filhol to Sir Hugo Bru;[3]
     I'm pleased the people of Poitou,
     Berry and Aquitaine,
     And Brittany rejoice for him.[4]

---

[2] *Lengua romana*, Romance, or vernacular, contrasts with Latin; it is the language of love poetry such as this.

[3] *Filhol* (the word means "Godson") must have been Jaufré's *joglar*, or performer. Hugo *Bru* ("the Swarthy") was probably Hugh VII, count of Lusignan, who went on the Second Crusade in 1147.

[4] Hugh of Lusignan announced his intention of departing on crusade in Bourges, the capital of Berry. The other regions mentioned surround Berry on every side. The poet reports that people everywhere congratulate Hugh for taking the cross.

12

Marcabru

Dire vos vuelh ses duptansa / I wish to speak firmly

Marcabru, the first great satirist in the troubadour tradition, probably came from Gascony, a region that stretches from Bordeaux to the Pyrenees. On the basis of internal evidence his compositions have been dated from 1130 to 1149. His first patron was Guilhem X of Aquitaine, the son of the first known troubadour; later, Marcabru spent time at the Spanish court of King Alfonso VII of Castile and León. He left a varied corpus of over forty songs in which he adopts conspicuously differing personae. The poems that follow illustrate the range of his tone: a tirade against love that is both moralistic and provocative; the earliest known *pastorela*, a dialogue between a rogue and a clever shepherdess who beats him at his own game; a crusade song; and a sympathetic portrayal of a girl who has been abandoned by her lover to go on crusade.

In the first poem, a hallucinatory rant about love, Marcabru seems to wear the mask of a preacher, but his insinuations prove to be erotic. This poem and others by Marcabru would be recalled a half-century later in a poem attributed to Raimon Jordan, but perhaps written by a woman. In that poem the speaker says, "Sir Marcabru spoke like a preacher / In a church or place of prayer / Who reproaches nonbelievers, / And he treated women just the same. / I tell you that there's no great honor / In maligning those who bear the children" (Poem 49, stanza 3).

1   I wish to speak firmly
About the purpose of this poem:
The language makes comparisons.
    Listen!
He who is slow to show prowess
Seems like a man who is gutless.

2   Youth fails, shatters and breaks,
But love is the sort
To start from the jump:
    Listen!
People seize what they can get,
Thinking they will incur no debt.

3   Love spreads like a spark
That mixes with soot,
Burning the wood and the straw.
    Listen!
Whoever gets caught by the fire
Doesn't know where to flee.

4   I'll tell you how love consumes us.
It sings to you; it ogles the other;
It talks to you; it flirts with another.
    Listen!
It will lie straighter than a line
Before you become its friend.

5   Once love lay straight;
Now it is twisted and notched
And has taken on bad habits.
    Listen!

When it cannot bite, it licks
More roughly than a cat.

6   Love has never been true
Since it parted honey from the comb,
But it knows how to peel the pear
    Listen!
Sweetly, like the lyre's song,
If only you stroke its tail.

7   He who strikes a deal with love
Ties his tail to the devil;
If another rod beats him, what does he care?
    Listen!
Nothing to do but scratch your hide
Until you've skinned yourself alive!

8   Love descends from a wicked line;
It has slain many without a sword.
God made no grammarian so smart
    Listen!
That love can't make him a dolt
If it catches him in its trap.[1]

9   Love has the habit of a mare
That yearns all day for a man to come
And mount her, league after league:
    Listen!
It won't offer you a rest
Whether you fast or feast.

10   Do you think that I don't know
If love is blind or has one eye?
It smoothes and polishes its deeds
    Listen!
And stings more softly than a fly,
But healing is harder for a guy.

11   Marcabru, son of Marcabruna,
Was engendered under a moon
That showed love falling, a seed from the husk.
    Listen!
He never truly loved a woman,
Nor has a woman loved him.

12   If a man lives by a woman's wit
It is right that he should suffer for it,
Just as the letter teaches.[2]
    Listen!
To you bad luck may come about
If you don't watch out!

---

[1]   The grammarian in love may refer to Peter Abelard, who died in 1142.

[2]   "Let women be subject to their husbands, as to the Lord: Because the husband is the head of the wife, as Christ is the head of the church. He is the savior of his body. Therefore as the church is subject to Christ: so also let the wives be to their husbands in all things" (Ephesians 5:22–4).

13

Marcabru

L'autrier jost'una sebissa / The other day I found a shepherdess

Marcabru's prototypical *pastorela* is often read in terms of the genre that developed when it was imitated by later poets such as Guiraut Riquier (see Poems 98–103). In its own time, however, it may be seen instead as a rewriting of Guilhem IX's adventure with the two ladies and a cat (Poem 6). Guilhem's narrator seems to recognize his two ladies as fellow aristocrats, but the narrator in Marcabru's poem is puzzled at first by what to make of the shepherdess, who seems, in her clothing both elegant and rustic, "a blend of social class" (*mestissa*).

Slowly, it dawns on him that she is Jewish. In stanza 12 the girl refers to the authority of "the ancient people," the *populum antiquuum* of the Old Testament (Isaiah 44:7). The man understands, and calls her *trefana,* "deceptive," using one of the few Old Occitan words derived from Hebrew. She then refers to the owl, a standard symbol for the Jews in Christian iconography, as a source of augury, and contrasts men who gape at an image—that is, Christians who adore the Cross—with those who pray for manna, as the Jews did in Exodus (16:31). A Jewish shepherdess recalls the shepherds who came to worship the Christ child at the Nativity, in contrast to the three kings, who were considered Christian. To Marcabru's other claims for a unique place among the troubadours may be added that he was perhaps the only one to create an intelligent, charming, and successful Jewish character.[1]

> 1 The other day I found a shepherdess
> Beside a hedge. Witty and full of happiness,
> She seemed a blend of social class.
> The daughter of a peasant woman,
> She wore a fur-lined cloak, a skirt,
> A cape, a coarsely-woven shirt,
> Woolen hose, and shoes.
>
> 2 I went to her across the plain;
> "*Toza,*"[2] I said, "you pretty thing,
> I'm worried that the wind will sting."
> "Sir," the peasant girl replied,
> "Thank God and Nurse, I don't care
> If winds come and blow my hair,
> For I am cheerful and strong."
>
> 3 "*Toza,*" I said, "you sound so pious.
> I have ventured off my path
> To offer you my company;
> A country girl like you can't tend
> So many sheep without a friend
> To serve as your companion
> In such a lonely place."
>
> 4 "Sir," she said, "whoever I am,
> I can tell reason from folly;

[1] See Paden, "Troubadours and Jews."
[2] *Toza* means "young girl" in Occitan. It is the feminine of *tos,* "lad," from Latin *tonsus,* "shaved," hence "shaver, one who has just begun to shave."

As for keeping company,
Sir," replied the peasant girl,
"Let that stay where it belongs.
Some girls think that such a song
Means something, when it's only show."

5 "*Toza*, with your noble demeanor,
He must have been a knight, the father
Who sired you, and your mother
Was clearly an elegant peasant.
The more I look, the prettier you grow;
The pleasure I'd take would make me glow,
If only you'd be human!"

6 "Sir, my conduct and ancestry
Follow the roots of the family tree
Back to the pruner and plow, you see,
And sir," replied the peasant girl,
"Some men act as though they're knights
But should work like them, by all rights,
Six days of the week!"

7 "*Toza*," I said, "a noble fairy
Must have endowed you generously
With grace and beauty
Finer than any peasant girl's;
And surely you'd be twice as fair
If only once we made a pair
With me on top and you below!"

8 "Sir, your praises lift me high,
Raising my worth into the sky,
And now your loving makes me sigh,
Sir," said the peasant girl,
"So you will get your just reward:
Gape wide, you fool, and take the road;
You waste your wait in the noonday sun!"

9 "*Toza*, a heart that's wild and turbulent
Can be tamed with patience;
I know, from passing acquaintance
That with such a peasant girl
A man can have companionship
And a loving relationship,
If one doesn't cheat the other."

10 "Sir, a man who's up to foolish play
Takes oaths and says that he will pay;
It's that kind of homage you throw my way,
Sir," said the peasant girl,
"But not for a paltry entrance fee
Will I trade my virginity
For the name of whore!"

11   "*Toza*, every living creature
Must return to its own nature.
Let us speak with words more graceful,"
I said, "my little peasant girl,
In the shelter by the pasture,
For there you will be safer
To do what is delightful."

12   "Sir, yes—but according to their nature:
A fool cuts a foolish caper,
A courtly man has a courtly venture,
And a peasant, a toss with a *toza*;
All around there's lack of order
For man has lost all measure,
So say the ancient people."

13   "Pretty one, I have never seen
A girl with a saucier look
Or a heart that's more *trefana*."

14   "Sir, the owl gives augury
That one man gapes at an image
While another hopes for manna."

14

Marcabru

Pax in nomine Domini! / Peace in the name of the Lord!

Marcabru's crusade song provides a clear image of crusading ideology. The preacherly persona urges his listeners to cleanse themselves of their sins by taking the cross; in fact, the Pope has offered plenary indulgences for all crusaders. If they refuse, the consequences will be dire. Here, the speaker in the poem threatens his audience with eternal punishment in hell if they fail to regain the Holy Land from the infidel. The date of the song is uncertain; we interpret the text as referring to events of 1137 (see stanza 8 and notes), but some scholars put it as late as 1149.

One manuscript of this poem (R: Paris, Bibliothèque nationale de France, fonds français 22543) introduces this poem with the following rubric:

Here begins a song of Marcabru, who was the first troubadour who ever was.

Scholars generally believe, however, that the first troubadour whose works have come down to us is Guilhem IX (see the headnote to Poem 5), not Marcabru, who was active in the following generation. Apparently, this manuscript promotes Marcabru to the role of pioneer for the sake of creating a moral and religious voice at the origin of troubadour poetry.

> 1 *Peace in the name of the Lord!*[1]
> Marcabru made the words and melody.
>   Hear me: I sing
> How the Lord, heaven's king,
> In his mercy has made for us nearby
> A washing bowl;[2]
> There has never been another
> But Jehoshaphat[3] across the sea
> And this one, the subject of my song.
>
> 2 Everyone knows we should wash ourselves
> In the evening and the morning—
>   I agree;
> We all have leisure to bathe.
> We should journey to the bowl
> While we are hearty and hale,
> For it will cure us of our ills.
> And if we should die before we go,
> We'll dwell not high but down below.
>
> 3 But stingy ways and worldliness
> Divide young people from their faith.
>   It is too bad
> That all want to go

---

[1] *Pax in nomine Domini!* Latin, echoing language in the Bible and the Mass.

[2] The bowl refers to crusade, with its cleansing effect upon the crusader's soul; either crusade in the Holy Land (stanza 4) or in Spain (stanza 7), including Santiago de Compostela (stanza 8).

[3] The valley of Jehoshaphat in the Holy Land is imagined as the scene of the Last Judgment in the Book of Joel (3:2).

43

Where their winnings will send them to hell,
Unless we make haste to the bowl.
Though they close their mouths and shut their eyes,
No one is so puffed with pride
That the Devil won't take him when he dies.

4 For the Lord who knows all that is,
Whatever will be or ever was,
  Has promised us
Honor and the rank of emperor;[4]
Those who go to the bowl
Will shine with beauty (did you know?)
Brighter than light from the morning star
If we avenge God for the terrible wrong
Done in Damascus by Saracens.[5]

5 Just like the lineage of Cain,
The very first of wicked men,
  Many nowadays
Refuse to show respect for God.
We shall see who his true friends are,
For it is the virtue of the bowl
That those who go there share in Christ.
Let us turn the bad ones back
Who believe in omens and fate!

6 Even if wine-swillers and lecherers,
Eager to dine by the fireside,
  And swaybacks on the road
Stay where they are in dreadful stench,
God will test cowards and the brave
In the cauldron of his bowl,
And those who keep themselves at home
Will meet a powerful foe.
They deserve to come to such an end!

7 I know the Marquis[6] is in Spain
With the knights of the Temple of Solomon;[7]
  They bear the weight
And burden of the pagans' pride,
And younger men are put to shame;
And Christ, for the sake of this bowl,
Will drive against the mightiest men,
Broken, craven, drained of daring,
Who love neither joy nor sport.

4 The just are prophesied to rule the earth (Wisdom 3:7–8; Apocalypse 5:9–10).
5 By worshipping the God of Islam.
6 Raymond-Bérenger IV, Marquis of Provence and count of Barcelona from 1131 to 1162.
7 The Templars, an order of crusading knights.

8   The French must be degenerate[8]
To refuse to do the work of God,
    For I know about
Antioch.[9] Here the river Vienne
And Poitou weep for the brave and bold.[10]
Lord God, may you in your bowl
Put to rest the soul of the count,
And may the Lord who rose from the tomb
Protect Poitiers and Niort![11]

[8]   Marcabru complains that the French have not responded quickly to the defeat at Antioch (see below) with a renewal of crusade.

[9]   Antioch in the Holy Land, scene of a Muslim victory in 1136 against Raymond, prince of Antioch, who was the younger son of Guilhem IX of Aquitaine, the troubadour.

[10] Guilhem X of Aquitaine, elder son of the first troubadour, died in 1137 while on pilgrimage to Santiago de Compostela, the washing bowl specifically intended in this stanza. On the death of Guilhem X see also Cercamon (Poem 16).

[11] Guilhem X, like his father before him, was count of Poitou and its capital, Poitiers; Niort was one of the chief cities of the county.

15

Marcabru

A la fontana del vergier /
Near the stream in the garden

Here Marcabru creates the appealing character of a young woman who is distraught because
her lover has left her to go on crusade. In stanza 4 she curses King Louis VII of France, the
husband of Eleanor of Aquitaine, for summoning men to crusade in 1146, in preparation
for departure in 1147. Some readers have understood the poem as implicit praise for the
fidelity of women whose lovers left them behind. It may be taken more straightforwardly as
expressing doubts about the crusading ideal.

1   Near the stream in the garden
On the green and grassy bank,
In the shade of an orchard plum,
Bursting with white blossoms
And the new old song of birds,
I found alone, with no companion,
The girl who spurns my affection.

2   She was alluring and fair,
The daughter of a castle lord,
And just when I thought the birds
And green leaves would cheer her,
And the sweet new season
Would make her hear me,
Suddenly her manner changed.

3   She wept beside the stream
And sighed deeply from within.
"Jesus," she said, "King of the world,
Because of you my pain grows deep;
Your battles in the Holy Land
Ravage my life, for the best men
Are serving you, as you command.

4   "My lover goes to be with you,
Handsome, gentle, noble, strong,
And I am left in great distress,
With longing, love, and tears.
Curses on King Louis,
For sending the summons
That pierces my heart!"

5   When I heard her grieving,
I walked toward her by the clear water.
"Pretty one," I said, "too much weeping
Will stain your face and lovely color;
Try not to fall into despair,
For he who makes the woods leaf out
Can give you plenty of joy."

6   "Sir," said she, "I well believe
That God will have mercy on me
As he has had on sinners before,
In heaven, many and evermore;
But here on earth he sends afar
The man who loved me and does not care
Now that he has gone away!"

16

Cercamon

Lo plaing comenz iradamen / In grief I begin this lament

Cercamon's name, which means "He searches the world," probably refers to the itinerant life of a *joglar*, or minstrel. His poems allude to events from 1137 to 1144 or later. Although his *vida* says he was a Gascon and Marcabru's teacher, scholars suspect that it was Marcabru who taught him instead. We have no reliable evidence on his place of origin.

This song is a lament for the death of Guilhem X of Aquitaine, the son of the first troubadour, who died during a pilgrimage to Compostela in 1137. Toward the end the lamentation for the dead evolves into praise and blame of his survivors. Among later troubadours the song became a model for the genre of the *planh*; it is a proto-*planh* but not a member of the genre itself, since the genre was not yet constituted at the time it was written.

Marcabru, too, grieved for the death of Guilhem, but did so in a song that principally concerns crusade (Poem 14). Compare also the song of Azalais de Porcairagues (Poem 27), in which she laments the death of Raimbaut d'Aurenga in 1173, even as she sings her love for another man. A later parallel is the *planh* of Sordel for Blacatz (Poem 90), which pretends to be a funeral lament but is actually an extended *sirventés*, or satire. Cercamon's song is identified in its first stanza as a *vers*, simply a lyric song.

1   In grief I begin this lament,
A song that saddens my heart;
I feel grief and sorrow and anguish,
For I see Youth fade,
Joy diminish, and Evil rise
Since the count of Poitou died.

2   The honor and glory have ceased
That once flowed from Poitou.
Oh, how the men of Bar[1] lament!
I am sorry to linger long in the world.
Lord God, if it pleases you, place
The baron I sing in Paradise.

3   I grieve for the count of Poitou,
Who was the comrade of Prowess;
Now that Merit and Giving have failed,
I am sad to dwell so long in the world.
Lord God, keep him far from hell,
For he had a noble end.

4   Glorious God, I cry to you,
For you take the ones I love.
You who created Adam,
Keep the count from the cruel grip
Of hell-fire; don't let him burn,
For the world leads us all astray.

5   I think this world my enemy.
It respects neither rich nor poor;

---

[1]   Those of Bar-sur-Seine in Burgundy, where Guilhem held fiefs.

All my friends are passing away,
And we who remain are wretched,
But I know that the bad and good
Will part at the true commitment.[2]

6   Courtly Gascons, widely famed,
You have lost his lordship.
You must find it harsh and cruel,
And Youth proclaims its misery
Since it finds no one to protect it
But Alfonso, who brought his followers joy.[3]

7   Normans and French mourn for him;
King Louis grieves for him too,
For he left him his land and his child.[4]
Such great honor has come to the king
He'll be put to shame if he doesn't appear
Riding against the Saracens.[5]

8   Men of Angoulême and Limousin[6]
Rejoice, and do not care who weeps.
If he had lived and God had pleased
He would soon have conquered them,
But God took him and they went free,
And grief has spread throughout Aunis.[7]

9   Cercamon sends this mournful song
With its worthy theme to Sir Ebló;[8]
Oh, how the Gascons grieve,
And the men of Aragon and Spain!
Saint James,[9] please remember the baron
Who lies before you as a pilgrim.

[2]   The last judgment.
[3]   Perhaps Alfonso VII of Castile, who ruled from 1126 to 1157.
[4]   The child was Eleanor of Aquitaine, left as a ward of King Louis VI of France.
[5]   Cercamon challenges Louis VI, now that he has gained Aquitaine, to use his resources in a crusade against the Muslims in Spain.
[6]   The regions around Angoulême and Limoges were frequently restive.
[7]   A region on the coast north of Bordeaux that was obedient to Guilhem.
[8]   Ebló, viscount of Ventadorn, an early troubadour (contemporary of Guilhem IX) whose works are lost.
[9]   Saint James (*Santiago*) of Compostela, the pilgrimage destination in northwestern Spain where Guilhem X of Aquitaine died.

17

Cercamon

Puois nostre temps comens'a brunezir / Since our season is turning dark

Cercamon begins this *vers* with an autumnal setting that prompts him to sing, by contrast, of love, but then he turns to gloomy feelings about the decline of poetry and society. At the end he cheers himself with the thought of his lady—in stanza 7 his joy of love turns green, or renews itself—and of the imminent crusade in which men could win indulgences for their sins. The song combines elements that would later become the specialized subjects of the *cansó*, or love song; the *sirventés*, or satire; and the crusade song.

1   Since our season is turning dark
And the branches have lost their leaves,
And I see that the rays of the sun are low
And shadows fill our days,
And we no hear no more bird songs or lays,
We must rejoice in the joy of love.

2   No matter how you serve this love
It will pay you back a thousandfold.
To those who do it well
Come honor and joy and all;
This love never lied or broke its word,
But I think it will be hard to win.

3   This love compels you to hope and try,
Since the prize is so heady and great;
It has no regard for those without taste,
For the stingy rich or the poor who are proud.
In more than a thousand there are not two
So true that they can win pure love.

4   These troubadours, with their truths and lies,
Bewilder the lovers and husbands and wives;
When they say that love is oblique,
They send husbands into a jealous pique;
They make the wives get thoughts in their heads,
And people are glad to hear what they've said.

5   These false minstrels[1] make people lose Merit
And Youth recoil in fright.
We may not ever see Prowess again,
For Stinginess stole the barons' keys
And locked them in the City of Decline,
And Depravity sets none free.

6   I see the world going into decline,
Which troubles me and makes me depressed,
For a worker[2] finds none to pay his wage

[1] *Sirven*, servants or minstrels, as in *sirventés*, the genre of songs sung by servants or minstrels, which will become the genre of social satire.
[2] *Soldadiers* will later mean "mercenary soldiers" and, eventually, simply "soldiers." But originally

Because of gossips with wicked tongues,
More evil than Judas, who bartered Christ.
They should be burned and buried alive!

7   We cannot scold them or change their ways,
So let us leave them. May God help us!
The joy of love returns for me,
And beauty I've not known before;
I see her little, but she makes me happy
And merry. May God let me rejoice!

8   Now we can wash and cleanse ourselves
Of heavy blame; if stained by sin,
To Edessa[3] we must make our way,
And leave the perils of the world;
By going we can put down the load
That makes men stumble, fall, and die![4]

9   I have made my song, and it won't grow old,
And neither will the theme I chose;
For good love never betrays or deceives,
But instead brings joy to all the bold.

10   Cercamon says: If it's anger you feel toward love
It's a wonder if passion survives,
For anger toward love becomes fear of loss,
Which lets you neither live nor die.

it meant "men who work for a wage," for *solidi*, Latin coins. Since Henry II was the first monarch who employed mercenary soldiers systematically, it seems that in Cercamon the word may mean "working men," including poets or minstrels who sang for wages. Nasty gossips (the *lauzengiers*) could damage the minstrels' trade with their slanders about love.

3   Edessa fell to Muslim forces in 1144, setting in motion the Second Crusade (1147–9). On the motif of cleansing oneself by crusade, compare Marcabru (Poem 14).

4   Those who took the cross were rewarded with indulgences for their sins.

18

Bernart Martí

Bel m'es lai latz la fontana / I like it near the fountain

We know little about Bernart Martí.[1] His poems do not provide traces of local dialect, nor do they enable us to date their composition; there is no *vida*. He is thought to have lived in the mid-twelfth century. A citation of the *pastorela* that he makes in our selection (stanza 3), along with his reference elsewhere to the *Vers del lavador*, the "Song of the Washing Bowl" (Poem 14), makes it clear that he admired Marcabru.

This song echoes Marcabru in its setting and vocabulary, but achieves memorable effects of its own.

1   I like it near the fountain:
Green grass and the song of a frog,
    How it strives
    On the sand
All night, when storms don't come;
And the nightingale starts his song
Under a leaf, on the branch;
    Under a flower I take pleasure
    In sweet and secret love.

2   A lady is perfidious
If she feeds three men with her love;
    Three
    Breaks the rules.
Along with her husband, I permit her
One courtly, worthy lover;
If she looks for more,
    I say she is dishonored,
    A proven whore!

3   But if her lover deceives her first
(Deception may bloom, but bears no seed),
    Let her trick him
    Without mercy,
And take care not to ruin herself![2]
If a man is false to his mistress
He deserves to be betrayed,
    Since he betrayed her first;
    So, "Gape wide, you fool!"[3]

4   God would have given me luck
In love, if only he'd made it easy;
    I caress,
    I woo,
No man likes it more!

---

[1]   *Martí* is the Occitan form of the name Martin.
[2]   By taking an unworthy lover.
[3]   The line repeats one from Marcabru's *pastorela* (Poem 13, stanza 8).

My heart is far from empty
Of love, when I take leave
    Of my beloved,
    But she is too far away.

5   She looks so shapely and slim
In her blouse of silk from Reims!
    When I see her,
    Good God!
I feel no envy of kings
Or counts,
For I get my way better than they
    When I undress her
    Behind a crewelled curtain.

6   I had set my heart on another love
Nearby, and it was sweet,
    But I dropped it
    Before doing damage,
Trusting the better won't trick me.
The sparrowhawk in graceful flight
Soars from the hill toward her;
    Freed from its leash,
    That's where it goes.[4]

7   A strong rein and halter
Are woolen threads to me
    (Some doubt it
    But it's true),
And so are a bridle and cinch.
Thus I go, weaving words
And refining tunes, as tongues
    In a kiss
    Entwine.

[4]   Compare the image of the hawk in Poem 4.

19

Peire d'Alvernhe

Rossinhol, el seu repaire / Nightingale, please go see

This native of Auvergne was active from 1149 to 1168. His earliest datable poems are the two that we translate, telling a fanciful adventure of a nightingale They were parodied by Marcabru, whom Peire admired. We know Peire traveled to Spain; he may have been the son of a burgher. The earliest troubadour to be cited by Dante (*De Vulgari Eloquentia*, 1.10), he was also mentioned by Petrarch (*Triumphus Cupidinis*, 4.48).[1]

1   "Nightingale, please go see
My lady in her home;
Tell her my concern,
And ask her to speak to you truly,
     And send me word
     How she is,
And ask her to think of me;
     Whatever she says,
     Don't let her
Keep you with her over there—

2   "Or keep you from bringing me
News of her and what she's doing,
For I have no family
I care about so deeply."
     The happy bird
     Goes away
Straight to where she lives,
     Diligently,
     Fearlessly,
Searching for her sign.[2]

3   When the well-born little bird
Saw her beauty shining,
He warbled, sweetly singing
As he does every evening;
     Then he fell silent,
     Sang no more,
Thought of her,
     How to tell
     Effectively
What she'd deign to hear.

4   "He who is your lover true
Has asked me to come to you
And here at your home to sing
In a way that would please you;

---

[1]   See Dante Alighieri, *De Vulgari Eloquentia*, ed. and trans. Steven Botterill (Cambridge: Cambridge University Press, 1996); Francesco Petrarca, *Trionfi, rime estravaganti, codice degli abbozzi*, ed. Vinicio Pacca and Laura Paolino (Milano: Mondadori, 1996).

[2]   *Ensenha*, "sign," perhaps "coat of arms," "address": Cf. *entresenha*, "secret sign," in stanza 4.

I shall learn
When I see
Your secret sign;
And I shall tell him
Once I know,
How he may dream.

5   "If my message brings him cheer,
You too should be happy,
For no man born of mother
Could love you more than he;
I shall go
And I shall die
Of joy, wherever I may be;
—No, I won't,
Not yet at least,
For I've not said what pact he seeks.

6   "This is what I plead:
If you put your hope in love
Do not hold back
When love has a chance,
For soon white
Falls over blond,
Like a flower on the branch;
It's a better plan
To do the deed
Before you change."

20

Peire d'Alvernhe

Ben ha tengut dreg viatge / The bird went straight

1   The bird went straight
    Where I had sent him,
    And she sent a message back,
    Responding to my plan:
            "I want you to know
            The way you speak
        Pleases me;
            So hear me,
            And tell your master
        My concerns.

2   "To me it's brutal
    That my lover has gone,
    For I never saw joy in any form
    That could so satisfy me;
            Our leave-taking
            Came too soon;
        If I were sure of him
            I would be
            More friendly;
        My doubts make me sad.

3   "I love him so deeply
    That always when I fall into sleep
    I go in his company
    To laughter, play, and joy;
            And the pleasure
            We take in silence
        No soul can know,
            As long as he lies
            In my arms
        Until he vanishes.

4   "I've always found him pleasing
    Since first I saw him and before;
    I wouldn't want to win the love
    Of one from higher lineage.
            This fantasy
            Is well made:
        It shelters me
            From wind and sleet
            And summer,
        From heat and cold.

5   "Good love has its ways:
    Like good gold that's refined,

It gleams with goodness
When its care is good;
So be sure
That love
Gets better every day;
One is bettered
And beloved
When gilded with joy.

6   "Sweet bird, please fly
To his home when morning comes,
And in plain words tell him
How obedient I am."[1]
Swiftly
He returned,
Well schooled
In surprising verses
And eloquent
With this great good news.

---

[1] Compare Guilhem IX of Aquitaine, *Pos vezem de novel florir / Since we see blooming again*,
stanza 5: "No man will ever be really true / To love, if he does not submit to it / And if, to
strangers and neighbors, / He is not accommodating, / And to all those of that dwelling /
Obedient." Riquer, *Trovadores*, no. 3; vol. I, p. 121; *The Poetry of William VII, Count of Poitiers,
IX Duke of Aquitaine*, ed. Gerald A. Bond (New York: Garland Publishing, 1982), no. 7. p. 28.

Summer

1150–1200

THE second half of the twelfth century saw some of the greatest poets among the troubadours, including Bernart de Ventadorn and the Comtessa de Dia for the love song, and Bertran de Born for satire. Bernart de Ventadorn and Bertran de Born were from the West, as most of their predecessors had been, and so were others such as Rigaut de Berbezilh, Giraut de Bornelh, Arnaut Daniel, Gaucelm Faidit, Maria de Ventadorn, Gui d'Ussel, and Peire Vidal. But the mode of troubadour poetry spread east to Provence with Raimbaut d'Aurenga (Orange) early in the half-century, and with Raimbaut de Vaqueiras later on. The first known woman troubadour, or trobairitz, was Azalais de Porcairagues, a friend of Raimbaut d'Aurenga whose home was near Béziers. The best-known trobairitz, the Comtessa de Dia, was from Die in northern Provence. Alfonso, the count of Barcelona, who became king of Aragon and count of Provence, also wrote Occitan songs, as did a lesser Catalan nobleman, Guillem de Berguedà.

Many of these poets traveled widely: Arnaut Daniel to Reims for the coronation of Philip Augustus, Giraut de Bornelh to Spain, Gaucelm Faidit to Romania, and Peire Vidal to the Holy Land on pilgrimage, to Hungary for a royal wedding, and to Malta on crusade. The Monk of Montaudon, in Auvergne, pretended in a song to have visited God in Paradise.

Figure 3. Ruins of the castle of Ventadour (in Occitan: Ventadorn) near the village of Moustier-Ventadour, arrondissement of Tulle, department of Corrèze. The round tower in the foreground dates from the thirteenth century; behind it, the remains of a chimney from the square tower of the fifteenth. The castle was the home of the troubadour Bernart de Ventadorn (Poems 28 to 32). According to his *vida* (our Selection 87) Bernart was the son of servants, but it seems more likely that he was the son of Viscount Eble III of Ventadour, who died in 1169. Maria de Ventadorn, who participated in a *partimen* with Gui d'Ussel (Poem 57), was the wife of Viscount Eble V of Ventadour. She retired with her husband to a cloister in 1221. (Photograph courtesy of Luc de Goustine)

21

Rigaut de Berbezilh

Atressi con l'orifanz / Like an elephant that falls

Rigaut de Berbezilh was probably a knight from Barbezieux, located in the department of Charentes, northeast of Bordeaux. Historical documents containing his name date from 1141 to around 1160. He made a specialty of interesting similes.

1   Like an elephant that falls,
    And cannot get up
    Until others with their cries
    Raise him to his feet again,
    So will it be with me;
    My offense is so heavy, so weighty,
    That unless the court of Le Puy,[1] and the pomp
    And merit of so many lovers can help me,
    I shall never get back on my feet;
    I beg them to beseech my lady,
    Or I shall never have her mercy.

2   And if the help of these lovers
    Fails to restore my pleasure,
    I shall leave my song forever.
    There is nothing else to do;
    I shall turn into a hermit,
    Alone and lonely—that's what I want,
    For my life is toil and torment.
    My joy is grief; my pleasure, pain.
    I am not like a bear that you can mistreat
    And beat without mercy, while he goes on getting
    Stronger and fatter, coming back for more.

3   I am sure that Love is so great
    That she could easily forgive
    If I erred by too much love,
    And acted like the magus[2]
    Who said that he was Jesus
    And tried in his pride to fly through the sky
    Until God brought his audacity down.
    My pride was nothing but love, that's why
    Mercy should come to my aid;
    Sometimes mercy is won by reason,
    But sometimes reason means nothing.

4   To all the world I make complaint
    Against myself and too much talk;
    If only I could imitate

---

[1]   The court at Le Puy, in the region of Velay (department of Haute-Loire), was also mentioned by Bernart Martí among other troubadours.

[2]   *Lo Magus*, Simon Magus, or "The Magician," was a first-century heretic who became legendary as a false Messiah. Some manuscripts read *Dedalus* or *Icarus*.

The phoenix, unique among its kind,
That burns itself up and is born again,
I'd set myself on fire for being such a fool
Speaking false words, deceptive and untrue;
I'd rise up again, sighing and weeping,
Beseeching the lady with beauty, youth,
And nobility. She only needs a little mercy
To have every good quality.

5   My song will be my spokesman
Where I don't dare to go
Or look straight into her eyes;
I'm so overcome and humbled,
I don't deserve a pardon.
Better-than-Lady, for two years I've fled
But return to you now, weeping, heartbroken,
Like the stag who turns back after making his run,
Facing the cries of the hunters, to die;
So I turn, lady, beseeching your mercy;
But you will not care, if you don't think of love.

6   My lord has within him so much good
That thinking of him, I cannot do wrong.

7   Handsome Beryl, dwelling in joy and fame,
I have all that I want when I think of your name.

Rögnvald, Earl of Orkney

Víst's, at frá berr flestum / For certain, wise girl

According to the Old Norse *Orkneyinga Saga*, or *Saga of the Earls of Orkney*, Rögnvald (the name corresponds to Ronald), who ruled this archipelago off the Scottish coast until his death in 1158, made a pilgrimage to the Holy Land. On the way he stopped in Narbonne, where he met Ermengarde, the young viscountess who had inherited the town on the death of her father. Ermengarde's followers suggested she marry Rögnvald. The saga describes a flirtation between them, but they did not marry. Nevertheless Rögnvald, who was an accomplished poet, composed skaldic stanzas in praise of her beauty.

If the saga is reliable in this episode, the events in Narbonne occurred in 1151. The historical Ermengarde was about twenty-two years old at that time; she had inherited the viscounty at about the age of four, and she had married when she was about fourteen (and perhaps, briefly, a first time before that), but by 1151 her husband had either disappeared (and the marriage been dissolved) or died, so, if we regard the saga as a historical source, as it appears to be, Ermengarde was marriageable when Rögnvald came to Narbonne. She would go on to rule the city in her own name for more than forty years, until her nephew usurped power in her old age.

In this, the first of Rögnvald's poems on Ermengarde in Old Norse, he compliments her on her hair, which flows like a river. He compares her favorably to other aristocratic women who wear golden tassels. Gold is "sea-king's corn," not the harvest of a farmer but that of a Viking like Rögnvald. Ermengarde is "the prop of a hawk's perch," the support of a hawker's arm, the helper of a sporting nobleman. Rögnvald depicts himself as one who appreciates both the red blood drawn by a falcon and the golden, silky hair of this beautiful girl. She is wise; he is a poet. She is like a flood; he sails the sea. The lovers glow with intelligence, vigor, and beauty.

> For certain, wise girl,
> Your flowing hair
> Is the loveliest among women
> Well tasseled with sea-kings' corn.
> The prop of a hawk's perch
> Permits her hair to fall to her shoulders—
> I reddened the claws of a ravenous hawk[1]—
> Golden, like silk.

---

[1] That is, I succeeded in the hunt; my hawk made a kill. The falcon seizes its prey in its claws, wounding and tearing it; see Frederick II Hohenstaufen, *The Art of Falconry, Being the De arte venandi cum avibus*, trans. Casey A. Wood and F. Marjorie Fyfe (Stanford: Stanford University Press, 1943), p. 627.

Raimbaut d'Aurenga

Ar resplan la flors enversa / Now shines the flower inverted

Raimbaut, count of Orange (north of Avignon, in the department of Vaucluse), died in 1173, perhaps at about the age of twenty-nine.[1] His will, which survives, shows that he was unmarried and left no legitimate children. His more than forty poems are marked by strong character, intelligence, and wit.

Writing this song in the style called *rim ric* or "rich rhyme," Raimbaut chooses difficult and unpoetic rhyme words, and then repeats the same words at the rhyme, in the same order, in every stanza, with a surprising and lively effect. Later it would occur to Arnaut Daniel to vary the order of the chosen rhyme words in a systematic permutation that produced the sestina (Poem 52).

1   Now shines the flower inverted
        Among sharp rocks and hills.
        What flower? Snow and ice and frost
        That sting and bind and cut,
        Killing cries and coos, calls and whistles[2]
        Among leaves, branches and shoots;
      But I rejoice, staying green[3] with joy,
      For I see blinded the wicked wantons.

2   Everything looks to me inverted:
        Valleys seem to me like hills,
        And I see a flower instead of frost
        And I feel that cold by heat is cut
        And thunder sounds like songs and whistles,
        And I see leaves on every shoot;
      I am so tightly bound in joy
      That nothing to me seems wanton—

3   Except for a bunch of rascals inverted,
        As though they were raised in the hills,
        Who hurt me more than hoarfrost,
        For each uses his tongue to cut,
        Speaking low, in whistles;
        Clubs don't help, or shoots
      Or threats, for it brings them joy
      To do what people call wanton.

4   If I don't give you a kiss inverted,
        Lady, it's not the plains or hills
        That prevent me, or ice or frost;
        But I find instead that impotence cuts
        Me off, Lady, and makes me whistle;
        Your pretty eyes to me are shoots

---

[1] The medieval name was pronounced in three syllables, *Ra-im-baut*. It corresponds to modern French *Rimbaud*.

[2] Winter quiets the cries of birds.

[3] That is, young.

That so whip my heart into joy
That I don't dare be mean or wanton.

5   I have gone about like a creature inverted
For some time now, searching vales and hills,
Wounded like one whom frost
Tortures and chops and cuts,
No more won by songs and whistles
Than a cleric is won by shoots.[4]
But now, thank God, I dwell in joy,
In spite of those lying, wicked wantons.

6   Let my verse travel inverted,
Not held back by valleys or hills,
Down to where none feel the frost
And cold has no power to cut.
To my lady may a minstrel sing and whistle
So clear that her heart will feel the shoots;
May he know how to sing with a kind of joy
That does not suit a singer who's wanton.

7   Sweet lady, love and joy
Keep us together despite the wantons.

8   *Joglar*,[5] I am having less joy,
For since I don't see you, I feel wanton.

---

[4] Raimbaut says that he did not love at first, any more than a priest turns amorous in springtime.

[5] "Minstrel"; apparently a secret name, or *senhal*, for a lady. For Pattison, a confidante; for Riquer, the word refers to Azalais de Porcairagues. See *The Life and Works of the Troubadour Raimbaut d'Orange*, ed. Walter T. Pattison (Minneapolis: University of Minnesota Press, 1952), p. 224; Riquer, *Trovadores*, vol. I, pp. 421–2.

24

Raimbaut d'Aurenga

Escotatz, mas no say que s'es / Listen! I don't know what it is

The vein of whimsical humor initiated by Guilhem IX in *Farai un vers de dreit nien / I'll make a verse about nothing at all* (Poem 7) continues here in the work of another lord, perhaps a half century later. Raimbaut turns the point of his wit against himself and his song even as he sings it. By breaking out of verse form entirely at the end of each stanza, he anticipates what would be called much later the "talking blues," in which the lyrics "are articulated in a rhythm approaching that of speech" (*Oxford English Dictionary*, 2nd ed.).

1   Listen! I don't know what it is,
    Lords, that I'm trying to start.
    Vers, estribot, sirventés,[1] it's not,
    And I cannot think what to call it;
    As for getting it done, I'm out of ideas
    Until I know how to complete it.
No one has seen such an attempt by a man or woman, not in this century nor in the last.

2   Although you may think it is folly
    I could not let it go
    Without telling the thoughts that come to me;
    No one ought to scold.
    I don't give a penny from Le Puy[2]
    For things in the world that I cannot see,
And I'll tell you why: if I started this for you and didn't finish, you would take me for a fool; I'd rather have six pennies in hand than a thousand sous[3] in the sky.

3   I beg my friends, don't be afraid
    Ever to disappoint me,
    If they won't help me right away,
    As they've offered to do eventually.
    No one can more easily trick me
    Than those who have conquered me.
I say all this for the sake of a lady who makes me languish with pretty words and long delays, and I don't know why. Can this be good for me, my lords?

4   It has been more than four months now,
    Yes, and it seems a thousand years
    Since she promised me and took a vow
    To give me what I hold most dear.

[1] A *vers* or song, like Guilhem IX's *Farai un vers de dreit nien* (Poem 7); the *estribot* is an obscure genre, perhaps involving use of a refrain; a *sirventés* is a moral or satirical song.

[2] A penny minted at Le Puy. Several troubadours mention a court that was held at Le Puy in Raimbaut's time.

[3] *Sols*, punning on "suns" and "sous," the coin.

Lady, sweeten my bitterness with love[4]
Since you hold my heart prisoner.
God, help, in the name of the Father and the Son and the Holy Spirit![5]
Lady, when will it be?

5 For your sake I am happy, then full of grief;
You make me compose, either joyful or sad;
I have taken my leave from three other women
Who, but for you, have no equal;
I'm so crazy a courtly singer
That they call me a minstrel.
Lady, you can do with me as you like, as did Lady Aima with the ladle,
who poked it where she pleased.[6]

6 Now I've finished my "Don't-Know-What,"
As I've decided to christen it;
Since I haven't heard such a thing yet,
That's the name I'll call it.
If someone wants to learn it by heart
He's welcome to perform it,
And if they ask him who wrote it, he can say that it was someone who
knows how to do whatever he desires.

---

[4] Punning on *l'amar*, which means both "the bitter" and "the loving."
[5] Raimbaut uses the ecclesiastical formula in Latin: *In nomine patris et filii et spiritus sancti.*
[6] The episode of Lady Aima and the ladle (if it was a ladle and not a shoulder-bone or a shoulder or a sword, and if the lady was not a lord) was celebrated by several troubadours, including Arnaut Daniel. Raimbaut provides the essential elements.

25

Raimbaut d'Aurenga and Giraut de Bornelh

Era.m platz, Giraut de Bornelh / Now I'd be pleased, Giraut de Bornelh

In this celebrated *tensó* or debate, Raimbaut defends the hermetic style called *trobar clus*, literally "closed composition," as in his Poem 23 and later in the work of Arnaut Daniel (Poems 50 to 53). Giraut de Bornelh champions the *trobar leu*, the "light" or "easy" style. The poem was written shortly before Christmas (stanza 9), perhaps in 1170.

1 *Raimbaut*
Now I'd be pleased, Giraut de Bornelh,
To know why you criticize
Trobar clus, and for what reason.
  Please explain,
  Since you so esteem
What all poets have in common;
In your view, they'd all be the same.

2 *Giraut*
Sir Linhaura,[1] I don't complain
If people compose as they like.
But in my judgment
  One is more loved
  And more esteemed
When he makes his song easy and light;
I hope you get my meaning right.

3 *Raimbaut*
Giraut, I do not want my work
To turn into a muddle; it is praised
By good men, both great and small.
  But the fools
  Will never praise it,
For they don't know or care
What is thought to be worthy and dear.

4 *Giraut*
Linhaura, if their thinking cost me sleep
And turned my days to torment,
It would seem I feared acclaim;
  Why do you compose,
  If you don't want
Everyone to know your tunes?
Singing brings no other gain.

5 *Raimbaut*
Giraut, if I prepare only my best
And bring it forth and sing it,
What do I care if it doesn't catch on?

---

[1] A poetic name for Raimbaut d'Aurenga: *linha aura*, "golden lineage," punning on his name and referring to his noble birth.

Never has ordinary fare
Been a dainty dish;
That is why gold[2] is worth more than salt,
And it is the same with song.

6   *Giraut*
Linhaura, you are so sure of yourself,
And as a lover so perverse
You cause me real anguish.
        As for my lofty song,
        Let a man with a stuffy nose
Garble it and sing it badly;
I have no desire to give it to the rich.

7   *Raimbaut*
Giraut, for the sake of the sky, the sun,
Or the light that shines,
I don't know what we're talking about,
        Or even where I was born.
        I get rattled
When natural joy gives rise to my thought;
But when not, my songs don't come from the heart.

8   *Giraut*
Linhaura, the lady I love
Shows me the red of her shield,[3]
And I say, God help me!
        What foolish,
        Outrageous thoughts
My presumption has caused me!
Did she not bring me nobility?

9   *Raimbaut*
Giraut, I'm sorry, by Saint Martial,
That you're leaving us at Noel.

10   *Giraut*
Linhaura, I'm headed for a royal court,
One that is mighty and great.

---

2   *Aur*, punning on his own name.
3   She defends herself against him.

26

Anonymous Trobairitz (perhaps Azalais de Porcairagues) and Raimbaut d'Aurenga

Amics, en gran cossirier /
My friend, I'm in anguish

This dialogue, or *tensó*, involves an anonymous woman poet who exchanges stanzas with Raimbaut d'Aurenga. Since Raimbaut died in 1173, this may be the earliest surviving text by a trobairitz. She has sometimes been identified on dubious grounds as the Comtessa de Dia, but the Comtessa seems to have lived later. It is also possible that the lady is a fictional character and that Raimbaut wrote the entire poem, which is attributed to him alone in the manuscripts. Perhaps the most attractive identification would be Azalais de Porcairagues, who lamented for the death of Raimbaut (see Poem 27) as she might have done if she knew him from poetic exchanges, such as this one.

1   *Lady*
　　　　My friend, I'm in anguish
　　　　Over you, and in great pain,
　　　　But I don't believe you care
　　　　About my suffering.
　　　　So why pretend to be a lover,
　　　If you leave all the grief to me?
　　　Why don't we share it equally?

2   *Raimbaut*
　　　　Lady, this is how love is:
　　　　When it chains two friends together,
　　　　They share the joy and share the pain;
　　　　That's what love demands.
　　　　But I believe, and it's no boast,
　　　That I have had the heartache
　　　On my side, though it's for your sake.

3   *Lady*
　　　　My friend, if you had a quarter
　　　　Of the heartache that troubles me,
　　　　You would know how bad I feel,
　　　　But you don't care about my hurt;
　　　　Even though I can't escape it,
　　　To you it's all the same
　　　Even if I lose the game.

4   *Raimbaut*
　　　　Lady, these gossiping fools
　　　　Have taken my wit and breath away;
　　　　I give up, not merely on a whim,
　　　　But because they're your sworn enemies.
　　　　I'm not at your side because their din
　　　Has assaulted you in deadly ways,
　　　And we cannot enjoy delightful days.

5   *Lady*

     My friend, I give you no thanks
     Because my hurt, you say, prevents you
     From seeing me, as I ask you to.
     But if you decide to protect me
     From hurt more fiercely than I want,
I will think that you're far more loyal
Than the noble knights of the Hospital.[1]

6   *Raimbaut*

     Lady, I am very afraid
     That I lose gold while you lose sand.[2]
     Because the words of tattletales
     Have turned our love to quarrystones,
     I must be always on my guard
Much more than you, by Saint Martial,[3]
Since you're the dearest one of all.

7   *Lady*

     My friend, I know you're fickle
     In matters of the heart;
     Though once you were a steady knight,
     Now you're nothing but a changer,[4]
     And I really have to tell you so
Since your mind seems to be elsewhere,
And you seem so cool to my despair.

8   *Raimbaut*

     Lady, may I never carry a hawk
     Or go hunting with a falcon
     If ever, since you gave me joy,
     I've pursued another woman;
     I'm no such deceiver,
But out of envy, lying schemers
Accuse me to blacken my name.

9   *Lady*

My friend, can I really believe you,
That you'll always be faithful and true?

10   *Raimbaut*

Lady, I will be so faithful to you
That I won't even think of anyone new.

---

[1]   Knights of the order of the Hospital in Jerusalem, a crusading monastic order.
[2]   A clever compliment, saying that he loses gold in her while she loses sand in him, with a double pun on his name: *aur*, "gold"; *arena*, "sand"; *Aurenga*.
[3]   Bishop of Limoges in the third century, believed to have been able to raise the dead to life.
[4]   Pun on *camjayre*, "changeable, fickle," but also "changer, one who changes money." To appreciate the vigor of this insult, compare the episode in Chrétien de Troyes's *Story of the Grail* in which Gawain is treated as a mere merchant, a horse-trader. Raimbaut responds by stressing his noble lifestyle.

27

Azalais de Porcairagues

Ar em al freg temps vengut / Now we've come to the cold time

We have only one poem attributed to Azalais of Porcairagues (today Portiragues near Béziers, in the department of Hérault), though she may have been the anonymous lady in the *tensó* with Raimbaut d'Aurenga (Poem 26). In English her name corresponds to Alice. She blends themes of death and love, grieving for the death of Raimbaut d'Aurenga even as she rejoices in the love of her lover. Since Raimbaut died in 1173, we can date the song in that year. Azalais is the earliest known trobairitz.

1 Now we've come to the cold time
   With frost and snow and mud.
   Little birds have fallen mute,
   Their summer songs have stopped;
   The hedges slowly lose their sap,
   No flower or leaf in bud;
   Nor do I hear the nightingale sing
   That stirs my soul in May.

2 I have taken a terrible blow
   That makes me feel bereft.
   Now I know we lose
   More often than we win;
   If I trip when speaking truth,
   My grief began in Aurenga.[1]
   It makes me stand astonished,
   My joy, diminished.

3 A lady in league with a powerful man,
   With anyone more than a vassal,
   Treats true love with abandon
   And lives the life of a fool;
   For as they say in Le Velay,[2]
   Love doesn't mix with money;
   And I say a lady who loves for wealth
   Is no better than a peasant.

4 My love is a man of great appeal
   Who rises above the others;
   He is no false deceiver,
   But gives his love to me.
   I say my heart belongs to him,
   And should someone deny it,
   God let fall the worst of luck!
   For good luck lies in loving.

5 O handsome man, I am pleased
   To be in league with you;
   I shall be sweet and welcoming

---

[1] Raimbaut d'Aurenga died in 1173, perhaps of influenza.
[2] The area around Le Puy, in Auvergne.

As long as we're discrete;
Soon will come a test
When I hand you my trust;
You gave me your word
To ask for nothing more.

6   To God I commend Belesgar[3]
And the city of Aurenga,
The castle and Glorieta[4]
And the lord of Provence,[5]
My countrymen who wish me well
And the arch that shows the battle.[6]
I've lost the man who held my life
And will forever be bereft.

7   *Joglar*, you with the merry heart,
Take my song with its theme of death
To Narbonne,
To the lady guided by joy and youth.[7]

---

[3]   In French *Beauregard*, "Fairview," a residence of Raimbaut d'Aurenga near Courthézon where he may have died.

[4]   An ancient palace of the princes of Orange.

[5]   Perhaps Raymond V of Toulouse, lord of both Raimbaut d'Aurenga and Azalais de Porcairagues.

[6]   The Roman triumphal arch that still stands at Orange, depicting violent scenes of battle between legionnaires and Gauls in the first century AD.

[7]   Ermengarde, who inherited the title of viscountess of Narbonne in 1143, ruled until 1192, when she abdicated in favor of her nephew; she died in 1197. See Poem 22.

28

Bernart de Ventadorn

Chantars no pot gaire valer / Singing can hardly be strong

Bernart de Ventadorn, one of the greatest love poets among the troubadours, is identified in his *vida* (Selection 87) as the son of a servant who "would fire the oven for cooking the bread" in the castle of Ventadorn. However, we have no way to confirm this information, which may be only a tale told for the sake of entertainment. On the other hand, we know that a son of the viscount of Ventadorn was named Bernart. This Bernart de Ventadorn, who may have been the poet, became a monk and died as abbot of Tulle.[1] The picturesque ruins of the castle of Ventadorn (in French, Ventadour) may be visited near the village of Moustier-Ventadour in the canton of Egletons, arrondissement of Tulle, department of Corrèze. See Figure 3.

Bernart's reflections on the role of the heart in love poetry fall in a tradition leading to the Italian *dolce stil nuovo*, or "sweet new style," of Dante and his friends. Love, even unhappy love, gives him a "good heart" (stanza 2), like the "noble heart" (*cor gentil*) of the Italian poets.

1   Singing can hardly be strong
If the song doesn't come from the heart,
And a song cannot come from the heart
Unless the heart has love that's true.
My songs turn out the best,
For I bring to joy of love refined
My eyes and mouth, my heart and mind.

2   May God never give me the power
To lose my desire for love;
If instead of getting love again,
Every day it brought me pain,
At least I would gain a good heart;
It brings me much more joy
To have a good heart and hope.

3   They blame love out of ignorance,
Foolish people, but they don't hurt love,
For love cannot just fall away
Unless it is common love.
That is not real love; that kind
Has only the name and the look,
And does not love if it cannot take.

4   To speak truthfully, I could tell you
Where the deception began;
It started with women who love for pay.
I call them sellers of sex.
I wish what I'm saying were false,

---

[1]   If Bernart was the son of a servant he was probably active from the late 1140s to 1173; if he was the son of the viscount, from 1173 until his death in 1234. See William D. Paden, "Bernart de Ventadour le troubadour devint-il abbé de Tulle?" *Mélanges de langue et de littérature occitanes en hommage à Pierre Bec* (Poitiers: Centre d'études supérieures de civilisation médiévale, 1991), pp. 401–13.

For the truth that I'm telling is vulgar;
It grieves me that I'm not a liar!

5   In pleasing and in longing
Is the love of two true lovers:
Nothing good will be forthcoming
If their wishes aren't the same;
So a man is a natural fool
Who scolds his beloved for what she wants
And tells her to do what she should not.

6   I think I've set my high hopes well
Since she is giving me her smile,
The one I desire and want to see.
Loyal and true, candid and sweet,
A lucky catch for even a king,
Pretty and charming, with body so pleasing,
She made me wealthy, starting from nothing.

7   There is nothing that I love or fear,
And nothing that can cause me grief
If to my lady it brings pleasure,
For it seems to me like Christmas
When she looks at me
With her warm, expressive eyes so slowly
That one day lasts a hundred!

8   This song is natural and true;
Good is he who understands it,
And better is he who hopes for joy.

9   Bernart de Ventadorn understands it;
He says it and does it and hopes for joy!

29

Bernart de Ventadorn

Can la frej'aura venta / When the cold breeze blows

The poet speaks to someone from his lady's land, possibly a messenger, and pours out his love for the lady. The opening image of the breeze from the land of the beloved recurs in the works of several other troubadours, including Peire Vidal (Poem 58); it seems to have been imitated from Arabic poets in Spain, including Ibn Zaydun, who died in 1071.[1]

1   When the cold breeze blows
From your land,
It seems I feel a wind
From Paradise
Bringing love of the noble one
Toward whom I lean,
On whom I've set my mind
And heart;
I've let all others go
Because she charms me so!

2   I am sure her lovely eyes
And open face
(May she never give me more)
Must have won me over.
I tell you, I have no reason to lie
Since I am sure of nothing;
But I would hate to change my course,
For once she said to me,
"A worthy man attacks
When a worthless man holds back."

3   As for women, it seems to me
That they go sadly wrong
Because the truest lovers
Are hardly loved at all.
I shouldn't speak about it
Except as they desire,
But it bothers me that a liar
Wins as much love or more
Through treachery
As a man who loves truly.

4   Lady, what do you intend to do
With me, who so loves you,
When you see me suffering
And dying of desire?
O noble, high-born woman,
Give me a pretty smile
To brighten my heart!

---

[1]   See Barbara Spaggiari, "Il tema 'west-östlicher' dell'aura," *Studi medievali*, 3rd ser., 26 (1985): 185–290; Arie Schippers, "La poésie de la nature en Al-Andalus," *La France latine*, n.s. 140 (2005): 115–28.

I am in great torment
And cannot escape it,
But I don't deserve the pain.

5   If it weren't for the peasants
And the wicked gossips
I would surely have my love,
But they all slow me down.
She gives me sweet company
When she has the opportunity,
So secretly, I'm sure,
I will get even more,
For the lucky live at ease,
While the unlucky labor to please.

6   I'm a man who will not scorn
The good that God will give him,
Since during the week
When I went to her,[2]
She told me plainly
That my singing brings her pleasure.
I wish that every Christian soul
Could experience the joy
That I had there and now have here,
For my song boasts of nothing more.

7   If she gives me her promise again,
Again I will believe her;
If not, then never again
Will I trust a Christian woman!

---

[2]   He went away from all other women, according to stanza 1.

30

Bernart de Ventadorn

Qan vei la lauzeta mover / When I see the lark beat his wings

This song became a classic in the troubadour repertory. It was widely imitated in form and rhymes, including an earthy dialogue between a troubadour named Arnaldo and Alfonso X, *el Sabio*, king of Castile (Poem 89).[1]

1 When I see the lark beat his wings
With joy in the rays of the sun
And forget himself and fall
In the warmth that fills his heart,
Oh, I feel so great an envy
Of anyone I see who's merry
I wonder that my heart
Does not melt with desire.

2 Oh, I thought I knew so much
About love, but how little I know!
I cannot stop loving her
Though I know she'll never love me.
She has stolen my heart and stolen herself
And me, myself, and all the world;
She stole herself and left me naught
But desire and a longing heart.

3 I despair of women.
I will never trust them again;
Just as I've always defended them,
I'll stop defending them now.
I see not a one of them gives me help
With the one who brings me to ruin,
So I fear and distrust them all,
For I know they all are the same.

4 Love is lost for certain,
And I never knew it at all;
If she who should have had the most
Has none, where shall I look?
Oh, it looks bad to whoever sees
Her let this yearning wretch,
Who will get no good without her,
Die because she will not help.

5 I get no help with my lady
From God or mercy or right,
And it doesn't please her to love me,
So I'll not tell her my plight;
If she discards me and denies me,

---

[1] Even Dante imitated it, in *Paradiso*, Canto 20, verses 73–5: Like a lark that soars in the air/
First singing, and then falls silent, happy/ In the last sweetness that gives it satisfaction ...

She'll kill me, and dead, I'll answer;
If she abandons me, I will go away
A wretch in exile, I know not where.

6 I have not had power over my life
Or been myself since the time
She let me look into her eyes,
Into a mirror that gives delight.
Mirror, since I saw myself in you,
My sighs have caused my death;
I lost myself, as handsome Narcissus
Lost himself in the spring.[2]

7 My lady resembles a woman
In this, and for it I reproach her;
She does not want what she should,
And she does what she should not.
I have fallen into ill favor,
And behaved like the fool on the bridge;[3]
This happened to me, I don't know why,
Except that I climbed too high.

8 Tristan,[4] from me you'll hear no more,
For I go in despair, I know not where.
I'll stop my voice from singing
And hide from love and joy.

---

[2] Narcissus appears again in Poem 68, stanza 2.
[3] According to a proverb the fool does not dismount, but rides onto a narrow bridge, and so falls into the river.
[4] *Senhal*, perhaps for Raimbaut d'Aurenga.

31

Bernart de Ventadorn

Non es meravelha s'eu chan / It is no wonder if I sing

1   It is no wonder if I sing
Better than other troubadours,
For I'm more drawn to loving
And better made for its command;
My heart and body, knowledge and mind,
And strength and power I give;
The rein pulls me so hard toward love
That I never look to other things.[1]

2   He must be dead who cannot feel
The sweet taste of love in his heart.
What is it worth to live without valor,
And bring only boredom to people?
May God never despise me so
That he lets me live a month or a day
If I make people turn away
And lose their desire for love.

3   In all good faith, without deceit
I love her, the fairest and best.
I sigh in my heart and weep from my eyes,
For I love her so much that I grieve.
What more can I do, imprisoned by Love
In a cell, while she keeps the key?
It will be opened only by mercy,
And no mercy comes to me.

4   This love strikes me so gently
In the heart with its sweet savor,
A hundred times a day I die in pain
And revive with joy a hundred more.
The bad in me wears a beautiful face,
For my bad is better than another man's good;
And since my bad is so good for me,
The good after grief will be good indeed!

5   O God, if only one could tell
Pretenders from true lovers,
And gossips and betrayers
Wore horns on their foreheads!
All the world's gold, and all of its silver
I would have had given, if only I'd had it,
Just so my lady would know for certain
How truly it is that I love her.

---

[1]   Compare this to the situation of the lover imprisoned on the Limoges Casket (see *Frontispiece*).

6   When I see her, you will recognize
The glow in my face, my color, my eyes,
For just as a leaf shakes in the wind
I tremble all over in fear.
I don't have the sense of a child
When love seizes me;
A man so completely conquered by love
Deserves a woman's pity.

7   Good lady, I ask you nothing at all
Except to make me your servant,
For I'll serve you as I would a good lord,
And never ask for another reward.
So here I am, at your command,
A frank, humble heart, courtly and glad!
You're surely not a lion or bear
Who'd slay me when I surrender!

8   To my Courtly One,[2] wherever she is,
I send this song; I hope she'll forgive me
For staying away so long.

---

[2] "My Courtly One" (*Mo Cortes*): a masculine *senhal*, or secret name, for the lady, referring to the same person as "she" in the same line. It could also refer to a male performer to whom Bernart sends the song, or a male patron.

32

Peire and Bernart de Ventadorn

Amics Bernartz de Ventadorn / My friend Bernart de Ventadorn

The interlocutor of Bernart de Ventadorn in this *tensó* is identified in various manuscripts as Peire, Peire Vidal, or Peirol. Some scholars believe that he was Peire d'Alvernhe.

1   *Peire*
      My friend Bernart de Ventadorn,
      How can you give up singing
      When you hear the nightingale
      Rejoicing night and day?
          Listen to the joy he feels!
      All night beneath a flower he sings;
      He is wiser than you about love.

2   *Bernart*
      Peire, I like my rest and sleep
      More than hearing a nightingale,
      And there is nothing you could say
      To make me go back to that madness.
          Thank God, I've cast off my chains,
      While all other lovers, including you,
      Continue making a hullabaloo.

3   *Peire*
      Bernart, he who cannot suffer
      Love is neither noble nor courtly,
      For whatever grief it brings,
      Love is better than other good things,
          For if it hurts, it heals.
      Without pain, nothing is dear;
      The joy will always dry the tears.

4   *Bernart*
      Peire, if I could make the world my way
      For two years or three,
      I'll tell you what—No longer would women
      Be courted at all;
          Rather, they'd be condemned
      To show to us so much honor
      That we would be wooed, not wooers!

5   *Peire*
      Bernart, it's just not proper
      For women to court. No, it's better
      For us to court them and beg their mercy;
      Any man who blames them and their ways
          Is more insane, I think,
      Than one who sows his seed in sand—
      When the teacher is bad, it all begins.

6   *Bernart*
     Peire, my heart aches
     When I think of that false woman
     Who did me in, I know not why,
     Except I loved her truly.
          I have endured too long a Lent,
     But I know, if I made it longer
     I would only find her meaner.

7   *Peire*
          Bernart, you must be crazy
     To abandon love so freely,
     The very source of dignity and worth.

8   *Bernart*
          Peire, whoever loves has lost his mind,
     For scheming women have ruined
     Joy and dignity and worth!

33

Alfonso II of Aragon

Per mantas guizas m'es datz / In many ways I am given

Alfonso II of Aragon ruled from 1162 to 1196. Later he came to be called Alfonso the Chaste. Becoming count of Provence, he traveled frequently from Barcelona to Aix and received troubadours generously in his court. He engaged in a dialogue with Giraut de Bornelh. A *razo* on a poem by Bertran de Born claims that Alfonso considered Giraut's love-songs the "wives" of Bertran's *sirventés*. Despite the apparent compliment, Bertran de Born became Alfonso's fierce enemy after Alfonso joined Richard Lionheart in the siege and capture of Bertran's castle of Autafort in 1183.

In the following song, one of two by Alfonso that survive, he speaks discreetly of a love that he says was reciprocated. In the first line we are reminded that the poet is a king who is accustomed to being served.

1 In many ways I am given
  Joy, delight and pleasure,
  For I hear singers rejoicing
  In orchards and in meadows,
  In foliage and flowers
  And in the fresh new season;
  But neither snow nor ice can harm
  My song, nor does summer help,
  Or anything but God and love.

2 But surely I'm not saddened
  By good weather or summer's light
  Or the sweet song I hear birds sing
  From their hideaway or by the green,
  For I, like them, am bound
  To the very best of all.
  My lady has wit and beauty,
  Joy, renown, and honor;
  All that I do, I do for her.

3 My heart overflows
  With bursting desire;
  I don't know if it is folly
  Or bravery or fear
  Or prudent good sense
  Or the star of love,
  But since the hour I was born
  Love never pressed me so,
  Nor have I felt such pain.

4 Her goodness so upsets me,
  Her prowess and her beauty,
  That I'd rather suffer grief
  And injury in peace
  Than enjoy ease and favor
  By loving another.
  If it pleases her, I'll swear

Forever to remain her vassal
And never serve another lord.

5   When I recall how we said goodbye
Once when I had no choice,
I feel happy and despairing,
For with sighs among her tears
She said, "Fair friend, please
Come back soon to me."
So I will go back quickly,
Since no other embassy
Gives me delight or savor.

34

Guilhem de Berguedà

Cansoneta leu e plana / I'll make a ditty, short and pretty

The eldest son of the viscount of Berguedà (the region around Berga in Catalonia, north of Barcelona), Guilhem de Berguedà was the lord of five castles and an important political figure. His more than thirty poems are mostly *sirventés*; he is best known for scathing personal attacks, but he also wrote amorous verses. Active from 1138 to 1192, he died unmarried and without known heirs. Although his native language must have been Catalan, he composed in flawless Occitan. Guilhem was a friend of another lord and troubadour, Bertran de Born.

In several *sirventés* Guilhem made the target of his invective Pons de Mataplana, the younger son of a Catalonian noble family that had its seat not far from Berguedà and Ripoll. When Pons died, however, Guilhem grieved for him in a *planh*. For reasons we do not know, Guilhem called Pons *Marquis*, which was neither his name nor his title.[1]

In 1172 Pons accompanied King Alfonso II of Aragon, who was also count of Barcelona, on an expedition that passed near Montpellier and Nîmes. While there he must have had the accident that Guilhem mentions in the second stanza of the *sirventés* below. Guilhem probably wrote the poem soon thereafter.

1   I'll make a ditty,[2] short and pretty,
Without a bit of pomposity,
All about my dear Marquis,
That traitor of Mataplana,
Stuffed to bursting with deceit.
Marquis, Marquis, Marquis, you sneak,
You're stuffed to bursting with deceit!

2   Marquis, a blessing on the stones
Of Melgur near Soméiras,[3]
Where you lost three teeth;
There's little harm done by the blow—
The stones remain, and their scars don't show![4]
Marquis, Marquis, Marquis, you sneak,
You're stuffed to bursting with deceit!

3   I don't give a rap about your arm,
Stiff as the joist of a beam,
So taut you can never bend it;[5]
You should apply a nettle-plaster
To loosen up that tendon.
Marquis, Marquis, Marquis, you sneak,
You're stuffed to bursting with deceit!

---

[1] A marquis was the holder of a march, or border territory. The border with Islamic territory had by this time moved farther south.

[2] A *cansoneta*, or little *canso*.

[3] Guilhem refers to Mauguio (Hérault), about twenty kilometers from Sommières (Gard).

[4] Pons must have fallen from his horse and broken three teeth. Elsewhere Guilhem mocked Pons for his large teeth; here he expresses amazement that his teeth did not damage the stones.

[5] Pons de Mataplana had a paralyzed arm.

4   Marquis, whoever gives you loyalty
Gets neither love nor fealty,
And always must take care
To walk with you only in the light,
And never go out with you at night.
Marquis, Marquis, Marquis, you sneak,
You're stuffed to bursting with deceit!

5   Marquis, you're not even safe at noon;
A man who joins you for a siesta
Better wear britches of leather,
For nary a Christian woman's son
Has kept more unsavory customs.[6]
Marquis, Marquis, Marquis, you sneak,
You're stuffed to bursting with deceit!

---

[6] In stanzas 4 and 5 Guilhem accuses Pons of sodomy, employing homophobia as a technique of character assassination as he does in other songs.

35

Guilhem de Berguedà

Arondeta, de ton chantar m'azir / Swallow, your singing unnerves me

In 1185 Guilhem de Berguedà accompanied King Alfonso II of Aragon and Richard Lionheart on an expedition against Count Raymond V of Toulouse, and was obliged to leave his lady. In this poem he imagines her sending a swallow as a messenger to remind him of her love.

1   "Swallow, your singing unnerves me;
    What do you want, what do you seek, why won't you let me sleep?
    You disturb me, and I don't know how to respond,
    For I've not been well since I crossed the Gironde;
    You bring no message from my Good Hope,[1]
    So I don't comprehend your tongue."

2   "My lord and friend, your lady bade me come
    In haste to you, for you are what she wants;
    And she says if she, like me, were a swallow,
    She'd have come to your bed two months ago;
    But since she knows neither land nor road,
    She sent me to learn the ways of your heart."

3   "Swallow, I should have received you more kindly,
    And honored and loved you, and served you better!
    God save you, he who encircles the world,
    Who made the sky, the earth, and the sea;
    If I've spoken rudely, I beg your pardon
    And pray that my words will bring me no harm."

4   "My lord and friend, the one who sent me here,
    Your lady, made me swear
    To recall for you the clasp of her tunic
    And the golden ring that is our secret,
    And also the time when she sealed with a kiss
    Her promise that you would have more."

5   "Swallow, I cannot leave the king,
    For I must follow him to Toulouse;
    But you should know, and all who complain:
    I'll unhorse my Jordan[2] near the Garonne[3]
    In the midst of a field before everyone.
    I mean what I say; I'm not merely boasting."

---

[1]   Identified by Riquer (*Trovadores*, vol. 1, p. 541) as Elis de Turena, a beauty who was also celebrated by Bertran de Born, among others.

[2]   Identified by Riquer (*Trovadores*, vol. 1, p. 542) as Raimon Jordan, a troubadour (see Poem 49) and rival of Guilhem de Berguedà for the affections of Elis de Turena.

[3]   The river that runs through Toulouse.

6   "My lord and my friend, God grant your wish;
As for me, when I get home
I'm sure to be plucked or skinned
. . . [4]
When she learns you will stay in a foreign realm,
It will be hard on her heart, brutal and cruel."

[4] A line is missing.

36

Guilhem de Berguedà

Mais volgra chantar a plazer / I'd like to sing more pleasingly

In 1190, intending to visit the court of Alfonso VIII of Castile, Guilhem expressed in this poem the fear that his lady might take another lover. He proposes a theory of pleasure that anticipates modern expressions of love. Most troubadours, like the Italian poets of the *dolce stil nuovo*, related the capacity for love to nobility of heart.

1   I'd like to sing more pleasingly,
    If I could, than other troubadours,
    For, thanks to God, Love has given me
    More pleasure and honor,
    I think, than any other lover;
    If I could be cured of one wound
    That I bear for her to whom I'm devoted,
    All my joy would be perfected.

2   This wound stems from fear
    That she might change her love,
    But I don't have a changing heart
    Or the leisure to make a change,
    For I am so loyal to her and true
    That I want her more than Paradise;
    So it will be deceit and a sin
    If she changes me for another man.

3   Good lady, you have wit and wisdom
    And every courtly merit;
    God grant you to have them in love
    So you know how to keep the best;[1]
    It is better to choose on the basis of pleasure,
    Since pleasure exalts and nourishes love,
    And no man feels happy with anything
    That doesn't please and satisfy him.

4   Now hear how much power in love
    Pleasure has, and how much it helps:
    A man may leave a grander lady,
    Who would do whatever he asked,
    For another less lovely because she charms
    Him, and he takes in her more pleasure;
    In true love pleasure has more worth
    Than either beauty or wealth.

5   I wish I could have a husband's place
    One night, and the night would last from Easter
    Until the feast of All Saints,[2]
    And the husband would go blind

---

[1]   As a feudal lord retains a knight, by appointing him to his court and keeping him in his company.

[2]   From spring to fall.

Or at least would always sleep,
And the whole world would never know;
If ever a prayer was answered,
God, please grant this one to me!

6   King of Castile, to catch sight of you
I would return from Paradise;
If I entered there without seeing you,
I would stay there forever in sadness.

37

Giraut de Bornelh

Reis glorios, verais lums e clardatz / Glorious King, true light and brilliance

Giraut de Bornelh was active from 1162 to 1199; perhaps he came from Excideuil in the Limousin, the area around Limoges. His surviving works, seventy-seven songs, are the most numerous of any twelfth-century troubadour. The *vida* calls him the "master of the troubadours" (*maestre dels trobadors*). He engaged with Raimbaut d'Aurenga in a dialogue on literary style (Poem 25), defending poetry that is "easy and light." Giraut traveled to Spain and participated in the Third Crusade of 1192–4 with Richard Lionheart.

Giraut's *alba*, or dawn-song, has close metrical resemblances to the monastic song beginning "O Maria, Deu maire" (Poem 3). It may be a contrafacture, or metrical imitation, taking the earlier hymn as its model. To think so, however, does not establish that Giraut's song was intended in a religious way; rather, the imitation, if imitation there was, may have added a pious nuance to a secular love song.

The poem begins in the voice of the watchman, who speaks first to God and then to his friend, the lover.

1   Glorious King, true light and brilliance,
       Powerful God, Lord, if you please,
       Will you help my friend?
       Since night fell I haven't seen him,
           And soon will come the dawn.

2   Fair friend, if you wake or sleep,
       Sleep no more but softly rise,
       For in the East appears the morning star
       That brings the day—I'm sure I see it,
           And soon will come the dawn.

3   Fair friend, I call you with my song,
       Sleep no more! I hear a bird that sings,
       Looking for light deep in the woods;
       I fear the jealous one will find you,
           And soon will come the dawn.

4   Fair friend, go to the window,
       Look out at the stars in the sky.
       You will know that I speak the truth;
       If you stay you may be hurt,
           And soon will come the dawn.

5   Fair companion, since I left you
       I have been on my knees, not sleeping or moving,
       But praying to God, Son of Holy Mary,
       To bring you back to me, your friend,
           And soon will come the dawn.

6   Fair companion, out on the terrace
       You begged me not to doze
       But to stay awake all night till day;
       Now you won't hear me or my song,
           And soon will come the dawn.

The lover answers:

7   Fair sweet friend, this stay is so rich
I wish dawn or day would never come,
For the noblest woman of mother born
Lies in my arms, and nothing else matters,
Not the jealous fool, not the dawn![1]

---

[1] The final stanza occurs in only two of the seven manuscripts that contain the poem. Some scholars doubt its authenticity, while others defend it. For us it is essential to the meaning of the song.

38

Giraut de Bornelh

Per solatz reveillar / To arouse rejoicing

Dante cites this poem in *De Vulgari Eloquentia* (II, 2) when he names Giraut as the poet of rectitude.

1   To arouse rejoicing,
Which has fallen asleep,
And to welcome merit
Home from exile,
I thought I should try—
But I can't make a song!
I've failed because
It can't be done.
The higher my will and passion go,
The more my pain and anguish grow.

2   It's hard to endure,
I tell you. You've heard
How joy and manners
Were once esteemed,
But now you must admit
You've seen decrepit peasants
Forced to ride stiff-jointed nags
Against their will.[1]
The scene, so ugly and odd,
Makes us blaspheme and lose God.

3   You've seen tournaments called
And rivals bearing handsome arms,
Then for the rest of the season
People recounting wonderful deeds;
Now it's grand to be a thief
Stealing sheep!
A knight should be ashamed
Who sets out to court ladies
After wrestling bleating sheep
Or robbing chapels and pilgrims!

4   You've seen eager minstrels
Going from court to court
Well dressed and shod,
All in honor of women;
Now we dare not tell
How low they've fallen.
Where the mischief started,
This evil gossip, with the ladies
Or the lovers, I don't know.
Both, I think, for deceit has brought us low.

---

[1]   Giraut complains of the decline of chivalry, which involves mock knights and aged mares instead of stallions.

<pre>
  5   Where have all the singers gone
           You saw so well received?
           Some who once led us
           Now need leaders themselves.
           I don't mean to harp,
           But now that merit is in decline,
           Some people go about alone
           Who once were heads of companies
      (Of how many men? I don't know),
      Splendid and armed from head to toe.

  6   I myself, a distinguished man,
           Could once address the nobles,
           But now I feel so much distress,
           I don't know what to think;
           Instead of noble songs,
           I hear people shout in court—
           For the count is just as pleased
           By silly tales of geese²
      As he is by artful songs
      Of times and years and mighty deeds.

  7   But to make hearts more noble
           That have grown too hard,
           Don't we need to remember
           Bygone men and what they did?
           It's bad to quit a business
           Once it has begun,
           Though it's true that wounds healed over
           Need be cured no longer;
      Let us take what we see, turn it and change it,
      Seize it, shake it, squeeze it, and drop it!

  8   Of this I can boast:
           My little house
           Has never been robbed.
           All men respect it;
           Both the brave and the cunning
           Know to defer.
           My distinguished lord
      Should pause to reflect,
      For it brings him no honor, praise, or glory
      If I celebrate them and complain about him.

  9   No more complaining. Why not? Come on!
           It will be a dirge, if thus I end my song.³

  10   So says Dalfin,⁴ who knows good songs.
</pre>

---

² Literally, "the goose of Bretmar" (the owner of the goose?); the tale is lost.
³ Occitan *planh*, "dirge, lamentation," became the name of the genre of the funeral lament.
⁴ Dalfin d'Alvernhe, count of Clermont and Montferrand, ruled 1181–1235; a patron of troubadours, he was a poet himself.

39

Giraut de Bornelh and Alamanda

S'ie.us quier cosselh, bel' ami' Alamanda /
If I ask you for advice, my fair friend Alamanda

The well-known troubadour Giraut de Bornelh apparently engaged in this dialogue with a woman named Alamanda who is otherwise unknown. Some scholars regard her as a fictional interlocutor, others as a real poet. Bertran de Born imitated this poem in a *sirventés* "to the tune of Alamanda," which may mean the tune composed by Alamanda or the tune about Alamanda, whether she was fictional or real.

1   *Giraut*
"If I ask you for advice, my fair friend Alamanda,
Don't tell me no, for I'm a troubled man.
Your lady's so false-hearted that she dares to say
I strayed far away from her command;
Once her love was mine, but now she takes it back.
    So what do you propose?
I am angry, and my heart burns
    When she pains me so."

2   *Alamanda*
"For God's sake, Giraut, a lover ought to know
His wish will not be granted the moment that he asks;
If one lover strays, the other should forgive,
Or they will only make their troubles worse.
If my lady tells you a mountain's really flat,
    Say oh, you hadn't noticed.
Take everything she gives you, both the good and bad—
    That's the way to win her loving back."

3   *Giraut*
"I cannot keep from scolding you for pride,
Donzela,[1] even though you are beautiful and blond;
You should let my anger go and care about my pleasure,
But all you women seem to think of neither.
What about me, so sad that I may die—
    Can't you tell me something?
Don't tell me I should wait, accept her every whim,
    Not if you really want to help."

4   *Alamanda*
"Giraut, if you want to speak philosophy,
I don't know what to say;
Though you think I should be happy because you say you're sorry,
I'd rather mow my meadow than watch another reap.
Should I lie about your antics for the sake of making peace?
    Now you're only trying
To keep her for yourself in time of need.
    Clearly, as you say, you are troubled!"

[1] An Occitan word meaning "Maiden." Alamanda is presumably a lady-in-waiting.

5   *Giraut*
"Donzela, I wish you didn't have to talk so much!
If your lady's tricked me more than a hundred times,
Are you saying I should always let it happen?
If I did, would you not think it was because
I couldn't get another girl? Now I want to slap you!
          Why don't you simmer down?
A she-ass[2] would have had a better plan
          Than this one!"

6   *Alamanda*
"I see the time, Giraut, when she'll repay you
For calling her fickle and capricious;
Don't think just for that I'm not a friend of yours,
But I don't think you'll find her quite so tame;
From now on she'll be slow to promise you
          Anything at all,
Even if she brings herself to seek
          A truce or peace."

7   *Giraut*
"Pretty one, for God's sake, don't take your help away,
For you know well what you promised me;
If I got a little touchy when I lost my temper,
Please don't let it harm me; if you have ever felt
The easy ups and downs of an angry man in love,
          Or if you yourself have ever been a lover,
Think about this truce. I am dead if I should lose her,
          But don't you ever tell!"

8   *Alamanda*
"My lord and friend, I'd already hoped to find a truce,
But my lady told me she was in the right
To punish you for wooing, like a fool,
One who's not her equal, either clothed or nude.
If she doesn't drop you, won't she seem an easy conquest
          If you pursue another?
I'll give you some assistance, even though I'm on her side,
          If you promise to stop acting quite so wild."

9   *Giraut*
"Pretty one, for God's sake, if she will believe you,
          Tell her for me that all I say is true."

10 *Alamanda*
"I'll do it, then, but once you win her back,
          Do not spurn the love that now you lack!"

---

[2]   Literally, "Lady Berenguiera," referring, we suppose, to a donkey by that name in the Old
French beast epic, the *Romance of Renard*, that was a teller of improbable tales. It may be,
instead, that Lady Berenguiera was a real lady known to Giraut and Alamanda.

40

Bertran de Born

Un sirventes on motz non faill / A sirventés where no word misses the target

Bertran de Born (active 1159–1215) was one of the great lords of Aquitaine, a vassal of the king of England, first Henry II (through his wife, Eleanor of Aquitaine) and later, after Henry's death, Richard Lionheart.[1] From his father and his grandfather Bertran inherited the castle of Autafort (the name means "High-Strong") in Dordogne, east of Bordeaux. Called "Hautefort" in French, the castle may be visited today. Much modified during the sixteenth and seventeenth centuries, it has been celebrated as the Versailles of the Midi.

As a poet Bertran sang the exhilaration of combat in more than forty poems, mostly *sirventés*. Conflict in his world sprang from many sources, among them inheritance practices that traditionally favored equal division among heirs in Aquitaine, whereas English law preferred primogeniture, or inheritance by the first-born son. Under these circumstances considerable ambiguity attended the rights to Autafort, which Bertran could claim alone as the eldest son. In the first of the poems below, he rejoices in having expelled his brother Constantine from the castle, which he did in 1182. In spring of the following year he joined a rebellion of the barons of Aquitaine against their lord, Richard Lionheart. The rebels justified their actions because Richard's elder brother Henry, called the "Young King," had been crowned king of England as a means to ensure his succession to the throne. When the Young King died suddenly in June 1183, the rebellion collapsed.

In Poem 40 Bertran defies Richard. In Poem 41 he laments the Young King's death. Richard besieged Autafort, took it, and gave it to Constantine to punish Bertran, but then Henry II reversed Richard's decision. In Poem 42 Bertran exults in the king's decision. In Poem 43, which can be dated only after these events, Bertran reflects on the meaning of youthfulness in women and men. In Poem 44 he once again sings the excitement of imminent conflict. His idealized vision of war expressed the perspective of the male aristocracy of his time.

1   A *sirventés* where no word misses
        I've made, and it cost me not even a garlic.
        I have learned a good trick:
        With my brother or cousin or kin
           I share my eggs and my coins;
        Then if he tries to steal my share,
           I throw him out on his ear!

2   All day long I struggle and fight.
        I fence and parry and carp,
        For they ravage and burn my land
        And cut my timber down
           And mix the wheat and chaff.
        Not a fox, not a cowardly foe
           Fails to turn against me.

3   Talairan[2] neither trots nor rears,
        Nor does he leave his fort
        Or react to lance or spear.
        He likes the cowardly life,
           And he's so full of sloth

---

[1]   The kings of England held Aquitaine from 1155 to 1453.
[2]   Elias Talairan, count of Périgord, a future ally of Bertran de Born in the revolt of 1183.

It pains me to watch him stretch and yawn
        While all the others ride away.

4   Guilhem of Gourdon,[3] you've put
     A dead clapper in your bell—
     So I love you, God save me.
     But those two viscounts,
             Because of your treaty,
     Think you're a fool and a dolt,
     And they want you in their army.

5   I keep all my thoughts locked up,
     Although Richard and Aimar
     Have caused me a lot of trouble;
     They've been keeping me on edge,
             But now I begin such a brawl
     That unless the king steps in,
             The boys will get theirs in the gut.

6   Near the wall of Périgueux
     I'll ride out on my bay
     As far as I can throw a mace,
     And if I find a puffing Poitevin[4]
             He'll find out how my blade goes in—
     On top of his head I'll carve out a slop
             Of brains mixed with mail.

7   All day I resole and recut the barons,
     And melt them down and heat them up.
     I had thought of clearing them out,
     For only a fool would let them upset him.
             Their mettle for me is twice as hard
     As iron was for Saint Leonárd,[5]
             So I would be a fool to care.

8   Barons, God save you and keep you
             And aid you and bring you assistance,
     Provided you say to Sir Richard
             What the peacock said to the crow![6]

---

[3]   Another future ally who has won Bertran's love by ignoring a treaty with the two viscounts of
       Limoges, Aimar and his son Gui, who shared the title.
[4]   A follower of Richard, count of Poitou.
[5]   The patron saint of prisoners, who easily broke their chains.
[6]   In a fable, the crow disguised himself in peacock feathers only to be found out and humiliated.
       The peacock told him, "He who climbs higher than he should / Falls farther than he would
       like."

Bertran de Born

Mon chan fenis ab dol et ab maltraire / For now and forever, I close my song in grief

In 1183 the abbey of Saint-Martial in Limoges was the site of a meeting at which the barons of Aquitaine agreed to rebel against the duke of the region, Richard Lionheart. Years later a candle burned on the altar in memory of Bertran de Born, the troubadour who in life had participated in that rebellion, and in his poems had defied the Truce of God. The rebellion sprang up early in 1183, but collapsed in June when its leader, Richard's older brother Henry, known as the Young King, suddenly died. Bertran grieved for Young Henry as a model of chivalric virtue.

1 For now and forever, I close my song in grief
   And suffering and think it is done.
   I have lost my joy and theme
   And the best king ever of a mother born,
         Generous, well spoken
         And a good horseman,
         Handsome
         And humble
         In conferring honor.
         My grief torments me
         So much I may choke,
         And I speak of it always.
         To God I commend him,
   To be placed in the seat of Saint John.[1]

2 King of the noble and emperor of the brave
   You would have been, Lord, if only you had lived,
   For you bore the name *Young King*,
   And you were the leader and father of youth.
         Now mail-shirts and swords
         And beautiful buckram,
         Helmets and banners,
         Doublets and lappets
         And joy and love
         Have none to sustain them
         Or bring them back;
         They will follow you,
         Disappear with you,
   Like all mighty and honorable deeds.

3 Noble hospitality, giving without stint,
   Fine conversation and a warm "Come in!"
   A great court, well paid and maintained,
   Presents and weapons and no one's offended,
         Dining to the sound
         Of viol and song
         With many companions

---

[1] Saint John the Apostle, believed to be the disciple "whom Jesus loved" (John 13:23), was said to enjoy a special place in Paradise.

             Daring and strong,
             The greatest of the great—
             I want them all to stop,
             To leave nothing worthy
             In the cruel world,
             After this unlucky year
          That began with so much promise.

4   Lord, in you there was nothing to change,
     For all the world had named you
     The best knight who ever bore a shield,
     The bravest and the finest in a tourney.
             Since the time of Roland
             No one has ever seen
             So excellent a king
             Or one so skilled in war,
             Or one whose fame spread
             So far throughout the world
             Or who gave it such new life,
             Or sought so much renown,
             Looking everywhere
     From the Nile to the setting sun.[2]

5   Lord, because of you I shall abandon joy,
     And all who saw you
     Must be sad and still,
     And never again let joy transform my grief.
             Bretons and Irishmen,
             Englishmen and Normans,
             Occitans and Gascons grieve,
             And Poitou suffers,
             And Maine and Tours.
             Now let France weep
             As far as Compiègne
             And Flanders and Ghent,
             All the way to Wissant.
     Let even the Germans weep!

6   Men of Lorraine and Brabant,
             When they go to tourneys,
     Will miss you and grieve.

7   I don't care a besant[3]
             Or the pop of an acorn
     For the world or those in it,

8   Because of the heavy death
             Of this good, worthy king
     Which afflicts us all.

---

[2] This should be read as hyperbole, since the Young King did not participate in any Crusade or otherwise visit Egypt. For the troubadours the Nile functioned as metonymy, representing the East.

[3] Originally a gold coin from Byzantium; but the word came to be used for any coin of small value.

42

Bertran de Born

Ges de far sirventes no.m tartz / Sirventés come to me so fast

After the rebellion collapsed, Richard made a tour of his territory to mete out punishment. With the assistance of King Alfonso II of Aragon he besieged Bertran in his castle of Autafort, took it, and awarded it to Bertran's brother and rival Constantine. But then Henry II, Richard's father, compelled Richard to reverse his decision, so he restored the castle to Bertran. In this satire, Bertran rejoices in Henry's favorable decision and declares his determination to keep Autafort.

1   *Sirventés* come to me so fast
I hardly have to work;
So subtle are my skill and wit,
I'm almost done before I start.
    I have so much luck
    That I escaped;
    No kings or counts
    Or cares disturb me now.

2   Since Count Richard and the king
Have pardoned me, I don't care
If Aimar, Amblart, and Talairan[1]
Never give me peace again.
    They'll need to make war
    To get even a garden
    Of Autafort;
    It's mine, and I'll keep it.

3   I'm so tough that shreds of war
Cling to me on every side.
A stye in your eye if you tear me away
Even if I start the fray!
    Peace gives me
    No harmony;
    I'm tuned to war,
    It's the law I know.

4   For Mondays or Tuesdays I don't give a rap,
Or weeks or months or years;[2]
In March and April I never stop
Scheming to think up tricks and snares
    Against my foes.
    The three of them
    Won't have the luck
    To get even a strap![3]

[1]   Viscount Aimar V of Limoges, Amblart of Anz, and Count Talairan of Périgord, three of Bertran's erstwhile fellow rebels.

[2]   Bertran defies the Truce of God, which forbade combat on certain days and at certain times.

[3]   Bertran's enemies will get nothing of value.

5   Let others try to clear their woods;
     I'm always in trouble
     Over crossbows, helmets and swords,
     Horses and spears and shirts of mail.
          I soothe myself
          And stay amused
          With wars and tourneys,
          Fighting and flirting.

6   My brother is so outrageous,
     He'd like my children's land.
     Fool that I am, I'd give it away,
     Then they'd say, "That weakling Bertran!"
          Had he done me no wrong,
          He'd meet a bad end
          Before I said
          He could talk to me.

7   As for Autafort, I care no more
          About right or wrong;
          I accept the decision
          Of my lord, the king.

43

Bertran de Born

Belh m'es quan vey camjar lo senhoratge / I like to see power changing hands

Bertran sings an ideal of youth, or youthfulness, that extends to dynamism in many forms, from politics to love to generosity. His ideal is opposed to the balance, measure, and economy that he imputed to upstart burghers.

1   I like to see power changing hands
When the old leave their houses to the young—
A man can leave his kin so many kids
That one, at least, should grow to something good;
Then I like it, for I think the world's renewed
Better than with flowers or songs of birds.
So if you can change your lady or your lord,
Old for young, I say you really should.

2   Old is a woman when her skin gets ugly,
And she is old when she doesn't have a knight;
I say she is old if she wants a pair of lovers,
And she is old if she lets a peasant take her;
I say she is old if she loves within her castle,[1]
And old when she stoops to magic tricks;
She is old when she finds that singers bore her,
And she is old when she wants to blather on.

3   Young is a woman who brings honor to her kin,
And good deeds keep her young if she does them.
She stays young when she has a nimble heart
And avoids contriving plots to win her fame;
She stays young when she keeps her body trim,
And young when she behaves as she should;
She stays young if she does not care to gossip
And avoids being cross with stylish youth.

4   Young is a man who pawns all he owns,
And he is young when he doesn't have a dime.
He stays young when he is generous to guests,
And young when he makes impressive gifts.
He stays young when he burns up chests and coffers,
And lays traps in tournaments and war.
He stays young if it pleases him to flirt,
And he is young when the singers like him well.

5   Old is a rich man who never pawns a thing,
And has too much bacon, wheat, and wine.
I say he's old if he serves eggs and cheese
When his friends are expecting to have meat.
He is old if he covers his cloak with a cape
And old if men call his horse his own;

---

[1]   If she chooses her lover for the sake of mere convenience.

Old when one day he does not like to flirt
And old when he can flee and pay no ransom.[2]

6   Take my *sirventés* both old and young,
Arnaut the singer,[3] to Richard for his use;
Tell him not to hoard up treasure that is old,
Since with young treasure, he can win repute.

---

[2]   Normally a knight taken captive in a tourney was freed for a ransom; in Bertran's eyes, one
who escapes without negotiating for payment fails to keep the system working.

[3]   Arnaut the singer was perhaps Arnaut Daniel, the author of Poems 50 to 53.

44

Bertran de Born

Miez sirventes vueilh far dels reis amdos /
Half a sirventés I'll sing about two kings

Relations between Richard Lionheart and Alfonso VIII of Castile came near the breaking point in June 1190, when Richard bestowed the province of Gascony on Berengaria of Navarre, his intended wife. Alfonso had an interest in Gascony himself, since Henry II had earlier given the land to Alfonso's wife, Eleanor, Henry's daughter. The two grants were not strictly contradictory, since Berengaria was to hold the province until the death of Eleanor of Aquitaine, Henry's wife, and Alfonso's wife was to hold it after she died. Nevertheless, the grants came close enough to create strained relations. Richard had confirmed Henry's gift himself. In this song Bertran expresses his intense hope for open conflict.

1 Half a *sirventés* I'll sing about two kings:
Soon we shall see more knights
Following Alfonso, the king of Castile;
He is coming, I hear, and wants mercenaries.
But Richard will spend silver and gold
By bushels and barrels; he will be glad
To spend and give, and he'll spurn Alfonso's treaty—
He wants war more than a hawk wants quail!

2 If both kings are noble and brave,
Fields will soon be strewn with pieces
Of helmets and shields and saddles and swords,
And bodies split open, down to their breeches;
We shall see stallions running wild,
And many a lance through chests and sides,
And joy and tears and grief and rejoicing.
The loss will be great, but the gain will be greater!

3 Trumpets, drums, standards and pennons
And ensigns and horses black and white
Soon we shall see, and the world will be good.
We'll take whatever the usurers have;
No driver of mules will travel in safety,
No burgher will go without fear,
Nor merchant coming from France.
He who happily takes will be rich!

4 But if the king comes, I trust in God
I'll be alive or cut to pieces;

5 If I am alive, it will be good luck,
And if I die it will be a release!

45

La Comtessa de Dia

A chantar m'er de so qu'eu non volria / I'll sing of him since I am his love

With four songs of undisputed attribution, La Comtessa de Dia, or countess of Die, is the most prolific trobairitz as well as the most celebrated. Her identification has proved difficult. The most persuasive candidate is Isoarde, the daughter of Isoard, count of Die, a town in the department of Drôme in northern Provence.[1] Isoarde of Die signed a legal document in 1212 and died by 1214. If she lived to an advanced age, she may have written love poetry around the 1180s.

This is the only song by a trobairitz that is preserved with its melody.[2]

1   I'll sing of him since I am his love,
But I feel so bitter I'd rather not.
I love him more than all the world,
But mercy and grace do me no good,
Nor does my beauty, merit, or wit.
I've been deceived and betrayed
For no reason, and in spite of my charm.

2   I comfort myself that I've done no wrong
To you, my friend, in any way.
I love you more than Seguin loved Valensa,[3]
And I'm glad to be better at loving,
Dear, since you're the more valiant one;
You're haughty to me in words and deeds
But to others, you're humble and kind.

3   I'm amazed at the pride that you show to me,
My love, and I am right to complain;
It's simply not fair for another to steal you
Because of something I might have said;
Remember how it was at the start
Of our love! May God never let
Something I did come between us.

4   The courage that I've seen in you
And your noble lineage keep me true;
For any woman seeking love,
Near or far, would turn to you.
But you, my friend, judge so well
That you can tell who is true;
Remember, then, the vows we made.

5   My merit should help me, and my lineage
And beauty, but most of all my heart.
So I send to you this song. Let it come
As my messenger to your dwelling place.
I would like to know, my fair and noble friend,

---

[1]   The daughter of a count could be referred to as a countess.
[2]   See Rosenberg, *Songs of the Troubadours*, p. 98.
[3]   Protagonists of a lost romance. Note that La Comtessa compares herself to the hero, not the heroine.

Why you are so fierce and cruel
And whether the cause is pride or malice.

6   But most of all, I want the messenger to say
That too much pride brings many people pain.

46

La Comtessa de Dia

Ab joi et ab joven m'apais / From joy and youth I take my fill

Here La Comtessa employs *rims derivatius*, or "derived rhymes," linking verses together in pairs.

1 From joy and youth I take my fill,
    And joy and youth fill me up;
Because my lover is a merry man,
    I am merry and pretty, too.
    And since I'm always true to him
It's only right he's true to me;
For my love for him has never waned
    And wane it never shall.

2 I'm pleased that he's a worthy man,
    The one who's worth so much to me,
And pray that those who set us up
    God will set in great delight.
    And if they say I do bad things
He should say no if I say it's not true;
For the man who hunts for switches
    May turn out to be the one switched.

3 So a lady who cares for her name
    Must surely give her care
To a worthy, noble knight.
    And when she sees his worth
    Let her open up to love,
For once the love of a lady opens,
No noble or charming man
    Will speak lightly of her charms.

4 My man is so high-born and handsome
    He makes merit rise even higher;
Sensitive, giving, and deft,
    He has the gift of wit.
    I pray that he'll believe in me,
Not in others who'd make him believe
That I could ever be false to him—
    Unless he were false to me!

5 Floris,[1] those who are valiant
Know your valor and worth;
So do not wait, if you please,
    To give me the weight of your love.

---

[1]   La Comtessa addresses her lover as *Floris*, using the name of the lover of Blanchefleur in an anonymous French romance; compare Poem 47, stanza 2.

47

La Comtessa de Dia

Estat ai en greu cossirier / I have been in heavy grief

1   I have been in heavy grief
For a knight who once was mine,
And I want it to be forever known
That I loved him too much.
        I see now that I'm betrayed
For not giving him my love.
Bemused, I lie in bed awake;
        Bemused, I dress and pass the day.

2   If only I could hold him
Naked in my arms one night!
He would feel ecstatic
Were I to be his pillow.
        Since I desire him more
Than Floris did Blanchefleur,[1]
I give him my heart and my love,
        My wit, my eyes, for as long as I live.

3   Splendid lover, charming and good,
When shall I hold you in my power?
If only I could lie with you one night
And give you a loving kiss!
        Know that I'd like
To hold you as my husband,
As long as you'd promise
        To do what I desired.

---

[1]   In the romance of *Floris and Blanchefleur* the young lovers are separated, reunited, and finally married. The anonymous French romance (*Floire et Blanchefleur*, written 1150–60) was translated into several languages, but not Occitan. La Comtessa compares herself to Floris, not Blanchefleur; compare her reference to Seguin and Valensa in Poem 45.

48

La Comtessa de Dia

Fin joi me don'alegransa / True joy gives me gladness

1 True joy gives me gladness
And makes me sing more merrily;
For me it is no heavy weight
Or cause for melancholy
To know that scandalmongers
Hate me every one;
Their nasty words don't make me fear,
But rather bring me double cheer.

2 In me they find no comfort,
Those tattlers speaking lies,
For no one can have honor
Who goes over to their side;
They are like a cloud
That spreads across the sky
Until the sun no longer shines.
Those are people I despise.

3 And you, you jealous gossips,
Don't think that I'll delay
To please myself with joy and youth
If only just to cause you grief!

49

Raimon Jordan (?)

No puesc mudar no digua mon vejaire /
I cannot keep silent; I must say what I think

Although the single manuscript attributes this song to Raimon Jordan, a minor troubadour of the late twelfth century, the sentiment in general and the last two lines in particular have persuaded many readers that it must have been written by a woman, unless the woman is a persona created by Raimon Jordan. If the poet was a woman, perhaps she was in the circle of Raimon Jordan, whom the *vidas* associate with Maria de Ventadorn (ca. 1165 to ca. 1221), the trobairitz and patroness of troubadours (see Poem 57). Whoever wrote the poem, it is remarkable for showing a woman's perspective on the troubadour tradition.

1   I cannot keep silent; I must say what I think
About something that stirs my heart;
It will be difficult for me to talk
About those ancient troubadours,
Now gone; but I say they gravely sinned,
For they threw the world into confusion
When they openly disparaged women.
Everyone who hears them goes along,
And all agree that what they say seems true;
And so they've led the world astray.

2   All these men who were good troubadours
Pretended to be loyal lovers,
But I am convinced no lover can be true
Who speaks ill of love;
Rather I say he must be a deceiver
Who behaves like a traitor
By candidly insulting
The object of his ardent hope.
For if a man owned all of France
But had no lady, he'd not have happiness.

3   A man of good lineage would never let
Another speak so foolishly of love
As do those who are deceitful, fickle
Lovers, and who all act the same.
Sir Marcabru spoke like a preacher
Who, in a church or place of prayer,
Reproaches nonbelievers,
And he treated women just the same.[1]
I tell you there's no great honor
In maligning those who bear the children!

4   No one should be surprised
If I speak this way and seek to prove
That just as men defend their brothers,

---

[1] See Poem 12.

Women should support their sisters;
For Adam was first father of us all,
And the same Lord God created us.
So if I choose to defend
Women, don't take me to task.
One woman should do honor to another;
That is why I've told you what I think.

50

Arnaut Daniel

L'aur'amara / The bitter breeze

The poems of Arnaut Daniel represent the pinnacle of *trobar clus*, the art of "closed composition" in which the sense of the song is disguised within elaborate patterns of rhyme and versification. Our translations, with their short lines of varying lengths, imitate the metrical form of the originals, in which each line ends in a rhyme. Arnaut was active from about 1180 to about 1195. His *vida* says he was from the castle of Ribérac (department of Dordogne), that he was a *gentils hom* (a well-born man), and that he studied letters—that is, Latin letters—but gave them up to become a *joglar*. In a poem he says he witnessed the coronation of Philip Augustus as king of France, which occurred at Reims in 1179. He was acquainted with Bertran de Born, whose castle of Autafort was about sixty kilometers from Ribérac (see note to Poem 43, stanza 6).

For Dante's encounter with the shade of Arnaut Daniel in *Purgatorio*, canto 26, see Poem 119.

1   The bitter breeze
    Makes the branchy bushes
      Brighten
  (The gentle one thickens them with leaves),
     And cheery
      Beaks
   Of birds among the branches
    Keeps stammering or mute,[1]
     Paired
    Or not paired;
   And so I strive
    To speak and make
     Pleasure
   For people, for the sake of her
  Who has turned me upside down
   And made me fear I'll die
 Unless she ends my agony.

2   It was so bright,
   My first look
     When I caught sight
  Of her, whose eyes I fear,
    That I don't give
     Two pence
   For nasty gossip;
    For others
     Rarely
    Hear my suit;
   That's why it's sport
    For me to hear
     Good cheer,
   Kind words unalloyed

---

[1] Winter makes leaves fall (spring makes them grow) and quiets the calls of birds.

From her, who gives me such delight
That to her service
I devote myself from top to toe.

3   Love, look out!
I'm so enthralled
    That I'm afraid,
If you scorn me, I'll scatter
   A set of
    Sins
You'd do better without!
   I'm a true lover,
    Dear,
   Always near,
But my stalwart heart
   Makes me hide
    What's true;
   With all this snow
I need a kiss to cool
   My hot heart—
No other balm will do.

4   If she whom I invoke
Protects me as she should,
    Lets me tell
(It's what lords do)
   The woes
    I have inside
Ranged in rows,
   My thought
    Clearly
   Will be disclosed;
For I'd be dead,
   Except that hope
    Makes me go on,
   And I beg her soon
To make me glad and cheerful;
    Enjoying any other joy
Isn't worth an apple.

5   Sweet face,
So lovely to see,
    I'll suffer
Your many proud whims,
   Because you are
    The goal
Of all my follies.
   Your beauty brings
    Brute rivals;
   Your jests
Don't deter me,
   Nor your riches
    Make me flee,

For I've never loved so much
With so little vanity;
I want you more
Than the monks of Domme love God.[2]

6   Now get set[3]
To sing
Songs
For the king who will bid you welcome;
Merit,
So blind
Here in France, is doubled there,
Where generous gifts
And groaning boards
Abound;
Go there in joy,
Behold his ring
If he shows it for homage.[4]
I've never been away
From Aragon a day,
When I wouldn't hurry home,
But here they've told me, "Stay!"

7   The rhyme is done,
For in my humble heart
I see
Her, whom I woo
Without a partner named Arnaut;[5]
As for any other thought,
I'm through.

---

[2]   Referring to the monastery at Domme in Périgord, Arnaut's native region.
[3]   Arnaut addresses his *joglar*, or performer.
[4]   The king of Aragon in question may have been Alfonso II, who ruled from 1162 to 1196, and was both a patron of poets and a poet himself (see Poem 33).
[5]   That is, without a rival who would be my peer.

51

Arnaut Daniel

En cest sonet coind' e leri / In this little song, playful and pretty

The famous image in the tornada of this song, in which Arnaut imagines himself doing impossible tasks, would be imitated by Petrarch:

> "And a doe, wandering and fleeing,
> I hunt with an ox, lame and sick and slow" (*Canzoniere*,
>   Poem 212)

> "And with the lame ox we shall go hunting the breeze"
>   [*l'aura*, Laura] (*Canzoniere*, Poem 239, a sestina).

1   In this little song, playful and pretty,
      I make words and carve and plane them,
      And they will be true and plumb
      When I'm finished with the file,
      For Love glosses and gilds
      My song, which starts with her
      Who guards and governs merit.

2   Daily I grow more resplendent
      Because I serve and praise the finest
      In the world, I tell you frankly.
      I'm hers from foot to summit,
      And even though the cold winds blow,
      The love that rains into my heart
      Keeps me warm when most it winters.

3   I hear and offer a thousand Masses,
      Burn candles made from wax and oil,
      Praying God to give me luck with her
      Who renders me defenseless;
      And when I see her auburn hair
      And smiling body, young and slender,
      I love her more than all Luserna.[1]

4   I love her and want her so lustily
      I fear I'll lose her for wanting too much,
      If loss can be wrought by greedy desire.
      With her body she holds me under
      And will never fly away;
      Truly, in interest she's made such a profit
      That she has a worker and tavern.

5   I do not want the empire of Rome
      Or for them to make me Pope,[2]

---

[1]   He would rather love her than a woman whose dowry would include the town of Luserna, a legendary Spanish city mentioned in medieval French epics.

[2]   The Roman Empire and the papacy were both vacant in 1191; perhaps the poem was written then, if Arnaut refers to these specific circumstances.

If I don't get the right of return
To her, for whom I burn and rhyme;[3]
If before New Year's she fails
To appease me with a kiss, she'll kill
Me and send herself to hell.

6   I don't give up on loving well
Because of damage I might endure;
Although she keeps me lonely,
I simply make words that rhyme.
I'm poorer in love than a plowman,
For the man from Monclí loved Audierna[4]
No better, not as much as an egg.

7   I am Arnaut, who gathers the breeze[5]
And hunts the rabbit with the ox
And swims against the stream.

---

3   *Rimar*, "to rhyme," but also "to split, crack." Arnaut's passion cracks the mold of conventional poetry.

4   The man from Moncli and Lady Audierna must have been lovers in a lost romance.

5   Arnaut uses *l'aura* (the breeze), as in Petrarch's beloved Laura. Dante echoes this line in *Purgatorio* when he has the shade of Arnaut say, "I am Arnaut, who weeps and walks while singing" (Poem 119).

52

Arnaut Daniel

Lo ferm voler qu'el cor m'intra / The firm intent that into my soul enters

In the *sestina*, a form that he invented, Arnaut chooses rhyme-words for their difficult sounds and unpoetic sense, and then puts them through systematic permutations in which each one occurs in every possible position in the stanza. If the first stanza rhymes the words in the order *abcdef*, the second moves to *faebdc*, and so on until each word has occurred in all six positions, and the poem ends.

1   The firm intent that into my soul enters
No beak can scratch out, nor can any nail
Of false flatterer, whose nasty talk will cost his soul;
And since he does not dare to strike with branch or rod,
At least in secret, where I have no uncle,
I'll rejoice in joy, in orchard or in chamber.

2   When I think of my lonely chamber,
Where, to my harm, I know that no one enters,
But I have no privacy from brother or from uncle,
My every member trembles, down to my nail,
As does a child who shrinks before the rod;
I'm so afraid she'll scorn to hear my soul.

3   I wish she'd take my body, not my soul,
And do it secretly within her chamber!
It wounds my heart more than a beating with a rod
That where she is, her servant cannot enter;
I'll stay as close to her as flesh and nail,
And do not fear rebuke by friend or uncle.

4   I never loved the sister of my uncle
As I love her, I swear it by my soul!
As close as is the finger to the nail,
If she pleased, I would be to her chamber;
With me, the love that into my heart enters
Can do its will, strong man with feeble rod.

5   Since there blossomed the dry rod[1]
And from Adam descended nephews and uncles,
No love as true as this that my heart enters
Has ever been, I think, in body or in soul.
Wherever she is, in city square or chamber,
My body[2] stays nearer than the length of a nail.

---

[1] The *seca verga*, or "dry rod," is a traditional symbol of the Virgin. Arnaut asserts that his love is the truest since the birth of Christ or the creation of Adam.

[2] Arnaut plays with the expression *mos cors*, literally "my body," but often used as here to mean "myself" or "I."

6   My body takes root in her, and nails
      Itself like bark around a rod;
      To me she is joy's castle, tower, chamber,
      And I love her more than brother, kinsman, uncle;
      In Paradise I know that two-fold joy awaits my soul,
      If ever for loving well anyone there entered.[3]

7   Arnaut sends his song of nail and uncle,
      For the pleasure of her who has the soul of his rod,
      To his Desire, whom fame in chamber enters.

---

[3] These lines may have suggested to Dante that he should include the soul of Arnaut in *Purgatorio* (Poem 119).

53

Arnaut Daniel

Sols sui qui sai lo sobrafan que.m sortz /
Alone, I know the supergrief that surges

1   Alone, I know the supergrief that surges
In my suffering heart from bitter superlove,
For my will, so firm and unmoving,
Has never torn me away
From her whom it craved at first sight and since.
Away from her, I am eager to speak;
Seeing her and loving so, I don't know what to say.

2   I'm blind to seeing others, to hearing them I'm deaf;
It's only her I see, and hear, and behold.
I'm not merely playing the prankster!
I yearn for her more than my mouth ever says.
Though I go among mountains, valleys, and fields,
Nowhere do I find all her virtues together;
God chose to select them and set them in her.

3   It is true that I've been to many good courts,
But here with her I find much more to praise:
Measure and wit and other good ways,
Beauty, youth, good deeds and pleasures.
Courtliness taught her and trained her.
She has broken so well with displeasing demeanor,
I think only good can be said about her.

4   No joy she brought could seem brief or short,
As I plead with her, please, to divine,
For it won't be through me that she learns it
Unless without words my heart opens;
Never the Rhône, with the water that swells it,
Feels the rush of the current
Of love's lake in my heart when I see her.

5   To take joy with another seems false and illicit,
For no other woman can equal her merit
Since she rises above all the others.
If I don't make her mine? Oh, she bit me so badly!
But my pain is pleasure and laughter and fun,
Since in thinking of her I'm a glutton and greedy;
O God, will I ever take pleasure with her?

6   I never took pleasure in tripping or tourney,
Nor did anyone ever gladden my heart
As this one does; sneaking deceivers
Said nothing about her—I alone have this treasure.
Do I say too much? No, if it doesn't disturb her.
My Beauty, by God, I'd lose speech and voice
Rather than say what would cause you displeasure.

7   I beg that my song may not disturb you,
      For if you deign to accept the words and the tune
      Arnaut little cares whom they please or annoy.

54

Gaucelm Faidit (?)

Us cavaliers si jazia / Once a knight was lying

Gaucelm Faidit hailed from the Limousin and was active from 1172 to 1203. A prolific poet, he left over sixty songs, including one in French.[1] He participated in the Third Crusade in 1192–3 (see Poem 55); during the Fourth Crusade (1202) he traveled to Romania.

It is not certain that Gaucelm Faidit wrote this *alba*, although it is typical of his style. One manuscript attributes it to him, but another to Bertran d'Alamanon, a minor thirteenth-century troubadour. Or it may have been written by another poet altogether, whose name we do not know.

1   Once a knight was lying
With the woman he loved best.
He kissed her many times and said,
"Dearest, what should I do?
The day comes and the night goes,
        Oh,
I hear the watchman crying,
'Away! Up![2] *For I see day*
      Coming after dawn.'"

2   "Dearest, if only it could be
That dawn or day would never come,
It would be a great mercy,
At least where a lover
Is coupled with his pleasure.
        Oh,
I hear the watchman crying,
'Away! Up! For I see day
      Coming after dawn.'"

3   "Dearest, no matter what they say,
I believe there's no greater grief
Than one that parts a lover from his love;
I know it's true for me.
Ah, so little night is left!
        Oh,
I hear the watchman crying,
'Away! Up! For I see day
      Coming after dawn.'"

4   "Dearest, I must take my road.
Wherever I am, I shall be yours;
For God's sake, don't forget me!
The heart in my body will stay
Here, so I shall never leave you.

---

[1] *Can vei reverdir les jardis*: see *Les poèmes de Gaucelm Faidit, troubadour du XIIᵉ siècle*, ed. Jean Mouzat (Paris: Nizet, 1965), no. 49, p. 403.

[2] *Away! Up!* The order of these two words is counter to common sense, an example of the figure of speech called "hysteron proteron" (Greek: "the second first"), a natural way to express urgency.

Oh,
I hear the watchman crying,
'Away! Up! For I see day
  Coming after dawn.'"

5 "Dearest, if I could not see you
  Soon, be sure that I would die;
  My strong desire would kill me,
  So soon I shall return to you
  For without you, I have no life.

Oh,
I hear the watchman crying,
'Away! Up! For I see day
  Coming after dawn.'"

Gaucelm Faidit

Del gran golfe de mar / From the great gulf of the sea

This poem of homecoming may have been written in 1192–3, when Gaucelm returned from the Third Crusade.

1   From the great gulf of the sea
And the dangers of mountain passes
And the perils of lighthouses,
Thank God, I have escaped!
So now I can relate
How many sicknesses
I've suffered, how many fears!
And since God wants me to return
With joy to the Limousin,[1]
Which I left with heavy heart,
I thank him for my return
And the honor that I've won.

2   I'm right to give thanks to God
Since he wants me, hale and strong,
To come back to my own country
Where a little garden is worth more
Than being grand in another land,
Enjoying prosperity!
The lovely welcome,
The honored deeds and the pleasing words
Of our lady, and her gifts
Of warm congeniality
And her sweet face
Are worth all any other land can hold.

3   Now I have a right to sing,
Since I see joy and flirtation,
Pleasant company and sport,
For that is your will;
The fountains and clear streams
Give me joy at heart—
Meadows and orchards, I love it all!
Now I fear neither sea nor wind,
Southwest, northwest, or west,[2]
And my boat doesn't bounce me about,
And I no longer fear
Galleys or pirate ships.

4   If one endures trouble
To win God
And save his soul,

---

[1] The area around Limoges.
[2] All these winds opposed the Crusaders' return from the Holy Land to France.

It is quite right, not wrong;
But others go to sea to rob
With wicked resolution
Where they undergo such dangers
That just when they think they are rising
They fall,
And despairing
Risk all—
Body and soul, silver and gold!

56

Gaucelm Faidit

Fortz chausa es que tot lo major dan /
It's a terrible thing that the greatest pain

Richard Lionheart was the preeminent leader of the Third Crusade (1191–2), since he far outshone his rival, Philip Augustus, who, as king of France, was lord of Richard's continental possessions. Although the Crusade failed to retake Jerusalem, and Richard himself was captured in its aftermath and held prisoner for a tremendous ransom by the Roman Emperor, he never lost the admiration of the public. When Richard died as a result of a trivial mishap in 1199, Gaucelm Faidit sang of the grief that many people shared. His song would be imitated years later by Daspols (Poem 108).

1 It is a terrible thing that the greatest pain
   And the deepest sorrow I have felt,
   The ache that brings me to tears again,
   I now must recount as poet and singer:
   He who was captain and father of valor,
   The great, daring Richard, England's king,
   Is dead! O God, what a loss, what grief—
   How strange to tell it, how harsh to hear it!
   Hard are the hearts of those who can bear it.

2 The king is dead. A thousand years have passed
   When there lived no man so brave, not one.
   Now never again shall we meet Richard's match—
   So giving, so rich, so brave a provider.
   Alexander himself,[1] who conquered Darius,
   Never gave or spent so much of his wealth;
   Nor did Arthur or Charles surpass him in worth,
   For he provoked others, if I may be frank,
   To hold him in dread or to offer him thanks.

3 I find this world of deception astounding.
   If he's courtly or wise, how can a man endure,
   Since good words and deeds seem to mean nothing?
   Why should we try even a little, or less?
   Death has made clear that she can wrest
   From us, from the world, the man who was best,
   And all honor, all joy, all goodness;
   And now that we've seen that we all face her wrath,
   We should be less afraid to meet with our death.

4 O Lord and King, now what will happen
   To arms and tournaments, crowded and busy,
   To splendid courts and generous giving,
   Since you are gone, who were their leader?
   What will happen to those who were courtiers,
   Who waited for prizes they thought would come quickly,

---

[1] Alexander the Great (died 333 BC), who conquered Persia and its king Darius among many other peoples, became a symbol of munificence among medieval writers.

But now must expect to be treated unkindly?
What will happen to those you gave power and wealth,
Who now think they should be killing themselves?

5   Long grief they'll have, and a wretched existence
And sorrow, forever, for that is their lot;
And Saracens, Turks, Pagans and Persians,
Who feared you more than man born of woman,
Will grow so great in pride and ambition
That Jesus' tomb[2] won't be ours until later—
But this is God's will; if his choice had been other
And you, Lord, had lived, then I am quite sure
That they soon would have fled from Syria.

6   There's no longer hope that a king or a prince
Will go there and know how to win it again.
But all those who come now, taking your place,
Should think how you sought the esteem of all others
As, while they lived, did your two brave brothers,
The Young King Henry and the good Count Geoffrey;[3]
Whoever it be who follows you three,
He'll need a high heart and firm intent
To do good deeds and lend a hand.[4]

7   O God, my Lord, who truly forgives,
True God, true Man, true life, have mercy!
Pardon him, for he must be needy.
Do not, O Lord, keep account of his failings;
Remember instead his devotion to serving![5]

---

2   The Holy Sepulcher in Jerusalem.
3   The Young King, Henry, died in 1183 while embroiled in a revolt against his father, Henry II, and robbing holy places in Aquitaine to pay his mercenaries (see Poem 41). Geoffrey had died, as meaninglessly as Richard, in a tournament in 1186.
4   That is, to assist in the crusades. Richard's successor as king of England, John Lackland, did not lend a hand; but the poet refers to all those who would succeed Richard on crusade. The Fourth Crusade, in 1204, weakened the Christian empire of Constantinople, but it failed in its goal to recapture Jerusalem.
5   Richard's failings included a streak of cruelty that led to the massacre of several thousand Muslim prisoners after the taking of Acre in 1191. His devotion to crusade held the admiration of many.

57

Maria de Ventadorn and Gui d'Ussel

Gui d'Ussel, be.m pesa de vos / Gui d'Ussel, I am concerned

Maria de Ventadorn, wife of Viscount Eble V of Ventadorn, was born around 1165, married no sooner than 1191, and retired to a cloister with her husband in 1221. The troubadour Gui d'Ussel was active in 1195–6. In this *partimen* Maria and Gui debate the equality between a man and a woman in love.

1   *Maria de Ventadorn*
> Gui d'Ussel, I am concerned
> Because you no longer sing.
> I'd like to make you start again,
>   So, since you know about these things,
> Please tell me if a lady in love
> Should do what her lover asks her,
> Just as he would do in return
> According to rights that lovers share.

2   *Gui d'Ussel*
> My lady Maria, I thought I had abandoned
> Debates[1] and all those things,
> But now, obeying your command,
>   I dare not refuse to sing,
> So I'll answer with a brief equation:
> The lady should treat her lover
> As he does her, with no thought of station,
> For lovers are equal, and neither is greater.

3   *Maria*
> Gui, a lover should request
> Gently what he desires;
> And a lady can command
>   . . .[2]
> And the lover must do whatever she asks,
> For she's both his lady and his friend;
> So a lady must honor her lover
> As her friend, but not as her lord.[3]

4   *Gui*
> Lady, we say to one another
> That if a lady wants to love
> She must honor her lover as he honors her,
>   For they love in equal measure;
> And if by chance she loves him better,
> Her words and deeds should make that clear;
> But if her heart is false and deceitful,
> Her pretty looks should hide her betrayal.

---

[1]   In Occitan, *tensós*, the name of the poetic genre of debates.
[2]   The line is missing in the base manuscript and unreliable in others.
[3]   The lady's lord (*senhor*) could be either her political superior or her husband.

5   *Maria*
      Gui d'Ussel, that's not the way
      Lovers speak at first;
      They all say, when they mean to pray,
      Clasping their hands and on their knees,
"Lady, please let me serve you humbly
As your man." Then, if she agrees,
I think he becomes a liar
If he presumes to be her equal.

6   *Gui*
      Lady, it's shameful to reason
      As a lady might do
      Who refuses to treat her lover as equal
      After making one heart of two;
Either you'll say (but not to your honor)
That the lover should love her more truly,
Or you will agree they are equals,
Since love is the reason he owes her.

58

Peire Vidal

A per pauc de chantar no.m lais / I'm about ready to give up on singing

Peire Vidal, according to his *vida*, was the son of a furrier from Toulouse. Active from 1183 to 1204, he traveled to Spain, to the Holy Land as a pilgrim, to Italy, to Hungary for the marriage of the daughter of Alfonso II of Aragon and King Emeric, and to Malta on crusade.

In a bitter mood, Peire complains of failures of leadership in the Church, France, the Roman Empire, and Spain, and then turns to thoughts of his lady. Scholars sometimes call such poems *sirventés-cansos*, "satire-love songs." Rather than show a blending of distinct genres, however, they provide evidence that these poets never differentiated sharply between genres.

1 I'm about ready to give up on singing,
   For I see that Youth and Valor are dead
   And Merit finds no way to be fed,
   Since people scorn and reject it;
   I see that Wickedness holds such sway
   That it conquers and rules the world,
   And I can hardly find a land
   Whose leader's not caught in the snare.

2 At Rome false doctors and the Pope
   Have so confounded holy Church
   That they anger God himself;
   They're so foolish and corrupt
   That heresies are spreading,[1]
   And since these priests were first to sin,
   Others follow, and do the same—
   But I don't want to stir things up.

3 The scandal got its start in France,
   With those who once were better;
   The king is not true or faithful
   Toward Merit or our Lord
   Since he left the Sepulchre behind.
   He buys and sells and bargains
   Like a peasant or a burgher,
   And brings shame upon the French.[2]

4 All the world is turning crooked—
   Bad before, worse today—
   And ever since the Emperor
   Broke with the guidance of God,
   We haven't heard that his merit grows.
   But if now like a fool he lets Richard,

---

[1] Heretical sects that were active in the south of France in the late twelfth century included the Albigensians, who would later be persecuted by the Albigensian crusade (1209–49), and the Waldensians, or "poor men" of Lyon.

[2] In August 1191 Philip Augustus cut short his participation in the Third Crusade, only four months after arriving in the Holy Land.

Who is locked in his prison, go,[3]
The English will say he's a joke.

5   The kings of Spain are a pain:
They insist on fighting each other
But send horses, bays or grays,
To the Moors because they're so afraid;[4]
By increasing the Muslims' pride,
They are conquered and subdued;
It would be better if kings agreed
To keep law, the faith, and peace.

6   Let no one think that I humble myself
Before great men who all turn bad,
For I have a true joy that guides me,
Keeps me glad with great sweetness,
And refreshes me with the faithful amity
Of the lady who most pleases me;
If you want to know who she is,
Ask for her in the Carcassés.[5]

7   She has never deceived or betrayed
Her lover, or put on artificial color,
And she doesn't need to, since her own
Is as fresh as a rose in spring.
She is lovely beyond all beauty,
And joins good sense with youth;
The courtliest men admire her,
And sing her praises with honor.

---

[3]   Richard was imprisoned by Emperor Henry VI from February 1193 to February 1194.

[4]   The Christian reconquest of Spain lasted, with many reversals, from 712, when the Muslims invaded the peninsula, until 1492, when they were expelled from Granada.

[5]   The region around Carcassonne.

59

Peire Vidal

Ab l'alen tir vas me l'aire / I breathe in the air

Peire expresses yearning for Provence, the region east of the Rhône, because his lady is there though he is not. This is not a song of patriotic feeling for the poet's own land, since he came from Toulouse, far to the west. He may have written this poem in Italy.

1   I breathe in the air
Blowing gently from Provence.
The soft breeze pleases me
And stirs my heart;
Words of praise for that sweet land
Make me smile
And gently yearn for more.

2   From the River Rhône to the hills of Vence,
From the sea below to the high Durance[1]
The land of perfect happiness
Shines in purest joy.
There among that noble people
I have left my heart rejoicing
With her who makes the sad ones smile.

3   I cannot weep on the days
When these memories return,
For in her being, joy is born.
Whoever praises her can say
Only what is true.
She is better and more worthy
Than any other, anywhere.

4   If I know how to speak or act
I owe her thanks, for she gave me
Wisdom and understanding.
My heart fills with joy and song;
Any good I ever do
Comes from her beauty, her charm,
Even when I lose myself in dreams.

---

[1]   The four borders of Provence: the Rhône to the west, its tributary the Durance to the north, Vence to the east, and the Mediterranean to the south.

60

Peire Vidal

Drogoman senher, s'agues bon destrier /
My lord Dragomán, if I had a good steed

1   My lord Dragomán,[1] if I had a good steed
My foes would know they were really in trouble;
Even now they only have to hear my name
To be stricken like quail scared by a hawk,
And they know that their lives are not worth a penny
Because I'm so feisty, so fierce, and so brave.

2   When I put on my shirt of mighty double mail
And gird on the sword that Sir Guy[2] gave me lately,
The very earth trembles wherever I walk,
And even the proudest of my foes
Yields to me the road or the path,
For they all fear the sound of my step.

3   In daring I equal Roland or Oliver,[3]
In loving, Berart of Mondisdier;[4]
I'm so noble that I'm known all over!
I'm besieged by errand boys who bring from ladies
Rings of gold and ribbons black or white,
And words that make me giddy with delight.

4   I am the perfect image of a knight;
Indeed that's what I am, for I know the ways of love,
Everything a lover needs to know.
No man was ever found to be better in a chamber,
Or so arrogant and haughty when he's armed;
Even when not seen or heard, I am loved and feared.

5   So if I had a horse, rapid and well trained,
The king of Aragon could take his ease;[5]
He could sleep softly and deep,
For I'd keep order in Provence and Montpellier,
And robbers riding on their wretched nags
Would never raid the Autavés or Crau again.[6]

6   If the king returns to Toulouse on the bank,
And the count marches out with his pitiful lancers

1   *Dragomán,* literally "Interpreter," as in English (the word comes from Arabic); a secret name, or *senhal,* perhaps for Peire's patron, Guilhem VIII, lord of Montpellier, who ruled the city from 1172 to 1202. Riquer takes it as referring to Alfonso II of Aragon (*Trovadores,* vol. 2, p. 874).

2   Perhaps Gui, the brother of Guilhem VIII of Montpellier.

3   Roland, the mighty warrior of the *Song of Roland,* and his companion Oliver.

4   A hero of the Old French epic celebrated for his courtesy and his triumphs in love.

5   Alfonso II, king of Aragon, was also count of Provence and an ally of Guilhem VIII of Montpellier.

6   Territories lying east of Arles and Tarascon, respectively.

Shouting "Aspa!" and "Orsau!"[7]
I'll be the first to strike a blow;
I'll hit them so hard they'll run back in a hurry
With me in pursuit, if they don't shut the gate.

7   If ever I catch the jealous men or tattlers
Who ruin people's pleasure with wicked advice
And beat down Joy in public and private,
They'll learn what kind of blows I strike;
If their bodies were made of iron or steel,
They would do them no more good than peacock feathers!

8   Lady Vierna, thanks to the lord of Montpellier
You will love a cavalier embroiled in battle here,
And, thanks to God, you've multiplied my joy.

---

[7]   Valleys in the Basque region, the homes of mercenaries who were hired by Count Raymond V of Toulouse. Raymond was involved in conflict with King Alfonso of Aragon from 1175 to 1185.

61

Raimbaut de Vaqueiras

Eras quan vei verdeyar / Now when I see the meadows turning green

Raimbaut, born in Vaqueiras (department of Vaucluse), was active from about 1180 to 1205 in the courts of Provence and northern Italy. He was knighted by his patron, Boniface, Marquis of Montferrat in Piedmont. Raimbaut participated in the Fourth Crusade and probably died in the Near East. As a poet he specialized in multilingual compositions.

This is the most famous representative of the *descort*, a genre in which the poet mixes elements of versification or melody in order to depict the confusion of the lover's mind. Raimbaut mixes languages, composing a series of stanzas, first in Occitan and then in Genoese, Old French, Gascon, and Galician-Portuguese, in which he babbles of his unhappy love. We have used bits of the original languages in our translation to express the multilingual effect. In the tornada Raimbaut runs through the languages again with just two lines for each one.

1   Now when I see the meadows turning green
And the orchards and the woods,
I'll sing a song of my discord
In love, and how it makes me spin;
Once a lady loved only me,
But now her heart has changed,
So what I'll do is make a quarrel
Of words and sounds and tongues.

2   *Io son quel que ben non aio,*
In Genoese, I have no luck
Nor ever shall in April or *Maio,*
Unless *Madona* makes it mine;
I certainly cannot describe
Her great *beutà* in her *lengaio;*
It's fresher than an iris bloom,
That's why I'll never leave her.

3   *Belle douce dame chiere,*
Sweet dear lady, in French
I surrender completely to you;
Never shall I have real *joie*
Unless I have you and you, me.
You must be a wicked warrior
If you kill me, *par foi,*
But still I will not break your *loi.*

4   *Dauna, io mi rent a bos,*
In Gascon now I yield to you,
The best of all and merry too,
If only you weren't so fierce, *tan hera.*
You have the prettiest face, *haissos,*
And color fresh, *hresq'e noera,*
(That means new), so I am yours;
If you are mine, my life's complete.

5   *Mas tan temo vostro preito,*
        In Portuguese I fear your wrath
        So much I'm all *escarmentado;*
        For you I suffer pain and grief
        And my body's wracked, *lazerado.*
        At night I lie in bed awake,
        But since my love brings nothing good,
        My hope is going, *meu cuidado.*

6   Fair Knight,[1] your ladyship (in Occitan)
        Is so dear to me, *tant car,*
        That (in Genoese) I'm quite dismayed.
        Woe is me, what to do, *que far,*
        If (in French) she whom I truly love
        Kills me and I know not *pourquoi?*
        Ma Dauna (in Gascon), faith I owe,
        And by the head of *Santa Quitera,*[2]
        My heart (in Portuguese, *corassó*)
        You've stolen with your charming speech.

---

[1]   The secret name, or *senhal*, by which Raimbaut names his lady. Many *senhals* for ladies are masculine: the troubadour might call his lady *Mon Desir* "my desire," and so on.
[2]   A Gascon saint.

Raimbaut de Vaqueiras

Altas undas que venez suz la mar / O high waves bounding across the sea

This poem in the voice of a young woman whose lover has left her resembles the *cantiga de amigo,* or "song about a lover," that was practiced by poets writing in Galician-Portuguese. Raimbaut was capable of composing in this language, as we see in Poem 61. In the Occitan poem below, he imitates a characteristic Galician-Portuguese form.

1   O high waves bounding across the sea,
The wind pushing you this way and that,
Do you have tidings of my Love,
Who sailed away and hasn't come back?
    O God, what love!
Sometimes it makes me laugh and sometimes cry!

2   O soft breeze that blows from distant lands
Where my Love sleeps and lives and lies,
Bring me a draft of his sweet breath!
I open my mouth wide in desire.
    O God, what love!
Sometimes it makes me laugh and sometimes cry!

3   It hurts to love a knight who lives so far away,
Whose games and laughter later turn to tears.
I never thought my Love would do me wrong;
I gave him all he asked of me in love.
    O God, what love!
Sometimes it makes me laugh and sometimes cry!

Raimbaut de Vaqueiras

Gaita be, gaiteta del chastel / Keep good watch, Guardsman of the castle

The form of this *alba* is reminiscent of Arnaut Daniel in its use of systematic internal rhymes.

1 Keep good watch, Guardsman of the castle,
  For I hold her Whom I love best
   To me Till dawn.
   Now day comes Though I didn't call it,
    And we must stop our play[1]
    Because of *dawn, the dawn,*
     Yes, dawn!

2 Keep watch, my friend. Wake and call and cry,
  For I am blessed To hold the one I love;
   But dawn makes me Its enemy,
   And the agony We owe to day
    Displeases me
    More than *dawn, the dawn,*
     Yes, dawn!

3 So keep watch, Guardsman in the tower.
  The jealous man, Your evil lord,
   Vexes me More than dawn;
   Down here We speak of love,
    But we're afraid
    Of *dawn, the dawn,*
     Yes, dawn!

4 Lady, goodbye! No longer can I stay;
  In spite of myself I must go away.
   How I despise Seeing dawn
   Come up So soon!
    It tries to trap us,
    Dawn, the dawn,
     Yes, dawn!

---

[1] *Joc,* "play, game," a near synonym of *joi,* "joy." Conversely *joi d'amor* means both the "joy" and the "game" of love. Compare Guido Cavalcanti, Poem 110, stanza 1.

64

Raimbaut de Vaqueiras

Kalenda maya /
When May Day comes

The *estampida* or, in French, the *estampie*, is "a lively rhythmical composition intended for either instrument or voice"; it probably originated "as a popular stamping dance."[1] It is thought to have originated in the North and to have traveled south to the troubadours, but the earliest known examples are in Occitan. Raimbaut's is the first and is considered by many the best. The melody for this poem has been preserved.[2] Although the notation does not indicate rhythm, the *estampida* is usually performed with a vigorous, driving beat. The lines are short, the stanzas elaborate.

1
      When May Day comes,
      Neither leaf of beech
Nor birdsong   Nor sword-lily
      Can ever please me,
      Noble, merry lady,
Until I get   A message quick
From beautiful   You, to tell me
Love's   Pleasure;
      And I lie,
      Drawing
Near you,   Lady true;
      And the jealous man
      Falls
With a wound   Before I go.

2
      O my lovely friend,
      God, don't let it be
That the jealous one   Gets a laugh on me;
      He would sell dear
      His jealousy,
If he parted   Two such lovers;
Never again   Would I be joyful,
And joy without you Would be no good to me;
      I'd go
      Away
And never be   Seen again;
      I'd die
      That day,
Good lady,   If I lost you.

---

[1]   *The Poems of the Troubadour Raimbaut de Vaqueiras*, ed. Joseph Linskill (The Hague: Mouton, 1964), p. 189.

[2]   Rosenberg, *Songs of the Troubadours*, p. 156.

3
But how could I lose her
Or get her back,
A lady   I never had?
A real lover, either he or she,
Is not just a matter of thought;
For when a lover   Becomes real
Honor   Grows
And the look of bliss   Makes people talk,
But I
Never held
You naked   Or another way;
I've wanted you,
Believed in you,
But not won you   Another way.

4
I would scarcely rejoice,
Fair Knight,[3]
If ever I left   You in anger;
My heart does not turn
Elsewhere, nor does
My desire,   For it desires nothing else,
Though I know it would please Those nasty gossips,
Lady, for there's no other way To cure their malady.
If a certain man
Saw
Or heard my pain,   He'd thank you,
For he
Has hopes
And thoughts   That make me sigh.

5
Lady Beatrice,
Your worth
Begins so well,   Surpasses others,
And grows;
As I believe
You adorn your manner   With merit
And fair words   Without fail;
You sow the seeds   Of deeds that please.
Knowledge
And patience
You have,   And sympathy;
You clothe
Your worth
Without quarrel   But with kindness.

---

[3]   A secret name, or *senhal*, for Beatrice, the daughter of Boniface of Montferrat, Raimbaut's patron. She is named in stanza 5.

6   Charming lady,
Everyone praises
And sings your value,   Which pleases;
If anyone forgets you
His life is worth little.
Why do I adore you,   Excellent lady?
Because I thought you   The noblest,
The most   Perfect;
I served you,
I wooed you,
As sweetly   As Eric did Enid.[4]
Sir English,[5]
I have built
And finished   This *estampida*!

---

[4] The loving but demanding husband and the loving, long-suffering wife in the French Arthurian romance, *Erec et Enide*, written by Chrétien de Troyes around 1170.

[5] In Occitan, *Englés*, perhaps a playful name for Boniface of Montferrat; see *The Poems of the Troubadour Raimbaut de Vaqueiras*, ed. Linskill, pp. 27, 190.

65

Raimbaut de Vaqueiras

Ges, si tot ma don' et amors / Although my lady and Love

1
    Although my lady and Love
    Have tricked me and scorned me,
    You must not think that I forget to sing
    Or imagine less value in my valor;
Or think that I am quitting worthy ways
Or the good deeds that so befit a knight,[1]
Or that wretched death threatens my life
As it did when I crossed the mountain pass.[2]

2
    Galloping, trotting, jumping and racing,
    Waking and toil and travail
    Will be my repose for the rest of my days,
    And I'll suffer the cold and the heat
Armed in wood and iron and steel;
My inns will be pathways and copses,
My songs, satires and discords,
And I'll fight the strong, defending the weak.

3
    But since it would be an honor for me
    To find a suitable lady,
    Charming and fair and worthy,
    Who did not delight in my grief,
Who trusted no gossip but tried to be true,
Who would not make me beg if I wanted to woo,
I'd make myself willing to tell her I love her
If she would love me, for that is my pleasure.

4
    But wait—my senses are fleeing!
    Here for a year I have been lost
    Because of a lady's changeable heart,
    But thinking of joy is so alluring
It cheers me up and rids me of care.
Despite Love, my wandering heart
And my lady (I've eluded all three),
I'll spur myself on and strive to stay free—

5
    To set out on other endeavors
    With lance and shield and sword,
    And to advance the cause of valor
    With kings and emperors.[3]

---

[1]   We know from another poem that Raimbaut was knighted in 1195 (*The Poems of the Troubadour Raimbaut de Vaqueiras*, ed. Linskill, p. 136).

[2]   "The reference is to the Alpine passes crossed by the poet on his journey from Italy to Provence" (*The Poems*, ed. Linskill, p. 136).

[3]   Raimbaut's patron, Boniface of Montferrat, enjoyed both royal and imperial connections (*The Poems*, ed. Linskill, p. 137).

At Montferrat and near Forqualquier,[4]
As a soldier for hire, I'll live on war;
And since Love brings me no reward
I'll drop it, and let her be at fault.

6   I've learned about love the difficult way:
Those who are fickle and change
Are loved best, and he who serves is dead,
So I'm far better off because I fled.

7   Lady Beatrice,[5] I hope and desire that God
May save and preserve your surpassing worth,
And your foe may be conquered and slain,
Since he likes neither joy nor pleasure nor fun.

---

[4] Raimbaut had been involved in conflict between his patron, Boniface of Montferrat, and the cities of Piedmont. In Provence, across the Alps, the inheritance of Forcalquier was in dispute. The chronology of these allusions seems to place the composition of this poem in 1196 (*The Poems*, ed. Linskill, p. 137).

[5] Beatrice, daughter of Boniface of Montferrat. If Raimbaut addressed her directly in life, he must have been in Italy at the time; but he may have addressed her directly only in the poem, intending to send it to greet her (*The Poems*, ed. Linskill, p. 137).

66

The Monk of Montaudon

L'autrier fuy en paradis / The other day I went to Paradise

The Monk of Montaudon left the monastery of that name near Aurillac (department of Cantal), in Auvergne, to become a troubadour. He was active as a poet from 1193 to 1210. In this fictional *tensó* or dialogue, he debates with God. He must have written the song during or shortly after the captivity of Richard Lionheart in 1192–4 (see note to stanza 6).

1   The other day I went to Paradise,
Where I was happy and glad
Because God was so kind
To me, he whom all things obey,
Mountains and valleys, land and sea.
He said, "Monk, why have you come?
How are things at Montaudon,
Where you have more friends?"[1]

2   "Lord, I've been being humble
In a cloister for a year or two,
But just for that I've lost the barons;
They take their love away from me
Because I love and serve you.
Sir Randon, who owns Paris[2]
And has never lied to me,
Regrets this, he tells me, as much as I do."

3   "Monk, I am not grateful
If you hide in your cloister
And make war and conflict
And trouble with your neighbors
Just to keep your power.
I'd rather hear song and laughter;
The world will be better,
And the winner, Montaudon!"

4   "Lord, I'm afraid I'll go astray
If I write *coblas* and songs,[3]
For a monk who breaks his oath
Loses you and your love;
That's why I gave up the trade.
I never enjoyed the world,
So I turned to reading psalms
And abandoned the road to Spain."

5   "Monk, you made a big mistake
When you failed to go

---

[1] The Monk implies that not many of his fellow monks at Montaudon have been received in Paradise.

[2] *Paris*, the name of a castle near Mende (department of Lozère), south-east of Aurillac; not related to either the capital of France or the town of Paris in Rouergue.

[3] Either "stanzas" in general, or the isolated stanzas that became an independent genre.

To the king of Oléron,[4]
Since once he was a friend.
I advise him to think again;
Oh, how many sterling marks
He wasted on your gifts,
For he raised you from the dust!"

6   "Lord, I would have gladly seen him
But for your bad decision
To let him be captured.[5]
You failed to remember
How the ship of the Saracens sails;
If that ship had arrived in Acre,
Evil Turks would be there still.[6]
Only a fool would follow you to war!"

---

[4]   As duke of Aquitaine, Richard Lionheart was lord of the island of Oléron off the French coast near Saintonge.

[5]   While returning from the Third Crusade, Richard was captured by an Austrian nobleman whom he had offended in the Holy Land. The Roman Emperor, Frederick VI, held him for an immense ransom. Richard remained in prison from late 1192 until early 1194.

[6]   In 1191 Richard captured a Saracen ship that was attempting to raise his siege of Acre. The fall of the city marked his first great victory of the Crusade. The Monk expresses resentment that God did not provide more reliable assistance for Richard and the Crusaders.

Fall

1200–1250

WITH the turn of the century, the women poets, or trobairitz, became more active. They had appeared on the scene in the twelfth century with Azalais de Porcairagues and the brilliant Comtessa de Dia. Now in the thirteenth century Castelloza made known the depth of her suffering, and a number of other women, all of the nobility, practiced verse. Often they wrote as a social amusement in the genres that use dialogue, the *tensó* and the *partimen*, or in independent stanzas called *coblas*. Relatively few poems by women survive, but those that do offer voices and perspectives that cannot be ignored. Because these poems have traditionally been overlooked or underrated, we have chosen to provide a generous representation of them.[1]

Among the troubadours active in this period, Peire Cardenal was outstanding. A scathing critic of clerical abuses and a satirist of human foibles, Peire lived to be more than a hundred years old. During this time the troubadours and trobairitz extended their influence all across the Midi. Bernaut Arnaut and Lady Lombarda hailed from Gascony in the West, while Falquet de Romans and Tibors sang in Provence to the East. The Dordogne in the North was represented by such poets as Elias Carel, while Raimon de Miravel worked further south, in the area around Carcassonne. Poets in Catalonia were writing in Occitan; a *planh* (Poem 78) by an anonymous trobairitz emerged from that region. Occitan verse also flourished in Castile (Arnaldo and Alfonso X) and in Italy (Domna H. and Rofin, Lanfranc Cigala and Guilhelma de Rosers).

---

[1]   The extant poems by women represent no more than two per cent of the total corpus. On the trobairitz see Bruckner, *Songs*; Rieger, *Trobairitz*; Paden, *Voice*.

Figure 4. Ornamented initial from the *vida* of Jaufre Rudel in chansonnier I (Paris, Bibliothèque nationale de France, ms. français 854, folio 121v). The initial depicts Jaufré Rudel expiring in the arms of the countess of Tripoli. It begins the narration in the *vida*, our Selection 86. (Reproduced by permission of the Bibliothèque nationale de France)

67

Anonymous

Dieus sal la terra e.l palai / God save the land and the great hall

The poem below is a *cobla*, or independent stanza, in the voice of a woman. Speaking to her faraway lover, she tells him she wishes she were free to be with him. To all appearances this stanza was composed independently of any longer context. The composition of *coblas* began in the last decade or so of the twelfth century.

> God save the land and the great hall
> Where you are and where you dwell!
> Wherever I am, my heart is there
> For no one can rule it here.
> I wish my body were also there,
> Though gossips would talk of it here;
> I'd rather have joy all-embracing
> Than this man who is so annoying.[1]

---

[1] *Enueijos* in the manuscript can be interpreted either as *enojos, enuejos*, "annoying, unpleasant," or as *envejos*, "envious." The latter interpretation might refer to the lady's husband, if not her lover, but the former could refer to a husband, father, brother, or any man who is an obstacle to her love.

68

Anonymous

Aissi m'ave cum a l'enfant petit / What happened to me recalls a little child

This anonymous Occitan poem develops an unusual simile of a child. It was imitated in Middle High German by Heinrich von Morungen, who was active from around 1190 to 1222.[1] The Occitan original was probably written at the end of the twelfth century or the beginning of the thirteenth.[2]

1   What happened to me recalls a little child
Who, seeing his own face in a glass,
Reaches out to grab it roughly,
Breaks the mirror in his folly,
And cries because of what he's lost.
In just this way a pretty face
Once made me rich; now tattletales,
By treachery, have taken her away.

2   That is why I feel downcast
And why I fear I'll lose her love,
And why I'm singing my desire;
The pretty one has so caught and held me
That I fear my eyes will lose my way,
Just as Narcissus saw his reflection
In the pool, loved it with all his heart,
And died for foolish love.[3]

3   I am impatient to get her pardon,
Since lying gossips parted us;
God give them grief, for without those traitors
I'd have great joy and great pleasure!
Remember, my pretty, the sweet moment
When you made me kiss your lovely face;
That's what keeps me happy in the hope
Our love will reach a joyful close.

4   Go, my song, to the pretty one;
Tell her, without joy I'm pale,
And only rejoicing will make me well.

---

[1] See István Frank, *Trouvères et Minnesänger: Recueil de textes pour servir à l'étude des rapports entre la poésie lyrique romane et le Minnesang au XIIe siècle* (Saarbrücken: West-Ost-Verlag, 1952), p. 112.

[2] The poem was discovered and edited in 1858 by Karl Bartsch, one of the giants of early troubadour scholarship. The manuscript he edited it from has never been found again.

[3] Compare the Narcissus image in Bernart de Ventadorn (Poem 30, stanza 6). These are the thoughts of a lover enchained, as on the Limoges casket (see *Frontispiece*).

69

Alais, Iselda, and Carenza

Na Carenza al bel cors avinenz / Lovely Lady Carenza

In this dialogue two sisters ask an older woman, Carenza, for advice.[1] We imagine the two sisters interrupting each other excitedly in their eagerness to ask their friend whether or not they should take a husband. Carenza responds that they should seek the husband who will leave them virgins; that is, she advises them to enter religion as brides of Christ.

In the absence of strong historical evidence, we suppose, as others have, that the poem may have been written in the late twelfth or early thirteenth century.[2] We do not know where it was written.

1 *Alais*
   Lovely Lady Carenza,
   Won't you give two sisters advice?
   Yselda
   Since you know how to judge what's wise,
   Please tell me what you think is best.
   Alais
   Do you think I should take a husband,
   Or, if I'd rather, stay a virgin?
   Yselda
   I don't think I want to have children;
   But not being married may hurt me!

2 *Carenza*
   Lady Alais and Lady Yselda, in complexion,
   Learning, merit, beauty, youth,
   Manners, courtesy and worth,
   You surpass the wisest maidens.
   My counsel is to sow good seed:
   Find a Husband with a wise head
   And bear fruit with him, the glorious Son;
   Wed to him, you will remain virgins.

3 *Alais*
   Lady Carenza, a husband would be cheery
   But if I had babies, I'd be weary.
   Yselda
   The breasts hang down so heavy,
   And the belly is stretched and ugly!

4 *Carenza*
   Lady Alais and Lady Yselda, keep me in mind
   When you come into the Aura divine;
   When you stand within his glory, pray
   To keep me close on Judgment Day.

[1] The "two sisters" mentioned in line 2 are identified twice in the text as *N'Alaisina Yselda*. These words have usually been interpreted as "Lady Alaisina Yselda," that is, one woman with a double name; but we think they are better read as *N'Alais i na Yselda*, "Lady Alais and Lady Yselda." We accept the latter solution, and accordingly distribute the lines of stanzas 1 and 3 between the two sisters, despite the element of arbitrariness in doing so.

[2] Rieger, *Trobairitz*, p. 165. Bruckner, *Songs*, p. 179.

70

Raimon de Miraval and Aesmar

Miraval, tenzon grazida / Miraval, I think we should make

Raimon de Miraval was the lord of Miraval (department of Aude), near Carcassonne. Active from 1191 to 1229, he left over forty compositions, mostly love songs. In this *partimen* (called a *tensó* in stanza 1) he debates with a certain Aesmar, perhaps Aesmar or Ademar lo Negre ("the Black") from Albi, who enjoyed the patronage of the kings of Aragon and Castile.

1   *Aesmar*
Miraval, I think we should make
An amusing *tensó*,[1] if you like,
So tell me, if you will,
Should a man abandon
His lady when she grows old,
And for no other reason?
Answer me, yes or no!

2   *Raimon*
Aesmar, I choose at once
The part of Merit and Worth:
A lover who has won a lady
Should not want to leave her,
Because pleasure is more sublime
When it lasts a long, long time.
How can we debate that?

3   *Aesmar*
Miraval, a woman looks strange
When her hair is turning white,
So I think she should stay with you,
Since you two will look alike!
An old man and woman make a perfect pair,
And youth goes well with youth;
So I don't court the older ones.

4   *Raimon*
Aesmar, since you intend
To turn our song into a quarrel,
I want people to know in Spain
That your lady's price
Makes her easy to get.
Leaving her won't harm you a bit;
Both of you, get over it!

---

[1]   A *tensó* is a debate or discussion; in this case, the poem corresponds to the more specific idea of the *partimen*, in which one poet proposes a set of alternatives, the interlocutor chooses to defend one of them, and the proposer is left to defend the other.

71

Isabella and Elias Cairel

N'Elyas Cairel, de l'amor / Sir Elias Cairel, I want you to tell

This *tensó* between a lady and a *joglar* is typical of the genre in its conversational manner. The subject evolves from one thing to another; the guiding purpose is to entertain. Elias Cairel, born in Sarlat (department of Dordogne), became an entertainer and traveled widely—to Greece, Italy, and Spain. He was active from 1204 to 1222. The identity of Lady Isabella, who was evidently an aristocrat, is uncertain.

1   *Isabella*

Sir Elias Cairel, I want you to tell,
Please, the truth about the love
We used to share:
Why have you now turned elsewhere?
Your song doesn't go as it used to do.
Never was I hard for you to find,
Never did you ask for so much love
That I failed to give it to you.

2   *Elias*

My Lady Isabella, valor,
Joy, merit, wisdom and wit
You used to uphold every day,
And if I praised you
In my songs, it was not to win your love,
But because I hoped for honor and profit!
That's what a minstrel does with a lady,
But every day you changed on me.

3   *Isabella*

Sir Elias Cairel, I never saw
A lover of your worth
Who changed his lady for money.
If I've spoken dishonorably,
I also spoke so well of you, I couldn't be believed.
Go on, then, and make yourself a fool again!
As for me, I am much improved,
But I'm through with longing and love.

4   *Elias*

My lady, I'd do a foolish thing
If I stayed in your power,
But even so, I don't despair
Though I win neither profit nor honor.
You'll stay the same as your people proclaim
And I'll go see my beautiful dame
With her lovely body, so slender and sweet,
Whose heart doesn't lie or practice deceit.

5   *Isabella*

        Sir Elias Cairel, you seem to be
        A pretender, as it seems to me—
        A man who pretends to be sad
        About a thing that gives him no pain.
    If you would believe me, I'd give you good counsel:
    You should go back to your abbey!
    I never dared to tell you before,
    But I talked with the Patriarch John.[1]

6   *Elias*

        Lady Isabella, I've never been
        In a refectory morning or night,
        But before long it will be your turn,
        For soon your color will fade!
    —No! You make me rude against my will.
    I lied, for I think no lady
    Anywhere has your beauty,
    Although it made me hurt.

7   *Isabella*

    If you please, Elias, I would like
    You to tell me who your lady is;
    Just tell me, and don't be fearful!
    If she's right for you, I'll be helpful.

8   *Elias*

    Lady, you ask me to play the fool,
    For I'd deserve to lose her love;
    I'm so afraid of those who defame,
    I dare not tell you her name.

---

[1]   Possibly a reference to John, the patriarch of Constantinople in 1199–1206. The text is corrupt and uncertain.

72

Castelloza

Mout aurez fag lonc estage / You've been away so long

After the Comtessa de Dia, Lady Castelloza (*Na Castelloza*), who left three songs of certain attribution and a possible fourth, is the most prolific trobairitz. We know little about her, but she seems to have been active in the early thirteenth century. Her *vida* says she was from Auvergne. Her name, which she alone seems to have borne, might be rendered "Castle Lady." We have no reason to doubt that it was a true name.

Castelloza strikes a consistently bleak note in her love poetry. In comparison to Bernart de Ventadorn, whose grief in love constantly alternates with joy, she illustrates depths of melancholy he did not plumb. In comparison to La Comtessa de Dia, she is a dark lady in song.

1   You have been away so long,
        Dear, since first you took your leave,
        It's cruel to me, and grave,
        For you promised me and pledged
        That as long as you lived
        You would never take another
        Woman. If now you have found her,
        You've murdered me, betrayed the hope
        I had placed in you: that with no reserve
        You would give me your love.

2   Fair friend, with a heart that's true
        I've loved you since our first pleasure;
        I know that I have been a fool
        Because I only hold you dearer
        And have not tried to flee;
        Though you treat me wrong, not well,
        I love you even more. I shall
        Not surrender. Love has so possessed me,
        I believe I could never live
        Happily without your love.

3   I am setting a bad pattern
        For other loving women,
        Since it is men who usually send
        Messages, words well chosen.
        Yet I think I am cured,
        Friend, when I pray to you,
        For keeping faith is how I woo;
        A noble woman would grow richer
        If you graced her with the gift
        Of your embrace or your kiss.

4   Let me be cursed if I've ever had
        A fickle heart or been untrue;
        Nor have I wanted anyone,
        No matter how noble, other than you.
        Now you find me pensive and sad

Because you seem to forget my love.
If joy from you doesn't soon arrive
You may discover that I have died,
For a lady can die from a slight infection
If a man doesn't come to lance it.[1]

5   For the suffering you've brought me,
The pain and hurtful gall,
My family gives you thanks,
My husband most of all.
If you've ever sinned against me,
In good faith I give pardon
And pray that you will come along
As soon as you have heard my song;
I am making you a vow,
To give you my prettiest smile.

---

[1]   That is, to relieve suffering by the medical technique of bloodletting.

73

Castelloza

Ja de chantar non degr'aver talan / I should never want to sing

1   I should never want to sing,
        For the more I do
    The worse I fare in love.
        Laments and tears
    Have made in me their dwelling
    Since I have put myself and my heart
    At his cruel mercy.
    If he doesn't take me soon,
    I will have waited too long.

2   O fair friend, at least one fair look
        Grant me, before
    I die of sorrow.
        Other lovers
    Think you are a beast,
    Since you give me
    No joy—still, I keep on
    Loving you in good faith,
    Always, with a steadfast heart.

3   I'll never bring you a deceitful heart
        Or a treacherous one,
    Even when I get the worst,
        For in my heart
    I know it is an honor.
    When I consider who you are,
    I remember your rank
    And know that you deserve
    A lady higher born.

4   Since I met you, I've done what you desired,
        But still, my friend,
    You did not treat me well.
        Your men have brought me nothing,
    And no messengers have come
    To say you'll ride my way.
    My friend, do no more!
    For there is no joy to give me hope,
    And I am nearly mad with grief.

5   If it would help, I'd remind you as I sing:
        I took your glove,
    Stole it with great fear.
        Then I was afraid
    I'd cause you trouble
    With the lady who retains you,
    So, my friend, right away

I put it back, for I knew
I had no right to keep it.

6   I know some knights who hurt themselves
          By paying court
      To ladies who do not court them,
          Because the knights
      Do not have wealth or rank.
      But I say, the more a lady falls
      In love, the more it befits her
      To court a knight, if she sees prowess
      In him, and a vassal's courage.

7   Lady Almuc,[1] I still
      Love what does me harm;
      For a man who has great worth
      Turns a fickle heart to me.

8   Fair Name, I do not give up
      Loving you forever;
      Forever I call on my faith
      And a steadfast heart.

---

[1]   Almuc de Castelnou exchanged *coblas* with Iseut de Capion in which she made a show of self-respect, in contrast to Castelloza's subservience. Almuc appears in a legal document of 1219 as the mother of a mature son.

74

Castelloza

Amics, s'ie.us trobes avinen / My friend, if I found you charming

1   My friend, if I found you charming,
     Humble, compassionate, and open,
     I would love you well, for now
     I find you wicked, proud, and mean
     Toward me, yet still I make songs
     To make your good name heard;
     I cannot stop making people praise
     You, even when you make me most angry.

2   I shall never be able to trust you,
     Nor love you from the heart;
     In truth, I'll think: would it do me good
     To show you a cruel and hateful heart?
     —No, I won't do it; I don't want you to say
     That I ever meant to neglect you;
     It would offer you some defense
     If I had committed negligence.

3   I certainly know that it pleases me,
     Even though people say it's not right
     For a lady to plead her own cause with a knight
     And preach to him all the time.
     But whoever says this doesn't know
     That I want to pray before dying,
     Since in praying I find sweet healing
     When I pray to the man who hurts me.

4   He's a great fool who reproaches me
     For loving you, since loving gives me pleasure;[1]
     He who speaks that way knows nothing of me,
     Nor did he see you through my eyes
     When you told me not to worry
     Because some day it might happen
     That joy would be mine again;
     Those words from you make my heart rejoice.

5   Since all other love means nothing to me,
     I want you to know that I feel no joy
     But yours, which delights and heals me
     When I feel the most pain and sorrow.
     With lamentations and lays, I hope to enjoy
     You, my friend, for I cannot convert;[2]
     I neither have joy nor expect to have help,
     Except what comes when I fall asleep.

---

[1] The male figure who discourages her love could be her father or another relative.
[2] Castelloza likens her love to a religion, and her lover to a god.

6   I don't know why I give myself to you,
     For I've tested with cruelty and kindness
     Your hard heart, which mine does not surrender.
     I'm not sending you this song, since I sing it myself;
     I shall die unless you let me enjoy
     Some happiness; if you let me die
     You'll commit a sin and go to torment,
     And I'll be more desired[3] at the Judgment.

[3]   God, whom she imagines as a lover, will desire her more than her lover does.

75

Castelloza (?)

Per joi que d'amor m'avegna / Whatever delight I get from love

This song is placed in the manuscript as though it were another one by Castelloza, but there is no attribution. Perhaps the scribe was merely inattentive. The song is consistent with Castelloza's tone and themes.

1   Whatever delight I get from love
    I care no more to feel it,
    For I don't think I please him
    Who never has obeyed
    My good words or my songs,
    And there's no tune bound in rhyme
    That says I could live without him;
    So I am afraid that I'll succumb,
    Since he lives with someone else
    And won't leave her for me.

2   I shall leave him; he scorns me,
    And my cares have done me in,
    But since he chooses to let me go
    He could at least agree
    To keep my heart in joy
    With light and playful banter;
    It should not matter to his lady
    If I stir him up a bit,
    For I don't ask him to stop
    Loving her or serving her.

3   Let him serve her but return to me,
    Not let me die completely;
    I fear his love will kill me
    That makes me languish now.
    O my friend, so strong and good,
    Since you're the best that ever was,
    Don't try to make me turn away!
    You still don't want to do or say
    What might help me one day stop
    Loving you and giving thanks.

4   I thank you, whatever else may come,
    For all my worry and my pain.
    No other knight should entertain
    Hope for me, for I want none;
    Fair friend, I do desire you,
    On you I fix my eyes;
    It pleases me to look at you,
    For I find no one else so fair.
    I pray to God to hold you in my arms,
    For only you can enrich me.

5   I shall be rich, if only you discover
How I can find the path to a place
Where we can kiss and embrace.
That is enough to stir my heart,
Which you have made hungry
For you, and most eager.
Dear friend, don't let me die
Just because I cannot win from you
A warm smile to give me life again
And put an end to my chagrin.

76

Bernart Arnaut and Lombarda

Lombards volgr'eu esser per Na Lombarda /
I'd like to be a Lombard for the love of Lady Lombarda

The *coblas* exchanged by Bernart Arnaut and Lombarda are transmitted in only one manuscript, where they are set within a *razo*, a prose commentary. Bernart Arnaut was a son of the count of Armagnac in Gascony, and eventually succeeded to the title; he died in 1226. In the *coblas* he addresses his neighbor Jordan, lord of l'Isle-Jourdain, for whom we also have historical evidence. Lombarda, the object of Bernart Arnaut's affections according to his *coblas*, answered him in *coblas* of her own. Her name means "Lady from Lombardy," or northern Italy, but it was presumably used as a name, not a geographical marker. The *razo* identifies her as a lady from Toulouse, but some scholars assume she, like the two men, came from Gascony.

Although the *razo* lacks historical authority, as all *razos* do, it is an interesting fiction that may bear traces of the truth.

Razo

Lady Lombarda was a lady of Toulouse, noble and beautiful and attractive and wise. And she knew how to compose well, and she made beautiful and loving stanzas. Bernart Arnaut, the brother of the count of Armagnac, heard about her goodness and worth and came to Toulouse to see her. He stayed with her in great intimacy, asked for her love, and became her close friend. And he made these stanzas about her and sent them to her in her home, and then he mounted his horse without seeing her again and returned to his land.

Bernart Arnaut

1 I'd like to be a Lombard for the love of Lady Lombarda—
Alamanda[1] doesn't please me so, and neither does Giscarda.
When she stares at me with lovely eyes so hard, a
Man might think she's after me, but I'm in doubt;
  She has so many pretty wiles,
  And my desires, and lovely smiles
 Stored up in her larder,
 That no one can get them out!

2 Sir Jordan, if I leave Germany for you,
And Normandy and Brittany, and France and Poitou, too,
The least you can do is set aside for me
Livorno and Lomagna, along with Lombardy.
  So if you help me,
  I will help you
 Win love from a lady who's so astute
 She'll run no risk of ill repute.

3   Mirror of Merit,
   Take comfort;
  My love's so discreet, no boor
  Will ever be able to trump it.

---

[1] *Alamanda* is a common Occitan feminine name; etymologically it means "German woman."

The *razo* continues:

> Lady Lombarda was astonished when she heard that Bernart Arnaut had gone away without seeing her, so she sent him these stanzas:

Lombarda

1   For the love of Bernart I'd take the name Bernarda,
For the love of Arnaut I'd be called Arnauda;
And many thanks, my lord, for naming me
With two fine ladies[2] so graciously.
         But I want you to say
         Which one keeps you gay;
       Which one do you hold dearer
       When you look into the mirror?

2   Mirrors and discretion are so out of tune
They nearly untune this ditty I croon,
Though when I'm attuned to my name in your rune,
My spirits ascend with your clever cartoon.
         But do give a thought
         To where you left your heart,
       For I don't know its home or its hut—
       All because you keep your mouth shut!

---

[2]   Alamanda and Giscarda.

77

Falquet de Romans (?)

Vers Dieus, el vostre nom e de sancta Maria /
True God, in your name and the name of holy Mary

Falquet de Romans was probably born in Romans-sur-Isère (department of Drôme), near Valence, on the Rhône, and near the northern border of the Occitan-speaking region. Active from about 1215 to 1233, he is called a *joglar* in his *vida*, but he seems to have been received in the company of great lords as a familiar acquaintance.

One manuscript attributes this poem to Falquet de Romans, another to Folquet de Marseilla, and a third to "Sir Folquet." The attribution to Falquet de Romans seems to be the most likely. A religious version of the *alba*, it may be compared to the early bilingual *alba* (Poem 2). The speaker of the poem may be an abbot calling his monks to matins, the service held at the first canonical hour, which sometimes began at dawn.

1   True God, in your name and the name of holy Mary
     I shall arise now, for the star of day
     Shines over Jerusalem and teaches me to say:
          Wake up and arise,
          Lords who love God,
          For day comes near
          And night fades away.
          We must praise God
          And adore him;
          Let us pray that he brings peace
          To all of our lives.
               Night goes and day comes
               In a clear and quiet sky;
               Dawn does not delay
               But comes, full and fair.

2   Lord God, born of the Virgin Mary
     To save us from death, to restore us to life,
     And to harrow hell, that the Devil held;
          You were lifted up on the cross,
          Crowned with thorns,
          Given gall to drink;
          Lord, this honored people
          Cries out to you for mercy,
          Begging that your pity
          Pardon their sins;
          Amen, O God, so be it.
               Night goes and day comes
               In a clear and quiet sky;
               Dawn does not delay
               But comes, full and fair.

3   Those who cannot pray to God must learn;
     Hear what I say, take heed, and understand:
     O God, you who are the beginning of all doing,
          I offer praise and blessings

165

For the good
You have done for me;
I beg, O Lord, that pity
May move you to save me,
And that the Devil
Will not find me or abuse me,
Deceive me or trick me.
> *Night goes and day comes*
> *In a clear and quiet sky;*
> *Dawn does not delay*
> *But comes, full and fair.*

4   God, grant me the wisdom and wit to learn
Your holy commandments, to hear and understand;
May your mercy guard me and defend me
From the earthly world,
That it not cast me down;
For I adore you and believe in you,
Lord, and offer you
Myself and my faith,
As it is fitting to do.
I cry to you for mercy
And for pardon of my sins.
> *Night goes and day comes*
> *In a clear and quiet sky;*
> *Dawn does not delay*
> *But comes, full and fair.*

5   I pray to the glorious God who sold his body
For our salvation, that he may fill us
With Holy Spirit and protect us from evil.
May he grant us his great gift
And lead us among the saved
On high where he reigns
And place us in his tent.
> *Night goes and day comes*
> *In a clear and quiet sky;*
> *Dawn does not delay*
> *But comes, full and fair.*

78

Anonymous

Ab lo cor trist environat d'esmay / With saddened heart wrapped in grief

This anonymous *planh*, or funeral lament, in a woman's voice has been dated from mid-thirteenth to the late fourteenth century, and set in either Provence or Catalonia. Its thematic elements relate closely to those of the Occitan troubadours and trobairitz, but details of its language reveal a composition by a speaker of Catalan.[1] We consider the work an expression of Catalan participation in the tradition of the Occitan trobairitz, perhaps from around the mid- or late thirteenth century. Although the Catalan language had become distinct from Vulgar Latin in speech as early as the eighth century, and Catalan prose flourished in the late thirteenth century, all the poetry that was written in the Catalan region in this period was written in Occitan.[2]

This is the only fully developed *planh* that we have by a woman, but compare the early song by Azalais de Porcairagues (Poem 27), who laments the death of one man and rejoices in the love of another. The anonymous Catalan woman's mourning may also be compared to that of the French poet, Christine de Pizan, who grieved for the death of her husband when he died in 1390.[3]

1   With saddened heart wrapped in grief,
Weeping and tearing my hair,
Sighing deeply in despair, I bid farewell
To True Love and all its counsel;
From now on, I don't want to love
Any man on earth, or to bear him good will,
Since—I tell you boldly—cruel death
Took the man I loved more than myself.[4]

2   And so, I'll act like one in despair
And every day I shall wear
A sad expression, and I shall make
Them understand, all those who come around,
That they should have no hope for me;
Let them look elsewhere
For a lady to love them or be their friend,
For I take my leave of joy and love.

3   If only I could leave the world
With God's blessing, as I take leave of love
(My family prevents me),
Since I am forlorn, I would not mourn;

---

[1] Bec, *Chants d'amour*, p. 119.

[2] Josèp Moran i Ocerinjauregui, "Inicio y desarrollo del Catalán escrito," *Medioevo Romanzo* 27 (2003): 311–19.

[3] For discussion of Christine's poem with the French text and a translation, see William D. Paden, "Christine de Pizan and the Transformation of Late Medieval Lyrical Genres," *Christine de Pizan and Medieval French Lyric*, ed. Earl Jeffrey Richards (Gainesville: University of Florida Press, 1998), pp. 27–49.

[4] Perhaps she can speak boldly because the man she has lost was her husband; otherwise, the poem could seem immodest. If it was her husband, her decision not to love again may be taken literally as the decision to remain a widow. Christine de Pizan made the same decision.

I pray that Death itself will come
Without delay to stop my weary heart,
For it took the man my heart laments
And makes me sigh day and night.

4   When I see people adorned and brightly dressed
Dancing and singing, happy and content,
It gives me pain, not pleasure or delight.
I don't think it should seem a wonder,
Since they open up my wound again
And make me remember the sweet demeanor
And bright clothing of the one—God keep him—
Who had, I think, no equal in the world.

5   It is right that I should never love again
And abandon love and its dwelling place;
For I don't believe you'll find another man
As good, as cheerful, or as well regarded.
He was honorable, worthy, and brave,
And so daring that his courage caused his death;
If after he died, I loved another man,
My heart would sorely go astray.

6   My sweet friend, though I am not buried,
I am as good as dead, and have been for some time;
God help me, for I feel nothing but pain,
So deep is my grief since I lost you.

79

Tibors

Bels dous amics, ben vos puosc en ver dir / My fair sweet friend, I can truly say

According to her *vida*, Tibors was a lady of Provence from the castle of Seranon, near Grasse. We know nothing else about her and have only a fragment of her *canso*.

> My fair sweet friend, I can truly say
> That I've never known a day without desire
> Since we met, and I made you my true lover;[1]
> Nor have I known a day, my fair sweet friend,
> When I didn't want to see you constantly,
> Nor have I known a time when I was sorry;
> Nor have I known a time, if you were angry,
> When I felt any joy until you returned;
> Nor have . . .

---

[1] The expression *fin aman*, "true lover," may suggest a conventional role in *fin'amor* rather than a simply (or even necessarily) sexual relationship.

80

Peire Cardenal

Ab votz d'angel, lengu'esperta, non blesza /
With the voice of an angel, with a tongue that never stammers

Peire Cardenal was the last great satirist in the tradition from Marcabru and Bertran de Born. A native of Le Puy (department of Haute-Loire), first a cleric, then a court poet, he left a corpus of over sixty compositions. According to his *vida*, he lived a hundred years. We know that he was active as a poet from 1205 to 1272.

In this *sirventés* Peire Cardenal satirizes the Dominican order and the Inquisition. He probably wrote it in 1229, or soon after.[1] The form and rhyme-sounds of the song are probably modeled on those of a *canso* by Peirol that has been dated before 1205.[2]

1   With the voice of an angel, with a tongue that never stammers,
      With subtle words smoother than an English weaver's weaving,
      Well considered, well spoken, and without repetition,
      Better heard—no one coughs—than learned,
          With groans and sighs they show the way
          Of Jesus Christ that we should take,
      Since he took it for our sake.
      As they travel,[3] they preach how we can find God,

2   Unless, like them, we eat shelled beans
      And soup so smooth a man could drink it down
      With rich hot sauce from a country hen,
      And sour soup on the side, with beets,
          And wine that couldn't be better
          For getting a Frenchman drunk.[4]
      If living well and eating and lying around
      Let a man win God, they may win him,

3   Along with those who drink small beer
      And, for love of God, eat plain bran bread,
      And reject the richness of an ox-tail soup
      Or flavoring with olive oil
          Or a fat fish fresh from the pond,
          Or a soup or a bubbling sauce.
      I counsel anyone who puts hope in God
      To eat at their feast if he can.

4   The first monastic order was made
      By men who wanted neither strife nor noise,
      But Dominicans deplore any silence after meals—
      They want to argue: which was the better wine?

---

[1] *Poésies complètes du troubadour Peire Cardenal (1180–1278)*, ed. René Lavaud (Toulouse: Privat, 1957), p. 163.

[2] *Peirol, Troubadour of Auvergne*, ed. S. C. Aston (Cambridge, UK: University Press, 1953), no. 20, p. 112. On the date see Peire Cardenal, ed. Lavaud, p. 46, and *Peirol*, ed. Aston, pp. 13–14, 179–80.

[3] Rather than withdraw to a monastery, as other religious orders did, Dominicans traveled to preach.

[4] The Dominicans came to the Midi with the French army led by Simon de Monfort.

They have set up a court to settle their disputes,
And they call a man Waldensian⁵ who dares to intervene;
They want to learn the secrets of a man
Just to make themselves be feared.

5   Their poverty is not a spiritual thing;⁶
They keep what is theirs and take what is mine.
They throw off hair shirts, finding them too harsh,
And wear soft robes spun of English wool;
    Never do they rend their robe in two,
    As Saint Martin was known to do;⁷
Rather, they gather up all the alms
That we once used to help the poor.

6   They wear large light robes with woven hoods
Of wool in summer, thicker in winter,
And when it's very cold, stout shoes soled
In Marseilles leather in the best French mode,
    Tightly sewn and skillfully
    (For poor sewing is a folly);
They go around preaching, with their subtle teaching:
Give our hearts and wealth to serving God.

7   If I were a husband, I'd take great offense
If a man without pants sat beside my wife—
Dominicans' skirts are as wide as womens',
And fire catches easily on grease.
    About the Beguines⁸ I won't say a thing,
    But some who are barren bear fruit;
Such miracles they do, and I know this is true:
These holy fathers may have holy heirs.

---

⁵ One of several heretical sects that were active in the South of France.
⁶ In contrast to the spiritual poverty that they profess.
⁷ When Saint Martin of Tours (perhaps in the fourth century) met a beggar, he divided his cloak in two and shared it with him.
⁸ Women in a holy order who lived in the world, often under the direction of Dominican priests.

81

Peire Cardenal

Clergue si fan pastor / The clergy pretend to be shepherds

Peire complains vigorously of clerical and papal meddling in politics, which, he claims, should be the domain of the secular nobility.

1   The clergy pretend to be shepherds,
When really they are killers;
If you watch them don their robes
They seem to be quite holy;
They make me think of Isengrin
The wolf, who one day wanted
To get into a sheepfold,
But he feared the dogs,
So he put on a sheepskin
And managed to deceive them;
He gobbled up and swallowed down
Everything he pleased.[1]

2   Emperors and kings,
Dukes and counts and viscounts
And knights, along with them,
Used to rule the world;
Now I see the clergy
In charge of running things
By stealing, by betraying,
By hypocrisy,
By force and by preaching.
They think it's a nuisance
If you put up resistance
Or fail to hand them everything.

3   The higher their rank
The lower their worth;
The higher their folly
The lower their truth;
The higher their lying
The lower their trust;
The higher their lacking
The lower their learning;
I mean the clergy who pretend—
From what I hear, God's not had
So many enemies
Since ancient times!

4   When I go to their refectory
I take it as no honor

[1]   Isengrin the wolf is a character in the medieval beast fables about Renard the Fox. Peire Cardenal refers to the Albigensian Crusade (1209–49), declared by the Pope and led by Simon de Montfort, a northern French nobleman (see Introduction). The crusade resulted in the deaths of many Albigensian believers and of others who resisted it.

Because I see traders
Sitting at high table,
And they are first to choose!
It is villainy enough
That they dare come in;
No one keeps them out.
At least I've never seen
A poor, begging trader
Sit beside a rich one—
For that much I excuse them!

5   Arab chiefs and sultans
Have no need to fear
That abbots or priors
Will assault them
And steal their lands—
That would be too hard.
Instead, they contemplate
How to win the world,
How they might have lured
Sir Frederick from his lair.
(Someone did attack him
Who had no cause to cheer.)[2]

6   If someone chose you, Clergy,
With no intent to harm,
He reckoned very poorly,
For you're the worst I've known!

---

[2]   After Frederick II Hohenstaufen, the Roman Emperor, fell out with Pope Gregory IX, he was attacked in his kingdom of Naples by his father-in-law, John of Brienne, who was assisted by papal troops. The attack failed, and John of Brienne sought refuge at the papal court in 1229.

82

Peire Cardenal

Un sirventes novel voill comensar / I want to begin a novel sirventés

Peire depicts himself in a comical confrontation with God, to whom he complains that he has sinned only because God created temptation. Compare the Monk of Montaudon, *L'autrier fuy en paradis / The other day I went to Paradise* (Poem 66).

1   I want to begin a novel *sirventés*
That I intend to recite on Judgment Day
To him who shaped me from nothing.
If he plans to accuse me of something
And tries to send me where devilry's hot,
"Mercy," I'll say, "Don't do it!
I tormented the wicked all my days
So keep me safe from tormentors, please."

2   I shall make his whole court marvel
When they listen to my plea,
For I say he wrongs his own
If he kills them and sends them to hell;
He who loses what he could gain
Deserves poverty, not means,
So he should be munificent and kind
When naming souls in passage to his court.[1]

3   You should never close your gate
And put Peter, the saintly porter,
To shame. Let souls who want to enter
Smile as they come in,
For no court is ever perfect
If one man weeps while another grins;
Even though you're a sovereign king,
Open the gates, or we'll complain!

4   You should disinherit the demons,
Since you'd win more souls more often.
Letting them go would make everyone glad;
As for yourself, you could furnish a pardon.
(For all of me he could cut them off,
Since we know he could absolve himself.)
Fair Lord God, disown them, please,
These unhappy and jealous foes!

5   I do not wish to despair of you,
Since I place in you my hope
That you will help me at my death,
And save my body and soul.
I shall propose a pretty choice:
Either put me back where I began,

---

[1]   In passage from life to death.

Or pardon me my wrongs—
I wouldn't have sinned if I hadn't been born!

6   If I suffer here and again in hell,
By my faith, it'll be wrong and a sin;
I do suffer here and can rightly complain:
For a single joy, I bear thousands of pains.

7   I beg you for mercy, my Lady Holy Mary,
Intervene for us in the presence of your Son;
Pray him to take the father and the children
And place them near the seat of Saint John.[2]

---

[2]   On the belief that Saint John enjoyed a privileged place in heaven, compare Bertran de Born's Poem 41, stanza 1. Some have thought that Peire means himself and his own children, but "the father and the children" seems to refer to the whole community of the dead. Similarly, "sister, cousin, or brother" could refer to all people (Poem 108, stanza 5). The underlying assumption is that the primary social unit is the family.

83

Peire Cardenal

Las amairitz, qui encolpar las vol /
These amorous ladies, if someone reproves them

Peire lampoons wives, husbands, the poor, and the rich, finding them all wicked, and depicts
himself as indifferent to their approval.

1 These amorous ladies, if someone reproves them,
  Defend their case just like Sir Isengrin;[1]
  One took a lover because she was noble,
  Another did it because she was poor;
  One married an elder, and she's just a girl,
  Another is older, and her husband's a boy;
  One has no cloth to make a brown cloak,
  Another has two cloaks and does it just the same.

2 War is too close if you've got it on your land,
  But it's even closer if you've got it in your bed.
  When a husband displeases his wife,
  That's worse than war between neighbors.
  If a man I know went farther than Toledo,[2]
  Neither his wife nor a cousin nor a kinsman
  Would ever say, "God send him back!"
  When he leaves he makes the sad ones laugh.

3 If a poor man steals a sheet,
  He's called a thief and put to shame;
  But if a rich man steals a figurine,
  He can go head high to the court of Constantine.[3]
  If a poor man steals a ribbon,
  He's arrested by a man who stole a horse.
  This justice is straighter than an arrow,
  That lets a rich thief hang a thief who's poor.

4 He makes a great feast, but he honors it little
  Who cooks an ox or a sheep that's stolen.
  I know one man who filled up his kettle
  At Christmas this way, but I won't say his name.
  That meat was meat that couldn't be clean,
  Illicit meat that the law forbids.
  A man who treats Christmas like that
  Does not have the wit of a child at the teat.

---

[1] Isengrin is the wolf in the beast-fables of Renard the Fox; here he appears as a dishonest
lawyer.

[2] Into Muslim Spain.

[3] Constantine, the Roman emperor whose conversion to Christianity in the fourth century
marked the end of paganism. Peire Cardenal imagines the rich thief being honored at a
legendary court in the remote past.

5   I sing for myself; it's for myself I pipe,
    For no one else understands my words;
    People comprehend what my songs say
    As little as they understand the nightingale.
    My language isn't Frisian or Breton,
    I'm not speaking Angevin or Flemish,[4]
    But Wickedness seals up everybody's eyes
    So they cannot tell the truth from lies.

6   If sinners don't heed my songs, that's fine,
    If the deeds they do are the deeds of swine!

---

[4]   Peire Cardenal treats Angevin, a western dialect of French, as equally incomprehensible as
      two Germanic languages (Flemish and Frisian) and one Celtic tongue (Breton).

84

Peire Cardenal

Una ciutatz fo, no sai cals / Once was a city, I can't say its name

In this *fabla*, or fable, Peire depicts his misadventures in a world gone mad. There is a close analog in Chinese, translated from an original tale from India, in which the exceptional man who does not go mad is the king. The story may have traveled west by oral tradition.[1]

Once was a city, I can't say its name
Where fell from the sky a peculiar rain
That drove all the men that it touched
Out of their minds.
They all went mad except for one   5
Who escaped, and he alone
Because he lay inside his house
Sleeping when it fell.
When he awoke and got out of bed
The rain had stopped.   10
He stepped outside to join the people
And found them acting crazy:
One wore a short cloak, another was naked,
Another was spitting straight up.
One threw stones, another sticks,   15
Another tore at his coat.
One hit and another pushed;
Another, who thought he was king,
Strode about with haughty pride.
Another jumped over benches.   20
One threatened, another cursed,
One swore, another laughed,
Another talked but made no sense
While another made faces.
But the one who still had all his wits   25
Was amazed when he saw
Those around him out of their minds.
He peered up and down the street
Looking for people with sense,
But no one sane remained.   30
The people amazed him
But even more, he amazed them
By acting with reason;
They thought he was crazy
Since he didn't act like them.   35
They all believed
They were sane and wise,
But he must be mad.
One hit his cheek, another his neck;

[1]   Alexandre Huber, *La fable dans la littérature provençale du Moyen Age* (Lausanne: Faculté des lettres, Section de français, 2001), p. 196.

He couldn't keep from falling down.   40
One pushed, another shoved;
He tried to escape from the crowd.
One tore at him, another pulled;
Struck, he got up, fell down.
Falling and struggling to his feet,   45
He fled with great strides to his house,
Muddy and beaten and half dead,
Relieved to get away.
This fable is like the world
And those who live there: 50
Our world is a city
Full of madmen,
For reasonable men know that good sense
Means loving God and fearing him
And obeying his commandments,   55
But now good sense is gone.
Rain has fallen here,
Greed and pride
And wickedness have come
And swept over all the people.   60
If God saves one man,
Others think he's weird
And spin him like a top
For not thinking, as they do,
That the sense of God is folly.   65
The friend of God, wherever he goes,
Knows the people must be mad
Because they've lost God's wit;
But the people think God's friend is mad
Because he's lost the wit of the world.   70

85

Domna H. and Rofin

Rofin, digatz m'ades de quors / Rofin, you're an expert in these matters

The lady who is identified in the manuscripts as *Domna H.*, "Lady H.," may have concealed her name out of a sense of modesty or discretion. If so, her choice to do so casts a revealing light on all of the trobairitz whom we know by name, and who evidently felt that no such modesty was required. On the other hand, women who were even more discreet may have written anonymously or not at all. Neither Domna H. nor Rofin has been identified with certainty, but they were probably an Italian lady and a *joglar*.

Domna H. proposes a quandary typical of the *partimen*, in which the first speaker offers a pair of alternatives; the second speaker chooses to defend one, leaving the first speaker obliged to defend the other. Domna H. asks which lover is more noble, one who keeps his promise to honor his lady's wishes or another who breaks his word and takes her by force. It is a provocative choice; in effect Domna H. dares Rofin to defend the man who rapes. When Rofin timidly (or slyly) picks the timid lover, Domna H. is obliged by the rules of the game to defend the rapist herself. She does so with an audacity that surpasses the boldness she summoned when she proposed the two alternatives. These qualities may explain the discretion that partially conceals her name.

1   *Domna H.*

Rofin, you're an expert in these matters,
So tell me right away, which one did better:
Suppose a lady who is noble and well born
And has two lovers
    Wants them both to swear an oath
Before she is willing to sleep with them,
Promising to do no more
    Than hug and kiss. And one makes haste
To do the deed and breaks his word,
While the other simply does not dare.

2   *Rofin*

Lady, folly overcame the one
Who was disobedient
Toward his lady, for it is not evident
That a lover, when love drives him on,
    Should ever defy his lady's words
And willfully compel her.
So I say the one who broke his faith
    Should lose the high joy of his lady
Without reprieve,
And the other one find mercy.

3   *Domna H.*

A true lover will not feel such fear,
Rofin, that he won't take his pleasure,
For his desire and overwhelming urge
Drive him so hard that he can't stop
    Or control himself
Despite the clamor of his famous lady;
For if love is earnest, lying about

And gazing heats him up
So much that he cannot hear or see
Or know if he does bad or good.

4   *Rofin*
Lady, I think it is a great mistake
In a lover who loves from the heart,
If any pleasure brings him joy
That does not honor his lady,
    For he should not want to avoid
Pain if it lets him honor her,
Nor should anything please him
    Unless it pleases her;
A lover who does not behave this way
Should lose his lady and his life!

5   *Domna H.*
Rofin, know that the shameful, gloomy one
Who lost his way when halfway home
Is one of those cowardly intruders,
Shameful and weak and irresolute;
    But the ardent one, in whom merit lives,
Knew how to advance his cause
When he took what he held most dear
    While his beloved was near;
A lady who distrusts a lover like him
Is wrong to trust a quitter.

6   *Rofin*
Lady, know it was character
And good judgment in this lover
And hope that his lady would help
That kept him from going wrong;
    The other man behaved like a born fool
Who dared to force his lady;
Whoever defends him knows little of love,
    For a lover, when lively true love
Drives him on, respects his lady and accepts
Whatever she says, as indeed he should.

7   *Domna H.*
    Now I know how it really is,
Rofin, since I hear you lay the blame
On the true lover and defend the wretch;
    For you would do just as wretched
Work! So let my Lady Agnesina[1] say
What she thinks about all this.

8   *Rofin*
    It doesn't matter what I swear,
For you can sort out what is right,

---

[1]   Lady Agnesina was perhaps Agnès de Saluzzo, of the Montferrat family; she will be the judge.

Lady, if you please, but it's dear to me
    That my Lady Agnesina, in whom merit lives,
Asks to enjoy the company
Of Lady Desirous of Every Good.[2]

---

[2]   *Na Cobeitosa*: perhaps Cobeitosa ("Desirous") of Este, who married Isnardo of Malaspina and died in 1257.

86

Anonymous

Vida of Jaufré Rudel

For about a hundred troubadours, we have prose commentaries: *vidas* or "lives" of the troubadours, and *razos* or "reasons" for the composition of individual songs. Most of them are
anonymous and were written around 1220 to 1250 in Provence or Italy; others were written
as late as the fourteenth century. Although they are transmitted in the manuscripts that
contain the texts of troubadour songs, they represent an accretion in the tradition, early
evidence of the gradual process by which the troubadours came to be treated as cultural
monuments.

The most famous of the *vidas* is the one for Jaufré Rudel. Elaborating on the theme of
Jaufré's own songs (see especially Poem 10), the prose writer created a powerful myth of love
from afar. Most scholars agree that the information in the *vida* was derived from the poetry
and does not provide independent information about the life of the poet. Typically, this *vida*
spins the narrative out of a succession of simple clauses, many of them joined by "and." The
effect of simplicity creates a naïve charm but does not express the syntactic and emotional
complexity of Jaufré's songs.

> Jaufré Rudel of Blaye was a very noble man, and he was prince of
> Blaye. And he fell in love with the countess of Tripoli without seeing
> her, because of the good that he heard said of her by the pilgrims who
> came from Antioch. And he made many songs about her with good
> tunes but poor words. And out of desire to see her, he took up the cross
> and set out to sea, but he fell ill on the ship and was brought to Tripoli,
> to an inn, near death. This news was made known to the countess,
> and she came to him, to his bed and took him in her arms. And he
> realized that she was the countess, and at once he recovered the senses
> of hearing and smell, and he praised God for sustaining his life until
> he had seen her, and thus he died in her arms. And she had him buried
> with great honor in the house of the Temple. And then on the same
> day, she became a nun because of the grief she felt at his death.[1]

For an ornamental initial depicting Jaufré Rudel's death, see Figure 4.

---

[1]   The actual countess of Tripoli at this time, Hodierna, was kept in a state of seclusion by
her husband, Count Raymond II. The Knights Templar were an order of crusading monks
quartered in Jerusalem next to the temple of the city.

87

Uc de Saint Circ (?)

Vida of Bernart de Ventadorn

Very little is known about the life of Bernart de Ventadorn, perhaps the most celebrated of all the troubadours (see Poems 28 to 32). His *vida* is erroneous in important details, and the basic facts that it gives about Bernart are impossible to confirm. We have no independent historical evidence on the poet, unless it is the existence of a certain Bernart, the son of the viscount of Ventadorn, who became abbot of the monastery of Tulle and died in 1234 (see discussion at Poem 28). If this man was the poet, the *vida* is thoroughly fictional. But if he was not, some elements of the *vida* may be true.

> Bernart de Ventadorn was from the Limousin, from the castle of Ventadorn. He was from a poor family; he was the son of a servant who was a baker, who would fire the oven for cooking the bread of the castle. And he became a handsome man and clever, and learned how to sing and compose well, and he became courtly and well taught. And the viscount of Ventadorn, his lord, became very fond of him and of his composing and his singing, and did him great honor.
>
> And the viscount of Ventadorn had a wife, young and noble and cheerful. And she became fond of Sir Bernart[1] and his songs and fell in love with him, and he with the lady, so that he made his songs and his verses about her, the love he had for her, and her excellence. Their love lasted a long time before the viscount and the other people became aware of it. And when the viscount became aware of it, he banished Bernart from his presence and had his wife locked up and guarded, and he made the lady dismiss Sir Bernart, so that he left and went far from that country.
>
> And he left and went to the duchess of Normandy, who was young and of great merit, and devoted herself to reputation and honor and praise. And the songs and verses of Sir Bernart pleased her very much, and she received him and welcomed him warmly. He stayed in her court a long time, and fell in love with her and she with him, and he made many good songs about her. And while he was with her, King Henry of England took her as his wife and took her from Normandy and led her to England.[2] Sir Bernart remained on this side [of the Channel], sad and grieving, and went to the good Count Raymond of Toulouse, and stayed with him until the count died.[3] And because of that grief, Sir Bernart entered the order of Dalon, and there he died.[4]

[1] It is curious that the *vida* calls Bernart "Sir," if he was in truth the son of a servant.

[2] The duchess of Normandy who married King Henry of England was Eleanor of Aquitaine. She became duchess when she married Henry in 1152, and queen of England when he became king in 1154.

[3] Count Raymond V of Toulouse (1148–94) was mentioned in several songs by Bernart de Ventadorn.

[4] The twelfth-century annals of the monastery of Dalon, in Dordogne, do not mention Bernart de Ventadorn. Another troubadour who did retire to Dalon was Bertran de Born. It is possible that this *vida* has adapted the motif of retirement to Dalon from the *vida* of Bertran de Born. See William D. Paden, "De l'identité historique de Bertran de Born," *Romania* 101 (1980): 192–224 (p. 219).

And I, Sir Uc de Saint Circ, have written what the viscount, Sir Eble of Ventadorn, told me, who was the son of the viscountess whom Sir Bernart loved.[5] And he made these songs that you will hear, written here below.

---

[5] The troubadour Uc de Saint Circ was active from 1217 to 1253. Viscount Eble IV of Ventadorn was active from 1169 to 1184. To judge by the last years in which each of these men is attested, Eble IV was about seventy years older than Uc of Saint Circ. If, as is usually believed, Eble IV was the son of the viscountess referred to here, it seems unlikely on chronological grounds that he could have told Uc this story. It may be that the name of Uc de Saint Circ was a late accretion to the *vida*.

Anonymous

Vida of Guilhem de Cabestanh

Guilhem de Cabestanh was a minor troubadour, a knight from Capestany near Perpignan who perhaps fought in the battle of Las Navas de Tolosa (1212). The tale of the eaten heart has analogues in Boccaccio's *Decameron* (fourth day, ninth story) and elsewhere.

Guilhem de Cabestanh was a knight from the region of Roussillon, which bordered on Catalonia and the area around Narbonne. He was very handsome and was esteemed in arms, in service, and in courtliness. And there was in his region a lady who was called My Lady Sermonda, the wife of Sir Raimon del Castel de Roussillon, who was very rich and noble and wicked and cruel and proud. And Guillem de Cabestanh loved the lady with true love and sang of her and made his songs about her. And the lady, who was young and noble and beautiful and pleasing, loved him more than anything else in the world. And this was told to Raimon del Castel de Roussillon, and he, like a wrathful and jealous man, investigated the story and learned that it was true and had his wife guarded closely.

And one day, Raimon del Castel de Roussillon found Guillem eating without much company and killed him and drew his heart from his body and had a squire carry it to his lodging and had it roasted and prepared with a pepper sauce and had it given to his wife to eat. And when the lady had eaten it, the heart of Sir Guilhem de Cabestanh, Sir Raimon told her what it was. When she heard this, the lady lost sight and hearing. And when she came around, she said, "Lord, you have given me such a good meal that I will never eat another." And when he heard what she said, he ran to his sword and tried to strike her on the head, and she went to the balcony and let herself fall, and she died.[1]

---

[1] The actual Saurimunda de Peiralada married Raimon del Castel de Rossillon (near Perpignan) in 1197. She outlived her husband and married again.

89

Arnaldo and Alfonso X of Castile

Senher, adars ie.us venh querer / My lord, I come now to ask

Alfonso *el Sabio* ("the Learned"), king of Castile from 1252 to 1284, was a remarkable man of letters. He encouraged the study of astronomy, codified Spanish law, established a school of translation from Greek and Arabic into Latin, and patronized the composition of the *Cantigas de Santa Maria*, a collection of over four hundred versified miracle tales written in Galician-Portuguese, the language favored for lyric expression in the Iberian Peninsula at this time.

Alfonso also found time to amuse himself and others. This poem is an exchange of witticisms between one Arnaldo (perhaps the troubadour Arnaut Catalan) and the king of Castile. Both men play upon the specific metrical form and rhymes from the song of the lark by Bernart de Ventadorn, *Qan vei la lauzeta mover / When I see the lark beat his wings* (Poem 30), reducing it to a scurrilous mockery involving a bird that was famous for flatulence.[1] Arnaldo addresses the king in Occitan; the king responds in Galician-Portuguese. The song has been dated about 1260, many years after the composition of Bernart's original. Clearly Bernart's song had achieved the status of a classic.

1   *Arnaldo*
My lord, I come now to ask
You for a boon, if you please:
I'd like to be your admiral
Over the bounding seas.
If you grant me this, in all good faith
I promise to drive your entire fleet
With the force of a windy fart,
And they'll sail with astonishing speed!

2   *Alfonso*
Lord Arnaldo, since you possess
Such power of wind, here's to you!
You plainly deserve that I should grant
This boon. But I say, Phew!
Why did no king grant this before?
Still, I'm not asking for renown or fame.
Since I have granted the favor you ask,
You shall be known as "Admiral Gas"![2]

3   *Arnaldo*
For this boon and this noble name
I owe you humble thanks indeed.
I'll also promise something else:
I'll produce a wind so courtly
That it will bring my lady,

---

[1]   This was not the first parody on Bernart's name, *Ventadorn*, that played on *ventar*, "to blow, to be windy," hence jocular *ventador*, "one who blows, one who is windy."

[2]   In the original, *Almiral Sisom*, literally "Admiral *Sisom*." The *sison* is a wading bird of the bustard family noted for its constant expulsion of fetid gases. The phrase *Almiral Sisom* puns on *Altretals se son* in Bernart de Ventadorn, "They're all the same" (Poem 30, stanza 3), that is, "Women are all the same."

The best in all the world,[3]
In the sweetness of the season
With a hundred other women.

4   *Alfonso*
Lord Arnaldo, you've gone too far,
Sending your lady across the sea
With those puffy sails,
For I don't think that there are three
In the world who have her merit.
I swear to you by Saint Vincent,[4]
He is no true lover who intends
To manufacture such a wind!

---

[3]   Arnaldo plays with formulas familiar in the troubadour tradition.
[4]   Perhaps Saint Vincent of Lérins, an island off Provence. Saint Vincent was a fifth-century monk who may be invoked because he sometimes sailed. If a learned listener recalled Saint Vincent's treatise on distinguishing truth from falsehood, particularly in the relation of Scripture and tradition, the allusion would heighten the contrast between Bernart de Ventadorn's original and this poem.

90

Sordel

Planher vuelh en Blacatz en aquest leugier so /
I shall grieve for Sir Blacatz to this sprightly tune

Sordel, to use the Occitan form of his name, was also known in Italian as Sordello and figures by that name in the poetry of Robert Browning.[1] He was born in Goito near Mantua.
After several risky undertakings he was forced by his enemies to leave Italy. He spent the
years from 1233 to 1245 at the court of Raymond-Béranger IV, count of Provence, before
returning to Italy with the triumphant expedition of Charles of Anjou.

In this mock *planh*, or funeral lament, Sordel pretends to lament for Blacatz, lord of
Aups in Provence (today in the department of Var), who died in 1237. In the original, the
poet uses identical rhymes throughout the stanza, perhaps in allusion to the assonance
that characterized early French epic poems like the *Song of Roland*. In the first stanza, for
example, all lines end with the sound *-ó* (*so, razó, bo,* etc.).

1   I shall grieve for Sir Blacatz to this sprightly tune,
     With sad and mournful heart, as I'm entitled to,
     For in him I've lost a lord, and a good friend, too,
     And in him we've also lost all valiant virtue.
     Our loss is so huge we've no hope to recoup
     Unless we take revenge upon the troop
     Of gutless barons—we'll tear out his heart
     And force it down their gullets to give them some spark!

2   The first one to eat, since so great is his need,
     Will be the Roman Emperor, whom the Milanese
     Have defied in the face of his mercenaries,
     So now, disinherited, he lives in poverty.[2]
     After him, the king of France will be the next to eat,
     Hoping to regain Castile and not be so naïve;
     But should his mother not like it, he won't get a treat,
     For he only does what pleases her, as we plainly see.[3]

3   I'd like the English king to eat plenty of this heart
     Since he has no bravery. This way he'll get the guts
     To take back the lands that the French king took
     Because he knew that his rival would be meek;[4]
     And the king of Castile for two will need to eat
     Since he wears two crowns, though for one he's far too weak;
     If he wants to eat, he will have to be a sneak,
     For if his mother knew, she'd beat him with a stick.[5]

---

[1] Browning, "Sordello" (1840).

[2] Frederick II Hohenstaufen, emperor of Rome, was threatened by the League of Milan.

[3] Louis IX of France, later known as Saint Louis, began his reign as a child; his mother, Blanche
of Castile, was regent.

[4] Henry III of England had failed to regain the continental possessions lost by his father, John
Lackland, to Philip Augustus of France.

[5] Ferdinand III of Castile and Leon was greatly influenced by his mother Berenguela, who was
the sister of Blanche of Castile.

4 I want the king of Aragon to eat some of this heart,
  For doing so will help him to escape the shame
  He got when he lost Millau and Marseilles;
  Otherwise, he never will regain his name.[6]
  Next this heart should pass to the king of Navarre,
  Who was far more valiant as a count, I hear;
  It's wrong, when God gives a man great power,
  If he loses it because he has too little heart.[7]

5 The count of Toulouse will need to eat a lot
  If he remembers what he had and thinks of what he's got;
  If he can't recoup his losses with another heart,
  I scarcely think he'll do it with the one that's now his part.[8]
  And the count of Provence will also have to eat
  If he thinks a man who has no land isn't worth a jot;
  So even if he fends thems off and tries to hold his own,
  He'll need to eat this heart to bear his heavy load.[9]

6 If the barons wish me ill for what I've said so well,
  Say I think no more of them than they do of me.

7 Fair Refuge,[10] if only in you I find compassion,
  I'll scorn any man who doesn't count me as a friend.

[6] James I of Aragon failed to help his cousin, Raymond-Béranger IV of Provence, to put down a revolt in Marseilles in 1230–43. James lost Millau in the department of Aveyron by the terms of the Treaty of Paris (1229), which eventually gave the king of France claim to regions involved in the Albigensian crusade.

[7] Count Thibaut of Champagne, the prince and French poet, became King Thibaut I of Navarre in 1234; in 1236 he rebelled against Louis IX, but only to fail.

[8] Raymond VII of Toulouse; following the terms of the Treaty of Paris, the county eventually reverted to the king of France.

[9] Raymond-Béranger IV of Provence (see stanza 4, note).

[10] A secret name, or *senhal*, for a lady, believed to be a certain Guida of Rodez.

Anonymous

Coindeta sui, si cum n'ai greu cossire / I am pretty, but my heart is aching

The *chanson de malmariée*, or song of an unhappily married woman, is a genre more frequently found in Old French than in Occitan.[1] The present example is typical in its use of a refrain and the invitation to sing in stanza 4. The theme is the woman's rebellion against an unhappy marriage, but the form is a dance-song, or *balada*.

> *I am pretty, but my heart is aching;*
> *I don't love or desire my husband.*

1   I'll tell you why I love so well;
> *I am pretty, but my heart is aching;*
> *I don't love or desire my husband.*[2]
Because I'm young and little, just a girl;
> *I am pretty . . .*
I deserve a husband who'd give me joy,
Who'd always laugh and play with me.
> *I am pretty . . .*

2   I swear to God I never loved him,
> *I am pretty . . .*
And I have no wish to love him now,
> *I am pretty . . .*
When I see him, I'm so ashamed
I pray that Death will take him soon!
> *I am pretty . . .*

3   But one thing I am sure is true:
> *I am pretty . . .*
If my lover gives his love to me,
> *I am pretty . . .*
That's the hope that keeps me bright;
I weep and sigh when he's out of sight.
> *I am pretty . . .*

4   I have set this ballad to a pretty tune,
> *I am pretty . . .*
So all may sing it, far and wide,
> *I am pretty . . .*
Learnèd ladies should join the choir,
And sing of the man I love and desire.
> *I am pretty . . .*

5   Here is what I have said I'd do:
> *I am pretty . . .*
Since my lover has so long been true,
> *I am pretty . . .*
Now I'll give him my love and desire
And the fervent hope to love forever.
> *I am pretty . . .*

---

[1]   See Bec, *Lyrique française*, vol. 1, pp. 69–90; examples, vol. 2, pp. 13–24.
[2]   The refrain recurs in its entirety three times in each stanza.

Lanfranc Cigala and Guilhelma de Rosers

Na Guilielma, maint cavalier arratge /
Lady Guillelma, a group of wandering knights

Lanfranc Cigala was active as a judge in Genoa from 1235 to 1257. An anonymous song tells us that Guilhelma de Rosers left her hometown of *Rogier* in Provence (probably Rougiers, in the department of Var) to go to Genoa. Perhaps the following *partimen* was composed there. It begins with an ethical conundrum, evolves toward increasingly playful give-and-take, and ends on a bawdy note.

1   *Lanfranc*
Lady Guilhelma, a group of wandering knights
Were traveling late, and the weather was bad,
When they said to each other they needed an inn.
Two barons overheard them, both of them lovers
Hastening along to visit their ladies.
One turned aside to help out the knights;
The other went straight ahead to his love.
Which one, would you say, did as he should?

2   *Guilhelma*
Lanfranc my friend, the most laudable,
I'd say, was the man who went straight to his love.
The other did fine, but as for his lady,
She could not see his love was sincere
As well as the lady who saw with her eyes
That her man had done as he promised.
I like a man better who does as he says
Than another who changes his mind.

3   *Lanfranc*
My lady, if you please, the other did as well,
I mean the knight who, by being civil,
Saved his fellows from death or danger.
Love moved him, since no courtesy lives
In any man unless it comes from love;
So I say his lady should thank him for saving,
By his love, those knights from discomfort
As they traveled along the road.

4   *Guilhelma*
Lanfranc, you never spoke more foolishly
Than you did in what you said just now,
For as you know well, his deed was heinous
Since polished manners meant more to him
Than the chance to serve his lady first;
He could have had her gratitude and grace,
Since he would have served her in many a place
With his love—he would not have fallen short.

5   *Lanfranc*
      My lady, I beg your pardon if I babbled nonsense,
      But now I see it's true, just as I thought:
      You women never like to see your lovers go
      On any other pilgrimage, but always just to you.
      Now, if a man sets out to train a horse to joust
      He must treat him calmly and with skill,
      But you ladies treat your lovers so unkindly
      That they lose their power, and you take the loss.

6   *Guilhelma*
      Lanfranc, I say on that very day
      That knight should have changed his way;
      For a woman who has breeding,
      Who is beautiful and noble, must have power
      To command generous service,
      Even when her lover is away! But both the men are right,
      For I am sure the one's so weak, his paltry strength
      Would falter at his time of greatest need.

7   *Lanfranc*
      My lady, I think I have the strength and daring,
      Though not against your will, to conquer you while lying,
      So I must have been a fool to have contended,
      But I hope you'll conquer me if you can.[1]

8   *Guilhelma*
      Lanfranc, I give you my consent,
      For I think I have got the heart and daring
      To take on the boldest in the land
      With the prettiest *con* a lady could defend![2]

---

[1]   In these final stanzas the poets engage in ribald word-play, systematically repeating the syllable *con*, which in Occitan means the same as it does in modern French, English "cunt." Lanfranc uses *contra*, "against"; *conten*, "contend"; *con que sia*, literally "however it may be," which we have rendered "if you can."

[2]   Guillelma continues Lanfranc's play on words. The last line of our translation corresponds to *C'ab aital gien con domna si defen*, which literally means "With such art as a lady may defend herself with"; but in this context *gien con* also suggests "pretty *con*."

Winter

1250–1300

THE end of the thirteenth century saw the flourishing of dance songs, or *bala-das*, and the nearly total eclipse of the trobairitz, as far as we can tell with our imperfect knowledge of their chronology. The sole possible exception, which we have included here, is Bietris de Romans, about whom we know little. The period is dominated by two prolific court poets, Guiraut Riquier of Narbonne, who served King Alfonso X of Castile, *el Sabio*, in Toledo for almost a decade, and Cerverí de Girona, who served King Jaume (James) I of Aragon in Barcelona. An Italian poet, Guido Cavalcanti, traveled to Toulouse and wrote about a lady he met there. The passion of erotic desire became more Christian and spiritual with Guilhem de Montanhagol, from near Toulouse. Hebrew poetry at this time included the powerful piety of David Hakohen, from Avignon, and the vigorous humor of Isaac Gorni, who was most active in Provence. A Jewish poet, Bonfils, engaged in an Occitan *tensó* with Guiraut Riquier and felt the brunt of his antisemitism.

Figure 5. A fifteenth-century geographical treatise, *Le secret de l'histoire naturelle contenant les merveilles et choses memorables du monde* (The Secret of Natural History, Containing Wonders and Memorable Things of the World), Paris, Bibliothèque nationale de France, ms. français 22971, folio 25. The illustration corresponds to the description of Gaul, or France:

> Gaul is a great and noble province. . . . Ever since Gaul received the sweet and holy oil of Christian belief, of all other peoples and nations they have been and still are the most merciful, kind, charitable and loving.

The illustration suggests that the loving character of the French may be seen in episodes from the pastourelle, or in Occitan the *pastorela*, such as Poems 13 and 98 to 103. (Reproduced by permission of the Bibliothèque nationale de France)

93

Anonymous

A l'entrade del tens clar—eya / On the opening day of spring, Tra la

We know nothing about the author of this dance-song, which we suppose was written in the thirteenth century. Like other *baladas*, it echoes the *malmariée*; compare Poem 91.

1 On the opening day of spring, *Tra la*
To start up joy again, *Tra la*
And mock the jealous ones, *Tra la*
The queen sets out to show
  How full of love she is.
Be gone, you jealous ones!
 Leave us, oh, leave us
To dance among ourselves.

2 She has sent to every place, *Tra la*
As far as to the sea, *Tra la*
For maidens and young men, *Tra la*
To come along and dance
  The dance of joy.
Be gone, you jealous ones!
 Leave us, oh, leave us
To dance among ourselves.

3 The king creeps up behind, *Tra la*
To try to end the dance, *Tra la*
For he is full of fear, *Tra la*
Someone might steal away
  The April queen.
Be gone, you jealous ones!
 Leave us, oh, leave us
To dance among ourselves.

4 But all his hopes are dashed, *Tra la*
Old men are not her care, *Tra la*
She wants a nimble lad, *Tra la*
Who knows how to please
  A lusty lady.
Be gone, you jealous ones!
 Leave us, oh, leave us
To dance among ourselves.

5 If you had seen her dance, *Tra la*
And show what she can do, *Tra la*
You could say in truth, *Tra la*
She has no earthly peer,
  The joyful queen.
Be gone, you jealous ones!
 Leave us, oh, leave us
To dance among ourselves!

94

Anonymous

Lassa, mais m'agra valgut / Unhappy me! It would have been better

The *chanson de nonne* or "nun's song," like the *chanson de malmariée* (Poems 91 and 93), is better known in French than in Occitan.[1] Like the unhappily married woman, the unhappy nun complains that she was committed to the cloister against her will—that she is an unwilling bride of Christ. Also like the *chanson de malmariée*, this poem may have been a dance-song.

It is difficult to say if this poem is written in Occitan or Catalan. If it was written during the thirteenth century, as seems likely, it may be regarded as an Occitan composition in Catalan orthography, in a Catalan manuscript, by a Catalan poet, with reference to a Catalan place. Like Poem 78, it illustrates the spread of Occitan poetry into Catalonia.

1   Unhappy me! It would have been better
        To be married
    Or to take a courtly lover
        Than to be made a nun.

2   Becoming a nun was wrong for me.
    As I see it now
        They greatly sinned,
    Those who made it happen;
        God send them a bad season,
    And hate them!

3   If only I had known—
        But I was a bit of a fool—
    If they'd offered me the town of Montagut,[2]
        I would not have gone into the convent!

---

[1]   For similar poems about nuns in French see Bec, *Lyrique française*, vol. 1, pp. 74–5; examples, vol. 2, pp. 69–90.
[2]   A town in Catalonia, east of Ripoll.

95

Anonymous

Quan vei los pratz verdesir / When I see the meadows turning green

The language of this anonymous song shows that it was originally written in Occitan, then translated into French, and then translated back into Occitan.[1] Thus it illustrates in a striking way the movement back and forth among languages that was characteristic of vernacular poetry at this time. It was probably written in the thirteenth century.

1   When I see the meadows turning green
     And flowers bloom again,
     Then I think and dream
     Of love that treats me so badly
     It has almost killed me;[2]
       So often I sigh
     Because I never have felt so hard a blow
       Without being hit.
        A, e, i![3]

2   All night I sigh and think
     And tremble in my sleep,
     Because it seems
     As if my lover wakens me.
     O God, how should I be cured
       If ever it really happened
     One night—if, by good fortune,
       He came to me?
        A, e, i!

3   Any woman who hopes for love
     Must have a steady heart;
     Some men will always take it up,
     And then in folly let it drop;
     But I do have a steady heart
       And loyal;
     Never did a woman of my station
       Behave so well.
        A, e, i!

4   A woman who has no lover
     Should beware of taking one,
     For love stings now and tomorrow
     And never gets its fill;
     It wounds and kills without a blow;
       The cure will never come
     To some, with any physician,
       Unless it's Love who brings him.
        A, e, i!

[1] Bec, *Chants d'amour*, p. 195.
[2] *Tuada*, "killed," is feminine, indicating that the speaker is a woman.
[3] Pronounce the vowels in the "continental" fashion: *a* as in "father," *e* as in "met," *i* as in "marine."

5   Messenger, get up early
And take a long day's journey;
Carry my song to my lover
Over in his country;
Tell him I'm very happy
     When I recall the song
He sang to me when we kissed
     Under my canopy.
       A, e, i!

6   Into my curtained bedroom
     He came like a thief;
Within my gilded bedroom
     He became my prisoner.[4]

---

[4] Compare the image of the lover as prisoner on the right side of the Limoges casket (*Frontispiece*).

96

Guilhem de Montanhagol

Ar ab lo coinde pascor / Now in harmonious spring

Guilhem de Montanhagol, from Toulouse, was active from 1233 to 1268. For services rendered to James I, the Conqueror, of Aragon, he was rewarded with certain lands. Later he attended the court of Alfonso X of Castile.

Guilhem may be regarded as a key figure in the transition from the love songs of the troubadours to Italian poetry of the *dolce stil nuovo*, or "sweet new style," because, like the Italians, Guilhem emphasized the morally ennobling nature of love.

1 Now in harmonious spring,
 When I see beautiful colors
 Of flowers in orchards and meadows,
 And I hear little birds that sing
 Sweetly on every side,
 I want to make in harmonies
 A song composed so it will please
 All those who are in love
 And most of all my lady,
 Who gives me skill in song.

2 Lovers surely must serve love
 Willingly, with all their heart,
 For love's not a sin, but a virtue
 That turns bad men into good;
 It makes the good ones better,
 And puts people on the way
 To doing good all day;
 So fidelity begins in love,[1]
 For anyone intent on love
 Cannot do any wrong.

3 Love has such nobility
 That ladies who have beauty
 Commit great folly
 If they do not love worthy men
 When they know the men love them;
 For they would take pleasure
 In joy and courtliness
 And songs and games,
 But this they fail to comprehend
 Unless love drives them to it.

---

[1] This line, *D'amor mou castitatz*, has been understood to mean, paradoxically, "Chastity begins in love." However, *castitatz* here must mean remaining true to one's beloved, or, more simply, fidelity. "Chaste marriage was a designation frequently used by medieval authorities, especially in the high and late Middle Ages, to designate a union in which the individuals were true to their marriage vows.... A reference to matrimonial chastity does not necessarily mean that absolute chastity is observed in marriage. It may just mean that the couple practiced sexual fidelity": Dyan Elliot, *Spiritual Marriage: Sexual Abstinence in Medieval Wedlock* (Princeton: Princeton University Press, 1993), pp. 4–5.

4 Love, I sing praise of you,
  For I love the fairest one,
  And she has so exalted me
  That even death would be an honor,
  So great is her power.
  If she ever gave me joy
  I know I would not die
  But live in happiness.
  If I don't have it, soon I will perish,
  For I love her so much my heart will break.

5 Whoever sees your fresh color,
  Lady I adore,
  And your flashing eyes and arching brows
  . . .[2]
  My love born in splendor,
  Anyone who looks at you
  Will shun poor demeanor,
  And I, with sighs, whom most you please,
  Die of desire, for it so presses me
  To contemplate your noble being.

6 True merit would fall into decline
  If the honored king of Castile[3]
  Did not sustain it;
  He does his deeds with such skill,
  There's nothing more he needs to learn.

---

[2] A line is missing in all manuscripts.
[3] Alfonso X of Castile, who ruled from 1252 to 1284, and was known as the Learned (*el Sabio*). Guilhem de Montanhagol addressed a number of songs to him. For a dialogue between the troubadour Arnaldo and Alfonso *el Sabio*, see Poem 89.

97

Guiraut Riquier

Ad un fin aman fon datz / A true lover once awaited

Guiraut Riquier, from Narbonne, may have been of bourgeois origin—neither noble nor peasant, but a townsman. He was active from about 1254 until his death in 1292. One of the most prolific troubadours, he left over a hundred compositions of various kinds. After serving the viscount of Narbonne he traveled to the court of Alfonso X of Castile in Toledo, where he spent nine years before returning to his native town.

Guiraut wrote out the texts of his poetry in a manuscript in his own hand. The original is lost, but the *chansonnier* known as C, in the Bibliothèque nationale de France (fonds français 856), contains a section that says it was copied from the autograph. Manuscript C includes rubrics or titles of Guiraut's poems, many of which specify the year or even the day when he finished writing them. Some scholars regard these dates as archival records of an authenticity that could not be stronger, but others consider them part of the poetic fiction.

Writing late in the troubadour tradition, Guiraut Riquier was keenly aware of the generic categories that had evolved over the years. In this poem he invented a pendant to the dawn song, or *alba*. He called it a *serena*, or evening song, about a lover's suffering at the end of the day.

Serena by Sir Guiraut Riquier, in the year 1263

1   A true lover once awaited
     A meeting with his lady
     At a given time and place.
     On the day he would get honor[1]
     In the evening, he walked deep in thought,
       And with a sigh he said,
       "Day, you grow long to my harm,
         And this evening
       Is killing me with waiting."

2   The lover was so eager,
     So ardent with desire
     For the joy he hoped to have,
     That he truly was afraid
     He might not live till evening,
       And with a sigh he said,
       "Day, you grow long to my harm,
         And this evening
       Is killing me with waiting."

3   Anyone beside him
     Could easily perceive
     His grief, he was so troubled
     And so close to weeping;
     He thought the day was cruel,
       And with a sigh he said,
       "Day, you grow long to my harm,

---

[1]   On this idea of honor, compare Raimbaut de Vaqueiras: "A real lover, either he or she / Is not just a matter of thought; / But when a lover / Becomes real / There's a great increase / In honor ..." (Poem 64, stanza 3).

And this evening
Is killing me with waiting."

4 Terrible torment is the fate
  Of anyone without a friend
  To help him, so take heed
  Of this lover, how he languished
  In longing that difficult day.
   And with a sigh he said,
    "Day, you grow long to my harm,
     And this evening
   Is killing me with waiting."

5   *And with a sigh he said,*
    "Day, you grow long to my harm,
     And this evening
   Is killing me with waiting."

98

Guiraut Riquier

L'autre jorn m'anava / The other day I was walking

The *pastorela*, known in French and English as the pastourelle, or poem about a shepherdess, was apparently invented by Marcabru in *L'autrier jost'una sebissa / The other day I found a shepherdess* (Poem 13). It thrived in many languages, most notably in French, where more than a hundred pastourelles were written in the thirteenth century.[1] It was represented by fewer songs in Occitan, but the tradition never died.

Near the end of the troubadour period Guiraut Riquier created a series of six *pastorelas*. In each one he says he met the same shepherdess. The poems are dated by the poet, in rubrics in the manuscript, over a period of twenty-two years. The shepherdess ages accordingly, changing from a young girl to a wife and mother.

The First Pastorela by Sir Guiraut Riquier, Written in the Year 1260

1 The other day I was walking
  Along the bank of a river
  Alone, to amuse myself,
  For Love had been treating me
  In such a way
  That I was thinking of a song.
  I saw a merry shepherdess,
  Pretty and pleasing,
  Watching her lambs;
  I turned toward her
  And found her bold
  In a becoming way,
  And she made me welcome
  At my first question.

2 I asked her,
  "Girl, have you ever been loved,
  Or do you know how to love?"
  She answered frankly,
  "Sir, I have given myself
  Without fear."
  "Girl, I'm delighted
  To have found you,
  If only I can please you."
  "Have you been looking, sir?
  I could believe it,
  If I were a fool."
  "Girl, do you doubt it?"
  "Indeed, sir, I do."

3 "Girl of good family,
  If you want my love
  I want yours."

---

[1] See William D. Paden, *The Medieval Pastourelle*, 2 vols. (New York: Garland Publishing, 1987).

"Sir, it cannot be:
You already have a sweetheart,
And I have a lover."
"Girl, that doesn't matter;
I love you—that makes me
The one for you."
"Sir, take another road
That will bring you
Greater good."
"But better's not my wish!"
"Sir, you're being foolish."

4   "Girl, I'm not being silly;
You make me so happy
That Love drives me on."
"Sir, I'm getting eager
To escape
This conversation!"
"Girl, I swear
You're too stubborn;
I'm asking humbly."
"Sir, I'm not forgetting
That I would be shamed
If I did what you want."
"Girl, I know I'm stronger!"[2]
"Sir, that would be wrong!"

5   "Girl, whatever I say,
Don't be afraid;
I won't put you to shame."
"Sir, then I'll be your friend,
Since your better judgment
Holds you back."
"Girl, when I feel
I'm close to going wrong,
I think of my lady, Good Conduct."[3]
"Sir, your friendship
Greatly pleases me,
For now you're being charming."
"Girl, did I hear you right?"
"Sir, it's you I desire."

6   "Tell me, merry maid,
What thought makes you say
A word so pleasing?"
"Sir, wherever I go
I hear people singing

---

[2]   The lover is momentarily tempted to take the girl by force. Rape never occurs in the more than twenty Occitan *pastorelas*, although it does in more than a dozen French pastourelles.

[3]   *Belh Deport*, "Good Conduct," is the *senhal*, or secret name, of Guiraut Riquier's lady, which he uses in other poems. When he cites the secret name here, the shepherdess recognizes him as Guiraut Riquier; in the following stanza she names him.

Songs by Guiraut Riquier."
"Girl, I still haven't heard
You say just the word
That I've been seeking."
"Sir, doesn't Good Conduct,
Who is your protector,
Save you from mistakes?"
"Girl, she doesn't help me."
"Sir, do you love her truly?"

7   "Girl, she would scare me,
But the noble Sir Bertran
Of Opian[4] protects me."
"Sir, I hadn't noticed;
But now you must be going,
And that makes me sad."
"Girl, many times again
I'll take this road!"

---

[4] A knight of Narbonne known to have been active in the affairs of the viscount from 1229 to 1242.

99

Guiraut Riquier

L'autrier trobei la bergeira d'antan, /
The other day I saw again a shepherdess I'd seen before

The Second Pastorela by Sir Guiraut Riquier, Written in the Year 1262

1   The other day I saw again a shepherdess I'd seen before.
I greeted the pretty one, and she greeted me;
Then she said, "Sir, why has it been so long
Since we last met? Does my love not tempt you?"
"Of course it does, Girl, more than I show."
"Sir, you seem to survive the pain."
"Girl, that is why I came back again."
"Sir, I could say, too, I've been looking for you."
"Girl, aren't you here to watch over your lambs?"
"Yes I am, sir, and you? Were you just passing through?"

2   "Girl, when we met I was smitten, truly,
But since then I've just been too busy."
"Sir, I can say the same for myself,
For if you speak truly, then I do, too."
"Girl, I'm glad you take it so well."
"Sir, I do as I should."
"Girl, please grant my wish."
"Sir, I'm eager to hear it."
"Girl, I wish to rejoice in your love!"
"Sir, you may do so after I leave."

3   "Girl, there's no other soul on earth
Who could make me rejoice so much."
"Sir, I'm sure what you say is the truth,
But anyway, ride away, take your road!"
"Girl, I don't want to; I'd rather dismount."
"Sir, now that you're down, what good does it do?"
"Girl, you must know that I want to love you!"
"Sir, just you hear, now, what I must say."
"Girl, tell me at once, and I'll listen."
"Sir, let's sit down. I bid you fair welcome."

4   "Girl, my lust for you has grown so great
That I must take you now!"
"But sir, your lady, Good Conduct!
Are you forgetting? Don't you love her?"
"Girl, yes I do; I'm already defeated."
"Sir, if she learns this, she'll be grateful."
"Girl, she stops me from many bad acts."
"Sir, that is why you win her praise."
"Girl, love for her brings me little rejoicing."
"Sir, in pleasure you don't seem to be lacking."

5   "Girl, my Good Conduct will not aid me,
Though nothing could make me so happy."
"Sir, I am sure she knows how to behave,
If her worth is as great as you say."
"Girl, it is so great that she makes me despair!"
"Sir, does she not offer to help you?"
"Girl, only enough that she kills me."
"But sir, people say you are wise."
"Girl, since I get no joy, what good does it do me?"
"Sir, your fickle heart makes you lose it."

6   "Girl, perhaps I shall die, since my heart is so true
And devoted, so faithful to her."
"Sir, all that I hear of Guiraut Riquier
Tells me she's right to offer no succor."
"Girl, don't believe all the rumors you hear."
"Sir, you've made your desire quite clear!"
"Girl, I love you so much, but you only play."
"Sir, you loved another as well yesterday."
"Girl, I'll be off since you do me no favor."
"Sir, away with you then, till I see you next year!"

100

Guiraut Riquier

Gaya pastorelha / A merry shepherdess

The Third Pastorela by Sir Guiraut Riquier, in the Year 1264

1 A merry shepherdess
 I found the other day
 On a riverbank,
 Keeping her lambs
 Out of the heat
 Beneath a shady tree.
 She was weaving a garland
 Of flowers and sitting
 High where it was cool.
 I dismounted on the path,
 For I wanted her love
 Come what may.
 She was so bold
 That she spoke right away.

2 I said to her, "May I
 Take pleasure with you,
 Since you're so inviting?"
 She said she was seeking
 A man of good family,
 And so she was thoughtful
 By night and by day.
 "Girl, you will have me,
 Not faithless or fickle,
 As long as I live."
 "Sir, I see it could happen,
 For in love you're impatient!"
 "Yes, Girl, I am hurting."
 "Sir, it's so sudden!"

3 "Girl, if you don't help me
 Before very long,
 My desire will kill me!"
 "Sir, patient waiting
 Wins us salvation;
 Take pleasure in hope!"
 "Girl, my love for you
 So pains and thrills me,
 I must have it now."
 "Sir, clearly
 You've not ever seen me!
 I'd be imprudent."
 "Girl, the sight of you wounds me."
 "Sir, does it not make you happy?"

4   "Girl, my love begins
     With so much pain
     That I need your help."
     "Sir, you've pursued me,
     Though timidly,
     For the past four years!"
     "Girl, I don't remember
     Seeing you before;
     Don't worry if I hurry."
     "Sir, I can tell you,
     You'll make people laugh!
     Do you think me a stranger?"
     "Girl, are you daft?"
     "No, sir, nor mute!"

5   "Girl, though I've tried to remember,
     I can't recollect:
     Are you the girl in my songs?"
     "Sir, although you may hurt
     I will see that you pay
     For your wicked designs."
     "Girl, whenever we meet
     Our talks seem to end
     On making amends."
     "Sir Guiraut, already,
     Riquier, you're ready!
     Don't pay—I've been silly."
     "No, Girl, you've been clever."
     "Sir, that gives me pleasure."

6   "Girl, I must be going
     To tend to my trade;
     Goodbye and God bless you!"
     "Sir, may you find
     Good luck and your road."
     "Girl, are you grieving?"
     "Yes, since you're leaving."

101

Guiraut Riquier

L'autrier trobei la bergeira / The other day I found the shepherdess

The Fourth Pastorela by Sir Guiraut Riquier, in the year 1267

1   The other day I found the shepherdess
I had met in other years
Watching lambs, and she was sitting.
She had a pleasing manner,
But she was greatly changed,
For now she held a little child
Sleeping in her lap,
And she was spinning, like a prudent woman.
I hoped that she'd remember me
Since we'd met three times before,
But I saw she didn't know me when she said,
"You there, why do you leave the road?"

2   "Girl," I said, "your charming company
Brings me so much pleasure
That now I need your help."
She said, "I am not the silly girl, sir,
That you assume I am;
My thoughts have turned to other things."
"Girl, you're making a great mistake,
For I've loved you faithfully and long."
"Until today, sir, it seems to me
I have never seen you."
"Girl, have you lost your memory?"
"No, sir. Try to understand me."

3   "Girl, without you
There's no cure for my malady.
It's been too long since you cheered me."
"Sir, Guiraut Riquier
Used to tell me that insistently,
But he never brought me shame."
"Girl, Sir Guiraut does not forget;
Now, don't you recollect?"
"Sir, he and his dear face
Please me more than you!"
"You've fled him, Girl, too frequently."
"Sir, if he comes, I think he'll conquer me."

4   "Girl, now my joy begins,
For I am certainly the one
Who brought you fame in song."
"Sir, you are not.
I'd never believe it in my life;
You don't even look like him!"

"Girl, Good Conduct, my leader and guide,
Three times now has stood at your side."
"Sir, you presume too much honor!
All this talking means nothing."
"Girl, don't you remember me?"
"Yes, sir, but only vaguely."

5   "Girl, I have given you fame,
But for me it's a strain;
Don't think I'll ask you again."
"Sir, I am satisfied
Now that I've taken revenge
For our last encounter."
"Girl, who is the father
Of this child? Was it just a fling?"
"Sir, a man who, I hope, will give me more,
For he married me in church."
"Girl, why does he leave you alone by the river?"
"Sir, because that is my pleasure."

6   "Could we reach an understanding
Together, charming girl,
If I concealed your part in it?"
"Sir, no more than the friendly agreement
We made the first time we met,
For I've kept away from you till now."
"Girl, I have tested you well,
And I find you thoroughly sensible."
"Sir, if I had been frivolous,
You would have scarcely made me wise."
"Girl, I'm going now to my work of the day."
"Sir, there's your road. Go find your way!"

102

Guiraut Riquier

D'Astarac venia / From Astarac I was going

The Fifth Pastorela by Sir Guiraut Riquier, in the Year 1276

1 From Astarac I was going
The other day toward l'Isle[1]
By the pilgrim road,
And near the path
Beneath an arbor
I saw (and didn't mind at all)
My shepherdess
Sitting with her daughter.
She recognized me easily,
Smiled, though she was grieving,
Looked surprised
And prayed that God be with her.
I dismounted right away.
She stood before me then
But took her place again
Once I greeted her.

2 I saw that she had greatly changed
From the beauty she had been.
I said, "Where are you coming from?"
"Sir, from Compostela.
As you can see,
I have been blessed."[2]
"Now that I've found you,
Tell me any news
That you know from there."
"Sir, the king of Castile
Is going against Granada,[3]
So go follow the trail!"
"Lady, what are you telling me?
I don't think I shall."
"Sir, you will fall behind
If you fail to take that road."

[1] Localities now in the department of Gers (capital Auch, west of Toulouse). Astarac was a castle, now destroyed; l'Isle-Jourdain is a town near Auch.

[2] Santiago de Compostela in the northwest corner of Spain, one of the leading pilgrimage destinations in medieval Europe. The shepherdess must be wearing a shell (a *coquille saint Jacques*), symbol of the pilgrimage to Compostela.

[3] Perhaps a reference to an expedition of Alfonso X of Castile against Granada in 1281, but if so the date does not match that of the poem according to the manuscript. Perhaps the shepherdess is misinformed; the poet's answer could be translated, "I don't think he is" (making such an attack). Another possibility is that the poem was actually written around 1281 and Guiraut gave the shepherdess a remark that made sense at that time, but later set the poem in a fictional time when the allusion did not work.

3   "Do you still insist,"
I said, "on needling me
Like this?"
"Sir Guiraut Riquier,
I'm not the shepherdess
To help you sing your song."
"Please, then, accept from me
My hospitality tonight
And just a little sport."
"Sir, by God, you must think me
Playful and light.
Don't even bother to ask!"
"Lady, I suppose that you
Don't care for me a bit."
"Not with love, sir,
And I don't regret it."

4   "From now on, in my songs
I'll complain bitterly
Because you are so harsh to me."
"Sir, by rights
Your songs should be of God,
If you think about it!"
"Lady, if you judge me right,
I am not so old
That I deserve your scorn."
"Sir, it's not reason
That keeps you from moderation,
Nor white hair, nor years."
"Lady, it appears
That you intend to scold me."
"Sir, it must not matter;
You do not seem to suffer!"

5   "Worthy woman, I have not yet
Said anything to trouble you;
Why do you reproach me?"
"Sir, I only wish
You thought the worldly way
To be harsh."
"Well, I would be surprised
If anyone saw glory[4]
In such a sermon."
"Sir, you only increase
My suffering when you speak,
And it doesn't help you, either."
"God save you forever!
I have nothing more to say."
"Sir, I do not care.
In God's name, go away!"

---

[4]   Guiraut finds no glory in the shepherdess's righteousness.

103

Guiraut Riquier

A Sant Pos de Tomeiras / To Saint-Pons-de-Thomières

The Sixth Pastorela by Sir Guiraut Riquier, in the Year 1282

1   To Saint-Pons-de-Thomières[1]
        I went the other day,
And I came, wet with rain,
To an inn two women kept
        Who did not seem familiar.
Still, I wondered.
The older one laughed
As she whispered to the younger
Some little joke I couldn't hear,
But they both offered me
Their warmest welcome,
And I was well lodged;
Then I remembered
Times now past
And I recognized the older one,
Which gave me pleasure.

2   I said, "Are you not she
        Who used to be
The shepherdess who made fun of me?"
She said without displeasure,
        "Sir, I shall no longer
Be unfriendly just for fun."
"Worthy woman, I think I see
You're still the kind of person
Who deserves to be reproached."
"Sir, if I had been frivolous,
Not long ago I had a chance
To find a market [for my charms]."
"Worthy woman, do you refer
To me, hard-pressed for shelter?"
"No, sir, I am the neighbor
Of a friend I do not love."

3   "Worthy woman, a girl like you
        Must have caught the eye
Of a lover who is eager."
"Lord God! He wants me
        To be his wife, but I
Don't intend to take him."
"Worthy woman, it's time to flee
From poverty,

---

[1]   In the department of Hérault, near Béziers.

If he's a wealthy man."
"Sir, we could live comfortably,
But I know he is the father
Of seven children."
"Worthy woman, you would be
Well served by his grown sons."
"Sir, I wish I would—
But he hasn't one as old as ten!"

4   "You must be mad—
        You've escaped from bad,[2]
And now you look for worse!"
"No, sir, I am quite sane,
        But my heart doesn't tell me
To get myself in trouble."
"Worthy woman, you seek
A twisted path; it will be your death,
If you ask me, within a year."
"Sir, here is one who comforts me,
For she's the gateway to my joy,
This girl who stands before us."
"Worthy woman, she must be
Your daughter; I can tell."
"Sir, you met us once near l'Isle
The other year."[3]

5   "Worthy woman, she will need
        To make amends
For all the grief you've caused me."
"Sir, first wait and see
        What her husband says,
Then go about your business!"
"Worthy woman, you've not been cured,
Nor have you forgotten
This mockery of yours."
"Sir Guiraut, I grow weary
Because you keep on singing
These same silly songs."
"Worthy woman, growing old
Makes you dislike singing."
"Sir, is aging so delightful
That you do not find it frightful?"

6   "Worthy woman, you will never
        Make me fear attack,
But this does sound as though you mock."
"Sir, I hardly think
        That you'd perceive

---

[2]   In Poem 4 we learned that the shepherdess had a husband. In Poem 5 (stanza 1) she grieves, apparently for the loss of her husband. Now she must be a widow, contemplating the prospect of remarriage.

[3]   See the preceding poem, stanza 1; that poem is dated six years earlier than this one.

Bad feelings on my part."
"Since I'm in your home,
You must forgive
Me everything."
"Sir, it doesn't please me
To speak angrily
Or make you feel discomfort."
"Lady, you never could,
For I cannot help but love you."
"Sir, even if you did not,
I would always honor you."

7 "Lady, our debate will please
The noble count of Astarac,[4]
Whom everyone must praise."
"Sir, he is so worthy
That all speak his name
With good will."
"Lady, if here you should see him,
Would you ask him in?"
"Sir, surely you would hear
What my heart says to do!"

---

[4] Bernart, count of Astarac (1249–91), participated in a debate poem with Guiraut Riquier. In the preceding poem the narrator sets out from Astarac.

104

Guiraut Riquier

Be.m degra de chantar tener / I should really cease to sing

The rubric identifies this poem as a *vers*, which means, in Guiraut Riquier's usage, what *sirventés* meant to Bertran de Born: a poem of satire or moral reflection.

The Twenty-Seventh Vers by Sir Guiraut Riquier, in the year 1292

1   I should really cease to sing,
Since a song needs good cheer;
Instead I find I am so drear,
On every side I feel pain.
Remembering my unhappy past,
Looking at my present sorrow
And considering tomorrow—
All give me cause to weep.

2   And so my singing cannot taste
Good to me, it's so bitter.
But God has given me the sense
To tell my folly as I sing,
My wit, my joy, my misery,
My gains and losses, truly;
I have nothing else to say,
Since I was born on a later day.[1]

3   No craft is now less welcome
In court than the happy art
Of making songs, for nobles like
To hear and see frivolity
And wailing mixed with shame;[2]
All that once before brought praise
Has been forgotten nowadays,
And the world is full of lies.

4   Because of the wicked pride
Of so-called Christians, far from love
And God's commands,
We are driven from his holy place[3]
With many other woes to face.
God seems to be opposed to us,

---

[1] Although this line has been fitted into a history of troubadour poetry marked by decline in Guiraut's time, it can also be seen as a topos in the tradition of *laudatio temporis acti*, the Horatian "praise of times past" or the "good old days," extending as far back as Eden. For similar themes in early troubadours, see Marcabru (Poem 12) and Cercamon (Poem 17).

[2] Possibly a reference to *baladas* such as the anonymous Poems 91, 93, or 94, or Cerveri de Girona, Poem 107, which is identified as a *viadeyra*.

[3] In 1291 the Latin Kingdom of Jerusalem, which had been founded in the First Crusade, was destroyed, and "the final shreds of crusader power vanished": John France, *Western Warfare in the Age of the Crusades, 1000–1300* (Ithaca, NY: Cornell University Press, 1999), p. 226.

To our unbridled desire
And reckless reach for power.

5 We must fear the dire peril
Of double death,[4] which threatens us
Since Saracens are arrogant
And God becomes indifferent;
Worse, we fight among ourselves,
So soon we'll be quite overwhelmed,
While our princes, it seems to me,
Neglect responsibility.

6 May the God of oneness,
Power, wisdom, goodness,
Grant his creatures light
To cleanse us of our sins.

7 Lady, Mother of charity,
Grant us out of pity
Through our Redeemer, your Son,
Grace and love and pardon.

---

[4] Death of the body in this world and death of the soul in hell.

105

Guiraut Riquier and Bonfilh

Auzit ay dir, Bofil, que saps trobar /
I hear tell, Bonfilh, that you know how to compose

This *tensó*, or debate poem, involves Guiraut Riquier and an otherwise unknown poet named Bonfilh ("Goodson"). Bonfilh is the only Jewish poet that we know who wrote in the troubadour language and manner. The trajectory of the debate is typical of many *tensós* in that it starts on a tone of sociability, but soon veers toward antagonism. In this case the antagonism summons up antisemitism on Guiraut's part. The text is transmitted in only one manuscript. A major lacuna swallows up half of stanza 3, all of stanza 4, and half of stanza 5, which breaks off at the end. Since the poem is not included in manuscript C, there is no rubric.

1   *Guiraut Riquier*
      I hear tell, Bonfilh, that you know how to compose,
      And you make stanzas; but I want to know, in short,
      Why do you sing? Are you afraid of something?
      Is there a woman who makes you do it,
      Or do you sing to ply the *joglar*'s trade
      And get paid by those who listen?
      Or do you sing to advance your fame?[1]
      Your song has merit if you know why you sing.

2   *Bonfilh*
      Guiraut, I sing to make my heart rejoice
      And for love of one who keeps me happy,
      And because I like honor and joy and youth;
      But I'd never sing only for money,
      Nor do I seek it; I'd rather give it to you,
      For I give generously, all for the love of my lady,
      Who is clever and worthy and pretty and gay.
      Because she smiles so sweetly to me, I sing.

3   *Guiraut Riquier*
      Bonfilh, I'd also like to ask you this:
      Since you sing and stay happy for love
      And a lady, tell me the truth,
      What is your faith? . . .

4   *Bonfilh*
      . . .

5   *Guiraut Riquier*
      . . .
      I really should stop,
      But it's not right for a betrayer
      To think he can follow our path;
      For your words and your deeds weigh heavily
      On Jesus Christ, whom you hurt so badly.[2]

---

[1]   Guiraut offers Bonfilh a series of alternatives, as in the special form of the *tensó* called the *partimen*. Bonfilh chooses to accept the first.

[2]   The accusation that the Jews betrayed Christ is common in medieval antisemitism.

6　　*Bonfilh*
　　Since you're leaving love to deliver a sermon,
　　Set speech aside and put on a white robe,[3]
　　Guiraut, and we'll have a spitting contest,[4]
　　For my lady declines to worship a cross.
　　If there were any love or courtesy in you,
　　You wouldn't think it foolish to use the word *tu*.[5]
　　Since love wants lovers to call each other *tu*,
　　You've simply no reason to stew.

7　　*Guiraut Riquier*
　　Bonfilh, no man has ever loved more strongly
　　Or had less interest in delivering a sermon
　　Than I, since it takes me away from women.
　　But I had to reproach you about the use of *tu*,[6]
　　And you wallow in your folly like a fool,
　　And you should not have called the monastic habit rustic,[7]
　　Or the admirable judgments of the man
　　From Opian . . .[8]

8　　*Bonfilh*
　　I leave this *tensó*; I'll answer you no more,
　　Since reason fails you and you speak villainy.
　　I let it drop out of respect for my lord Bertran[9]
　　Of Opian, who is prosperous in love.

9　　*Guiraut Riquier*
　　I don't like your answer or your company
　　From this hour on, for my worth has been diminished;
　　And my wisdom, once great, has been reduced,
　　For when your value drops, mine does, too.

---

[3]　The white robe of the Cistercian monk. Cistercians practiced a vow of silence but were active in suppressing heresy, often by means of public debates.

[4]　"Spitting contest" (*esputamen*): Bonfilh makes a humorous blend of Latin *disputatio*, "disputation," with Occitan *espudar*, "to spit on," and the suffix *-amen*, expressing the action described by the verb.

[5]　The line is puzzling, perhaps because of the lacuna. Apparently, Bonfilh thinks lovers should call one another *tu* and reproaches Guiraut Riquier for disagreeing, but Bonfilh seems to be alone in this opinion. Troubadours ordinarily employ the polite second-plural *vos* when speaking to their lady; Guiraut Riquier does so even in adressing the shepherdess in his *pastorelas*, as Marcabru does in his. In the fourteenth-century *Roman de la Reine Esther*, by the Jewish poet Crescas Caslari, King Assuérus addresses Esther as *vos*: see Suzanne Méjean-Thiolier and Marie-Françoise Notz-Grob, *Nouvelles courtoises occitanes et françaises* (Paris: Livre de Poche, 1997), p. 154, line 441.

[6]　Perhaps Guiraut reproached Bonfils about the use of *tu* in the lost portions of stanzas 3 or 5. Bonfils responded in stanza 6.

[7]　In the preceding stanza Bonfilh meant to say *vest blanc vestimen*, "put on a white robe," but pronounced *vest* as *vist*, and Guiraut misunderstood *vist blanc* as *vilan*, that is, *vilan vestimen*, "peasant garb." It was characteristic of Jewish pronunciation of Occitan to blend the vowels *i* and *e*, as Bonfilh already did in his playful coinage *esputamen* (Latin *disputamen*).

[8]　The text is incomplete.

[9]　Bertran d'Opian, a knight of Narbonne who was active from 1229 to 1242, perhaps acted as judge of the *tensó*. Guiraut also mentions him in three other poems, including his first *pastorela* (Poem 98).

Cerverí de Girona

Al fals gelos don Deus mala ventura / God give bad luck to that lying, jealous man

Guillem de Cervera, from the town of Cervera de la Segarra northwest of Barcelona, adopted the professional name Cerverí ("the man from Cervera") as a *joglar*, and added "de Girona" because King James I of Aragon gave him land near that town. Active from about 1259 to 1285, he was the most prolific troubadour. He wrote 114 lyric songs, five longer narrative poems, and a large collection of proverbs in verse.

This song in the voice of an unhappily married woman, like Poems 91 and 93, may be called a *malmaridada*. In the manuscript the poem is identified as a *Gelosesca*, or song about jealousy. Since Cerverí refers in stanza 5 to Peter III the Great, king of Aragon, as *Infante*, or heir to the throne, this poem must have been written before Peter's accession in 1276.

Gelosesca

1   God give bad luck to that lying, jealous man
        Who ruins my pleasure with my lover!
        He's been a torment since I took him, and he lives too long.

2   At least I can say, and I'm certain of this,
        That he won't live four days more,
        For I'll smear an ointment on his wrists
        That will kill the jealous wretch.
        Then I'll tie around his neck
        My lover's letter for a curse,
        And my mother will conjure up a hex.

3   Hear how this jealous man behaves:
        When he goes to bed—it hurts me to say it—
        He gives me his back, swarthy and tough,
        And as rough as the leaf of an oak,
        And he snores without stopping, and snorts.
        I hope to wear black for him soon;
        I've never seen a creature so crude.

4   A woman with a hateful, lying husband
        Is far from joy but close to wrath and rancor;
        No thanks to my luck, I know this too well.
        My family gave me a wrinkled old codger
        Whose sweat makes me sick and disgusted.
        If you see him and want to avoid an encounter,
        Just tell him, "God give you good pasture!"[1]

5   The Ladies of Thistles and Surpassing Worth
        Preserve honor, and the Infante has a noble plan
        To maintain merit and justice and peace.[2]

---

[1] That is, "Get out of my way!" as though speaking to a domestic animal.

[2] The poet plays on *cart*, "thistle" in Catalan, and *cardon* in Occitan. Cardona lay in the province of Barcelona; the place-name is the basis of Cerverí's word-play. The Lady of Thistles is the wife of his lord, Ramón Folch V, viscount of Cardona. The viscount died in 1276; his wife, born Sibilla d'Empúries, died in 1317. The second woman Cerverí salutes is his own lady; his secret name for her is *Sobrepretz* (Surpassing Worth). We know nothing about her. Cerverí also pays tribute to the Infante, Peter III (the Great) of Aragon, who lived from 1240 to 1285. He was heir to the throne until his accession in 1276.

Cerverí de Girona

No.l prenatz lo fals marit / Don't marry that liar

The rubric identifies this dance song, or *balada*, as a *viadeyra*, or song for the road. Some of its rhymes (*lit*, "bed," and *amich*, "lover," in stanza 7) are impossible in other troubadour genres, but are specifically approved for the *viadeyra* by the *Leys d'amors*, the early fourteenth-century poetic treatise. The song resembles the Galician-Portuguese *cantiga de amigo*, or "song about a lover," which was also imitated by Raimbaut de Vaqueiras (Poem 61).

This is a viadeyra

1 Don't marry that liar,
  Delicate Anna!

2 Don't marry that phony,
 He's stupid and crude,
  Delicate Anna!

3 Don't take that bad husband,
 He's drowsy and dumb,
  Delicate Anna!

4 He's stupid and crude—
 Don't give him your love,
  Delicate Anna!

5 He's drowsy and dumb—
 Don't take him to bed,
  Delicate Anna!

6 Don't give him your love—
 Let me be your friend,
  Delicate Anna!

7 Don't take him to bed—
 Let me be your lover,
  Delicate Anna!

Daspols (Guilhem d'Autpol?)

Fortz tristors es e salvaj' a retraire / It is a terrible sadness and cruel to explain

A late manuscript attributes two poems to "Daspols," which is perhaps a corruption of D'Autpol. Guilhem d'Autpol is the author of two other songs and the lord of Hautpoul (department of Tarn), where the ruins of his family's castle are still visible. Guilhem d'Autpol was active from 1231 to 1289.

Daspols (or Guilhem d'Autpol) was one of three troubadours who composed funeral laments, or *planhs*, for the death of King Louis IX of France. Louis died in Tunis, where he was on Crusade, in 1270. Considered a virtual saint in his lifetime, he would be canonized in 1297; he is known to this day as Saint Louis. In his *planh* Daspols studiously imitated the lament for the death of Richard Lionheart that Gaucelm Faidit had written in 1199 (Poem 56).

Only a year after Louis's death the county of Toulouse would revert to the crown of France, following the provisions of the Treaty of Paris (1229).

1   It is a terrible sadness and cruel to explain
That with joy I sing of my heartfelt pain
At the death of our lord the king,
Nobleman of France, emperor of merit;
And so I sing, aggrieved and joyful,
Because God wanted him for his own,
Since he had served promptly and well;
If not, God would never have let him die,
And so, my dismay and loss are great
When I hear that the king of France is dead.
O God, what a sorrow it is!

2   The king is dead; but I cannot explain
The loss that Christians feel, or their weeping
At living without shepherd or ruler.
May God, our powerful Father, guide us
For if the king is in the glorious kingdom,
He has left us in torment here below;
The hurt will not leave my heart
Since I cannot follow him in death.
My pain is strong and more earnest
Since I must live and not go to my death.
O God, what a sorrow it is!

3   O holy Church, death could never steal
A more loyal servant in the world
Than this king. God did him such honor
That he never delayed in doing good,
For he put heart, body, wit, and friends
In the service of the cross and us.
May God, who came to take away our death
On the cross, hear my prayers
And pardon the king his errors and sins,
Since great good died with his death.
O God, what a sorrow it is!

4   Tongue cannot tell our hurt or loss;
        Each of us must live in fear,
        For we know death takes the worldly best
        And has stolen the noble king.
        If the honored, courageous king had lived,
        He soon would have slain the proud Saracens,
        Made them surrender their fiefs and lands
        And deny and renounce Mohammed;
        He would have opened the ports and roads.[1]
        See how we are diminished by his death.
            O God, what a sorrow it is!

5   Noble king, because of you all Christendom,
        Monks and learnèd doctors, clerics and laymen,
        Must renounce joy to adore the Cross,
        Nor do I excuse sister, cousin, or brother.
        Wherever you were, our merchants and their goods
        Were safe from plunderers and thieves;
        So as long as they live, grief must not leave
        Our hearts. When I consider
        What our Savior will be when he returns,[2]
        My life is worth less than my death.
            O God, what a sorrow it is!

6   Noble King Philip,[3] no man should renounce
        Doing good deeds while he has strength.
        You will not believe a traitor or a liar
        If you resemble Louis, your father,
        For he was noble and true and loving,
        And just and worthy, a loyal king.
        You will not listen to false advisers
        Or approve whatever they say;
        You will do justice for weak against strong,
        And in you they will find no sin, no death.[4]
            O God, what a sorrow it is!

7   May God, who came to earth to take on human flesh
        From the Virgin—Lady, for love of you—
        Put the soul of the king in an honorable place
        Near her who is like a mother to him,
        In paradise, among his companions,
        For he lived, full of mercy, in the service of God
        And in God's service he died;
        So we can praise, without contradiction,
        All his good deeds, whatever the comfort,
        Since all living faithful grieve at his death.
            O God, what a sorrow it is!

---

[1]   Louis would have opened Christian pilgrimage routes that had been closed by Muslims.
[2]   At the Last Judgment, the poet hopes to be saved.
[3]   Philip the Bold, king of France 1270–85, the son and successor of Louis IX.
[4]   Philip will be sinless and therefore will not suffer the death of the soul in hell.

8   I shall make my lamentation heard at Posquières,[5]
      Since Jesus Christ causes Our Lady
      To be praised at Vauvert; may God pardon the sins
      Of Louis, the French king, who is dead.
          O God, what a sorrow it is!

---

[5] Posquières (department of Gard), near Vauvert, where Saint Louis prayed before departing on crusade.

Guido Cavalcanti

Una giovane donna di Tolosa / A young lady from Toulouse

The Italian poet Guido Cavalcanti, who was born about 1258 and died in 1300, was Dante's friend and one of the poets of the *dolce stil nuovo*, or "sweet new style." At an uncertain time Guido undertook a pilgrimage to Santiago de Compostela. Although he never reached his destination in northwest Spain, he did reach Toulouse. There he met a woman who reminded him of his beloved in Florence. He wrote of this lady in two poems, a sonnet and a ballata.

The sonnet form was invented in Italian by a Sicilian poet, Giacomo da Lentini, early in the thirteenth century. Seen in relation to Occitan practice, it is an extension of the *cobla*, which like the sonnet was short and was frequently involved in poetic exchanges (see Poems 67, 69, 76, 113). Like the *cobla* in comparison to the *cansó* or love-song, the sonnet was less august and more conversational than the *canzone*. The major innovation of the sonnet was the practice of fixed form, in contrast with the constant variation of forms among the troubadours.

Sonnet

A young lady from Toulouse,
Fair and noble, chaste but joyful,
Is so precisely like
My lady in her gentle eyes

That she has made my soul
Eager; it leaves my heart
And goes to her but has such fear
It cannot say she owns it.

It looks into her lovely eyes,
And takes from Love delight
In seeing its lady clearly there;

Sighing then, it returns to my heart,
Mortally wounded by a piercing dart
The lady flings as they part.

Guido Cavalcanti

Era in penser d'amor quand' i' trovai /
I was thinking of love when I came upon

The Italian *ballata* resembles the Occitan *balada* (Poems 91, 93, 94, 107). Both are named for dance forms, whether or not they were actually danced or even musical. Like Poems 91 and 107, this one begins with a short initial stanza called the *respos* in Occitan, the *ripresa* in Italian.[1]

Ballata

1   I was thinking of love when I came upon
Two young country girls.
One was singing, "It is raining
Games of love on us."[2]

2   They seemed so pleasing,
So calm and courteous and kind
That I said, "You have the key
To every virtue high and noble.
O country girls, don't hate me
Just because my heart is broken,
As it has been, if not killed,
Ever since I saw Toulouse."

3   They turned their eyes to see
How my heart had been assailed,
And how a spirit born to weep
Had slipped out of the wound.[3]
When they saw me so dismayed,
One of them laughed and said,
"Just see how the force of love
Has conquered this one here!"

4   The other, moved to pity and mercy,
Playfully wearing the guise of love,
Spoke: "The wound I see in your heart
Was struck by eyes too great for you
And left within you such a glow
I cannot bear to see it.
Tell me, are you able
To remember those eyes?"

5   To the disturbing question
This country girl had asked,
I said, "I remember, in Toulouse

---

[1] See Paden, "Petrarch, Poet of Provence."
[2] For the image of rain compare Arnaut Daniel: "The love that rains into my heart" (Poem 51, stanza 2). Guido uses the word *gioco*, literally "game," as a near synonym of *gioia*, "joy." Occitan *joc* and *joi* have the same semantic overlap, as in Poem 63, stanza 1.
[3] The poet's soul goes out from his heart, as it does in the sonnet (Poem 109).

A lady, beautifully dressed;
Love called her Amandetta;[4]
She came to me so suddenly—
Her eyes pierced me
Even to the point of death."

6 Most politely she responded,
The one who at first had laughed,
Saying, "This lady who planted her image
In your heart suffused with love,
Looked intently through your eyes
And made Love emerge.
If you suffer great pain,
Ask Love to be kind."

7 Go to Toulouse, my little *ballata*,
Softly enter a church, La Daurade,[5]
And there ask to be taken
Courteously by a lovely lady
To the one I have begged you to see.
If she receives you
Say ever so softly,
"I have come to you for mercy."

---

[4] Italian form of Occitan *Amandeta*, the diminutive form of *Amanda*.
[5] An ancient church in Toulouse, beside the Garonne river. It was demolished before the Revolution.

111

David Hakohen

Bow down, my soul, and kneel before my rock of refuge

The Jewish minority in the population of southern France had been present since before the fall of the Roman Empire. To our knowledge only one Jewish poet participated in the Occitan poetic tradition, when Bonfilh shared in a *tensó* with Guiraut Riquier (Poem 105). An extensive body of poetry survives, however, that was written in Hebrew, primarily in the thirteenth century and in Provence.[1] Despite the divisions between Jewish and Christian society, this poetry was part of the broader lyric world in which the troubadours sang.

The Hebrew poet David Hakohen probably lived in Avignon in the late thirteenth century. The following poem is a prelude to a prayer; its form is that of a *muwashshah*, or classical ode. Paradoxically, David Hakohen says he will pray in silence. We have adapted our version from the translation by Carmi in the *Penguin Book of Hebrew Verse*.

Silence and Praise

1   Bow down, my soul, and kneel before my rock of refuge;
     Praise the Lord and bless Him!

2   My lips are too low to sing his high praises.
     My years are too few to recite his glorious works.
     All my days would not suffice to tell his mighty deeds.
     Therefore, with song and tears, my mind's libation,
     Seek the Rock, look eagerly for the Lord.

3   When my mind tries to fathom the abyss of his ways
     And my words move on the vault of his heavenly praise,
     I am struck blind by his flashing swords.
     They turn over and over as I turn beyond the limits of my reason.
     My thoughts cannot attain the knowledge of the Lord.

4   Though he stand still, no pursuer can overtake his glory.
     His light casts darkness: you cannot see his splendor.
     All majesty, all precious things are His, and blessed in his hands.
     Then who am I and what am I to burden Him with innumerable songs?
     I shall be silent, and by my silence shall thank the Lord.

5   Mutely, I proclaim that greatness is His.
     I have become a byword for hoping in dumb silence;
     Yet I shall wait until the Rock decrees my redemption.
     I shall glory in wearing the yoke of his statutes
     And the yoke of exile, as I uphold the love of the Lord.[2]

6   Now bless God, all his hosts of cherubs;
     Let each one praise his name, in the company of his loved ones.
     He is terrible above the hosts who stand about Him.
     Let each one, at his station, bow down as I pour forth my supplications.

---

[1]   See Paden, "Troubadours and Jews."

[2]   The kings of France expelled Jews in 1182, 1306, 1322, and 1394; the kings of England expelled them from Gascony (under English control) in 1287, and from England in 1290; the king of Spain expelled them in 1494, and the king of Portugal in 1497.

And when my soul blesses the Lord,
Let his ministers, too, ['bless the Lord who is blessed'].[3]

<hr>

[3]   The brackets are Carmi's, indicating a conjectural reading.

Anonymous

En un vergier sotz fuelha d'albespi / In an orchard under hawthorn blooms

This anonymous *alba* is set in the form of a dance-song, or *balada*. It provides little evidence for its date, but, like many other dance-songs and poems that make use of a refrain, it may have been written in the late thirteenth century.

1 In an orchard under hawthorn blooms
 The lady held her lover by her side
 Until the watchman cried he saw the dawn—
 O God, O God, the dawn! It comes so soon!

2 If only God had wanted, the night would never end
 And never would my lover go away,
 And the watchman would not see the dawn or day!
 O God, O God, the dawn! It comes so soon!

3 Fair, sweet lover, let us have a kiss
 Down in the meadows where the little birds sing;
 Let us do it all, despite the jealous one!
 O God, O God, the dawn! It comes so soon!

4 Fair, sweet lover, let us play another game
 In the garden where the little birds sing
 Until the watchman plays upon his pipe;
 O God, O God, the dawn! It comes so soon!

5 I drank a draft of my lover's breath
 On the breeze that came from over there
 Where he dwells—courtly, gay and fair;
 O God, O God, the dawn! It comes so soon!

6 The lady is pleasing and graceful;
 Many admire her beauty,
 But her heart seeks love that is loyal.
 O God, O God, the dawn! It comes so soon!

Anonymous

Quan lo rossinhols escria / While the nightingale makes his cries

This anonymous piece may be a fragment, but it seems to concentrate the theme of the *alba* in a single stanza, or *cobla*. We have no way to ascertain its date.

> While the nightingale makes his cries
> With his mate all night and day,
> I lie with my beautiful lover
>> Beneath the flower
> Until the watchman in the tower
> Cries, "Lover, time to rise!
> I see dawn coming and bright day!"

Isaac Gorni

From its very first day, the city of Arles was known as a city of strength

Isaac Gorni, or Ha-Gorni, was a Hebrew poet active in the late thirteenth century who traveled from city to city, entertaining Jewish communities and cultivating their generosity. His name means "threshing floor" (Hebrew *goren*), in Occitan *aire*, alluding to his birth in Aire-sur-l'Adour (Landes) in Gascony. His eighteen surviving poems, all transmitted in a single manuscript, suggest that he traveled from Arles to Aix, Manosque, Carpentras, Apt, and Draguignan, all in Provence, but also farther afield to Narbonne, Perpignan, and Luz in the Pyrenees.

The poem is the opening passage of a blistering attack on the nobles of Arles, who had apparently failed to offer Isaac Gorni the generosity, patronage, and protection that he felt he deserved. Our versions of this and the following poem are adapted from the translations by Carmi in the *Penguin Book of Hebrew Verse*.

Gorni Pleads His Cause

From its very first day, the city of Arles was known as a city of strength
And was honored as the seat of [David's] royal kin.
A mother city in Israel, it was famed as a stronghold in times of need;[1]
It stood in the breach.
And when Gorni found himself in distress, its citizens proclaimed a solemn fast,
As if for the fall of the city of Ariel [Jerusalem].
But the rulers of Arles—against them I shall cry out,
For they claim that my soul lusts for the lovely ladies!
And in truth, I spurn them, I abhor the very sight of them.
If I see them in my dream, sleep deserts me.
If I meet them in the street, I quickly step aside.
If ever I did look behind me [at a woman], may I be turned into a heap of rubble![2]
Call me Peleg,[3] for in my time womankind was divided, and all withdrew from me.
For days of loving have turned into days of wandering.
In vain do the girls still parade [before me],
I have estranged myself from beauty and charm.
I am in constant revolt against love. In the heat of my passion, at night,
Ice strips off my clothes [and bares my shame],
Snow comes down and covers my bones.
My heart has already been broken.
I now lead a pure life in the company of the pure, the blameless, and the loyal;
To them I give my loyalty.
Lord, do not hand me over to my enemies!
Why should Poetry perish on the day I perish?
For as long as I live, she lives too. But once I have died,

---

[1]   There were Jews in Arles as early as AD 449. In succeeding centuries, when Jews were expelled from other regions they fled to Arles and other cities in Provence where they were protected by the authority of the pope.

[2]   Like Lot's wife (Genesis 19:26).

[3]   One of the sons of Eber, the eponymous ancestor of the Hebrews (Genesis 10 and 11); his name means "division." He was so called, according to tradition, because in his time the earth was divided after the Tower of Babel had failed to unite humanity.

She will follow me down to Sheol[4] and there spread her couch in the darkness.
If I have sinned against you only, have mercy on my precious song;
Do not let them destroy me!

Isaac Gorni

I shall now lament my desires

Here Isaac Gorni imagines his own death and his legacy of sexual desire, making light of the Christian tradition of reverence for saintly relics. As a mock *planh*, or funeral lament, for himself, the poem may be compared to that of Guilhem IX of Aquitaine (Poem 8).

The Fate of the Adulterer

1 I shall now lament my desires,
The silenced beat of my drum.
Friends, my own sins deprived me of favors,
So great were my offences.
My merry harp was tuned to mourning
And my flute to the sound of weeping and lament,
When my desire died and my passion vanished,
When the gracious gifts of love came to an end.

2 The day was far gone, the shadows had fled,
No wind stirred in the gardens.
And my heart was filled with a sudden dread of death—
What hope is there for an ass like me?
Oh, my passion will set fire to the earth's foundations,
Clouds will hover above my grave.
And if I should die while still young,
My complaints will accompany me down into Sheol.

3 In days gone by, I was a hunter, hot in the pursuit of desires.
In all the provinces, [my lust] was likened to [the fires of hell].
But all those loves that had no virtue to them
Have now turned against me and fearfully disfigured me.
The dust of my grave will be sent to foreign merchants,
To be blended in cosmetics for pleasure-loving girls.
From the boards of my coffin [they will concoct powders] for barren women,
To have them bring forth sons and daughters.
Of my maggots they will compound ointments for stammerers and mutes,
To make them speak seventy tongues.[1]
My hair will serve as strings in musical instruments,
Which will then play sweetly even without a player.
My sash will be made into a loincloth for the adulterer,
To put a stop to his fornicating and whoring.
And all my belongings will be declared holy relics,
And my clothes will be treasured as keepsakes.
Oh, who will grind my bones as fine as dust
Before they are turned into icons?

4 May my words endow the fool with wisdom,
And the young and wise with understanding!

---

[1] Compare the babble that may represent Arabic in Guilhem IX, Poem 6, stanza 2.

Tribolet (?)

Us fotaires qe no fo amoros / A fucker who was not in love

This exercise in obscenity is perhaps the work of a troubadour named Tribolet, otherwise unknown. The repetition of the sexual verb expresses the strength of desire in an exaggerated and comical way. An ambiguous pronoun in the refrain enhances the poem's significance. Is it a bawdy hyperbole about heterosexual love? Or does it suggest the mixed rebellion and self-condemnation of a homosexual man in a homophobic culture? The reader cannot be sure.

We have no evidence for the date of the poem other than the manuscript, which was compiled in the last thirty years of the thirteenth century. The poem may have been written in the same period.

1   A fucker who was not in love
With any girl, but wanted to fuck
Always had a hard on, and was eager
To fuck any woman he could fuck.
He always had so strong an urge to fuck
That he was called Sir Fucker,
A fucker, alas! unhappy and sad,
And he said, "He dies badly and lives worse
Who doesn't fuck the one he loves."[1]

2   This fucker was so anxious to fuck
That the more he fucked, the sadder he got while fucking
To think he wasn't fucking more. He would have fucked
As much as the two best fuckers in Lombardy,
For as he fucked, he said, "I'd be happy to be fucking!"
He was called Sir Fucker,
A fucker, alas! unhappy and sad,
And he said, "He lives badly who doesn't fuck
Night and day the one he loves."

---

[1] "The one he loves": *le qui ama* (lines 9 and 18). *Le* appears to be masculine. If it is, the lover has sex with women but is unhappy because he does not have sex with the man he loves. However, Carapezza interprets *le* as a form of the feminine, normally *la*; he takes *le* as comparable to *celes* (line 4), here translated "any woman," for normal *celas*. On the other hand, the feminine is normal in *neguna*, "any girl" (line 2). For *le* as a masculine pronoun beside normal *lo*, see François Zufferey, *Recherches linguistiques sur les chansonniers provençaux* (Genève: Droz, 1987), p. 372; this form may reveal French influence according to C. H. Grandgent, *An Outline of the Phonology and Morphology of Old Provençal*, rev. ed. (Boston: Heath, 1905), p. 101.

Bietris de Romans

Na Maria, pretz e fina valors / Lady Maria, your virtue and pure worth

We have no historical information about Bietris de Romans. She may have been from Romans-sur-Isère (department of Drôme), near Montélimar and about forty kilometers from Die in Provence.

Since she addresses this love poem to Lady Maria, some scholars read it as a poem of lesbian desire. Others have argued that Bietris was not a woman at all but a man; they interpret *Bietris* as a scribal error for *Alberis*, that is, Alberico da Romano, an Italian nobleman and occasional troubadour, who, they claim, wrote this poem, which they regard as a conventional expression of male desire. Still others, preferring to avoid such violence to the sole manuscript attribution to Bietris, have sought to define the desire of one woman for another, as it is expressed in the poem, as a specific form of female friendship. It may also be that a female poet wrote the poem in the voice of a male persona. If, despite these alternatives, readers find the lesbian reading the most direct and reasonable one, then this is "the sole extant example of a medieval love poem written in the vernacular by one woman to another."[1]

1 Lady Maria, your virtue and pure worth
 And joy and wisdom and pure beauty
 And grace and virtue and honor
 And kind speech and conviviality
 And sweet face and gay manner
 And sweet gaze and loving glance—
 These things put you before all others
 And draw me to you without deceit.

2 So please, I beg you, let true love
 And delight and sweet humility
 Help me plead my case,
 And grant me, pretty lady,
 What gives me greatest pleasure.
 In you I have my heart and desire,
 And through you I've known joy,
 And for you I often sigh.

3 Since your beauty and virtue surpass
 All others, and no one goes before you,
 I beg you, please, to enhance your fame,
 Say no to lovers who try to deceive.

4 Lovely lady, surpassing all in joy,
 Worth, and gentle speech, I send you my stanzas,
 For in you are charm and delight
 And the virtue one seeks in a lady.

---

[1] Herman Braet, "Bietris de Roman," in Wilson, *Women in the Middle Ages*, vol. 1, p. 95.

Aftermath
1300–1350

IN the fourteenth century the Old Occitan language shifted into Middle Occitan. Early in the century poets such as Rostanh Berenguier (Poem 118) wrote in the manner of the troubadours. A new group also emerged known as the School of Toulouse, whose poetry was mostly religious; definitely written, not oral; read, not sung; and transmitted in manuscripts distinct from the troubadour *chanson-niers*. One of these new poets was Arnaut Vidal, perhaps a graduate in law, whose poem in praise of the Virgin won the first competition organized by the *Consistori de la Gaia Sciensa* (Poem 120). The most prolific member of this school was the priest and friar Raimon de Cornet (Poems 123 and 124). We have included two anonymous poems, one a Hebrew *piyut*, or liturgical song (Poem 121), and the other an apparently autobiographical account of the sufferings of an Occitan poet who was afflicted with leprosy (Poem 122). The Italian connection, dating from Sordel and Guido Cavalcanti in the thirteenth century, continued with Dante's fictional encounter with the shade of Arnaut Daniel in Purgatory (Poem 119), and culminated in Petrarch's mutation of Occitan poetry into Italian (Poems 125 and 126).

Figure 6. Sketch from Petrarch's personal copy of the Roman naturalist Pliny, depicting his beloved Vaucluse (*Vallis clausa*, "closed valley") in Provence, east of Avignon (Bibliothèque nationale de France, ms. latin 6802, folio 143 verso). At the village of Fontaine-de-Vaucluse, the Sorgue river rises from underground sources in a powerful spring. The sketch shows the spring gushing from the base of a rocky cliff; at the top, a chapel appears that is no longer there. Trees, reeds, and a heron with a fish in its beak make up the rest of the landscape.

Petrarch inserted the sketch near a passage in which Pliny mentions the Sorgue, and inscribed it *Transalpina solitudo mea iocundissima*, "My most pleasing Transalpine solitude." Petrarch made the sketch from memory; he bought the manuscript in Mantua in 1350, and it never left Italy.[1] The word *Transalpina* implies that Petrarch considered the scene from the point of view of Italy, but the phrase as a whole, and the sketch itself, imply an emotional center in Provence. In Poem 125 the poet invokes the memory of meeting Laura, perhaps in this place, if Laura was a real person and not a poetic fiction.

(Reproduced by permission of the Bibliothèque nationale de France)

[1]   Pierre de Nolhac, *Pétrarque et l'humanisme* (Paris: Champion, 1907), vol. 2, p. 271.

118

Rostanh Berenguier

Tot en aisi con es del balasicz / Just as the look of the basilisk

Rostanh Berenguier was a poet of Marseilles in the early fourteenth century, a protégé of the Grand Master of the Order of the Hospital, that is, the Hospitallers, an order of crusading knights that was named for a pilgrim hostelry in Jerusalem. The following poem, which is reminiscent of Rigaut de Berbezilh (Poem 21), anticipates Petrarch in its use of mythology and its themes of clarity and the lady's look. Although Rostanh Berenguier is not usually treated as part of the canon, we feel that he was a greater poet than has been acknowledged.

1   Just as the look of the basilisk[1]
       Wounds more deeply than any sword
       And makes its victims shriek and shout,
       So does the look of my lady deceive;
       For she looks at me sweetly, and her sweet look
       Wounds me and breaks my heart,
       So that my heart neither lives nor dies
       At once, but lingers in the hope of death.

2   Now they will say I am sad for no reason,
       For no reason my heart lives in dismay,
       I'm a fool and an idler, since I grieve
       And lament as I sigh. My grief is my reason
       For a true lover must patiently agree
       To every grief and every delay
       To the degree that delaying pleases his lady;
       My joy goes away for reasons far too clear.

3   A gift quickly given may seem a beggar's gift.[2]
       We clearly see, wherever we go,
       That what costs the most is valued highest;
       Just as we clearly see that lavender
       That keeps its scent is thought to be precious;
       It is held dear, priced high, desired
       Overseas, and treated as a treasure,
       While here at home fools use it for garlands.[3]

4   Thus I shall live, languishing in sunny spots,
       If she declares that I must pay for having seen her;
       In my defense, I say I've been her lover
       With faithful heart in song and lay;
       If she goes and leaves me unprotected,
       It is not right that she dally with another;
       For ten years, day and night, from hour to hour
       I have remained her servant until now.

---

[1] A reptile, according to the bestiaries, that was hatched by a serpent and could kill with a look.

[2] A gift too easily given may seem worth less than it is.

[3] Lavender had been used for medical purposes and as perfume since Antiquity.

5   Of little good have been my worth and wooing,
Or the rejoicing of birds or the lily flowers
Or the pleasure God sends us in May
When we see the meadows and woods turn green;
It is better for me, as I see it now,
That grief pierce my heart and kill me,
Or that I become a recluse in a tower
Than suffer such bitter, heavy grief.

6   Lady Fair Comfort, your luminous beauty
And the sweet look that wounds my heart
Make me sing like a dying swan[4]
A joyful song that overcomes my woe.

---

[4] The swan was fabled to sing most beautifully just before it died.

119

Dante

The Divine Comedy
Purgatorio, Canto 26

In *The Divine Comedy* the highest circle of Purgatory, the one nearest to Paradise, is reserved for the lustful. Their punishment is to be purified in fire. Among them are love poets including Guido Guinizelli, whom Dante the pilgrim, making his own journey through the realms of the afterlife, hails as his poetic father and the model for his poetry of love. The shade of Guido Guinizelli points out the shade of another poet who influenced Dante, the troubadour Arnaut Daniel. (For Arnaut's own work see Poems 50 to 53.) When Dante addresses the shade of Arnaut, the troubadour answers him in Occitan. (Other troubadours who appear in *The Divine Comedy*, including Bertran de Born, speak Italian.)

We present the passage first in its original languages and then in translation. For purposes of clarity we have italicized the passage written in Occitan.

> "O frate," disse, "questi ch'io ti cerno
> col dito," e additò un spirto innanzi,
> "fu miglior fabbro del parlar materno.
> Versi d'amore e prose di romanzi
> soverchiò tutti; e lascia dir li stolti
> che quel di Lemosì credon ch'avanzi.
> A voce più ch'al ver drizzan li volti,
> e così ferman sua oppinïone
> prima ch'arte o ragion per lor s'ascolti.
> [...]
> Poi, forse per dar luogo altrui secondo
> che presso avea, disparve per lo foco,
> come per l'acqua il pesce andando al fondo.
> Io mi fei al mostrato innanzi un poco,
> e dissi ch'al suo nome il mio disire
> apparecchiava grazïoso loco.
> El cominciò liberamente a dire:
> *"Tan m'abellis vostre cortes deman,*
> *qu'ieu no me puesc ni voill a vos cobrire.*
> *Ieu sui Arnaut, que plor e vau cantan;*
> *consiros vei la passada folor,*
> *e vei jausen lo joi qu'esper, denan.*
> *Ara vos prec, per aquella valor*
> *que vos guida al som de l'escalina,*
> *sovenha vos a temps de ma dolor!"*
> Poi s'ascose nel foco che li affina.

As the episode begins, Guido speaks to Dante.

> "O brother," [Guido] said, "the shade I'm pointing to
> With my finger"—and he gestured to a spirit up ahead—
> "Was a better craftsman in the mother tongue.
> He surpasssed all others in poems about love

And in stories of romance;[1] let the fools talk on
    Who think the one from the Limousin[2] came in first.
They turn their thoughts to words instead of truth,
    And thus they arrrive at their opinion
    Without listening to art or reason . . ."

Guido then disappears. Dante addresses Arnaut, and Arnaut answers in Occitan (here in italics). He speaks of Italian poetry and begs Dante to pray for him. Dante finishes the canto.

Then, perhaps to give his place to another
    Close behind him, he disappeared into the fire
    Like a fish that sinks to the bottom of a pond.
I moved a little closer to the one he meant
    And told him my desire had prepared me
    To give a gracious welcome to his name.
With willing heart he then began to speak:
    "Your courtly way of asking so pleases me
    That I neither can nor will refuse you.
I am Arnaut, who weeps and walks while singing.[3]
    With grief I look back on my foolish past,[4]
    With joy I watch for hopeful days to come.
Now I implore you, by the goodness
    That guides you to the top of these stairs,
    Think in good time on my terrible pain."[5]
Then he hid within the purifying fire.

---

[1]   We do not have romances written by Arnaut Daniel. Dante means that "Arnaut was superior to all who wrote either in Provençal or French": *Dante Alighieri: The Divine Comedy*, ed. Charles S. Singleton. 3 vols. in 6 (Princeton: Princeton University Press, 1970–5). Singleton, *Purgatorio*, part 2: *Commentary*, p. 642.

[2]   Giraut de Bornelh, born near Limoges, the center of the area called the Limousin.

[3]   The shades in the circle of lust sing a hymn attributed to Ambrose, *Summe Deus clementie / O highest God of clemency*, in which they pray that the lust in their loins be burned away. Cf. Arnaut Daniel: "I'm afraid . . . I'll scatter a set of sins" (Poem 50, stanza 3); "I want you more than the monks of Domme want God" (Poem 50, stanza 5).

[4]   Compare Guiraut Riquier, who finds only grief in the past, present, and future (Poem 104, stanza 1).

[5]   The shade of Arnaut may be thought to be warning Dante by his example, or to be requesting Dante's prayers for his salvation, as Guido did.

120

Arnaut Vidal

Mayres de Dieu, verges pura / Mother of God, Virgin pure

Arnaut Vidal of Castelnaudary (in the department of Aude), west of Carcassonne, completed a romance in verse, *Guilhem de la Barra*, in 1318. His only surviving lyric poem is the following praise of the Virgin, in which he tells us that he was a member of the collegial church of Notre-Dame in Uzeste (department of Gironde), south of Bordeaux. Arnaut's poem won the first prize awarded by the newly founded *Consistori de la Gaia Sciensa* in Toulouse in 1324. The rubric identifies the poem as a *sirventés*. The meaning of the term had evolved from a poem of satire, political or personal, into a poem of moral reflection. By the fourteenth century it had become a poem of religious expression.

A sirventés that was made by Arnaut Vidal of Castelnaudary; and he won the Violet of Gold at Toulouse, that is, the first one that was awarded, and this happened in the year 1324.

1 Mother of God, Virgin pure,
I turn toward you pure in heart
And sure in hope
That I may be sure
    To cleanse my soul
Until it dwells
Where joy dwells.
I pray you, O Virgin, in just measure
Pray God not to measure me,
For in justice it is a somber place
My soul deserves, a somber dwelling;
And I pray not to feel rancor
Or lose the joys of heaven!

2 Virgin with no peer for charm,
For love of us, you so charmed
God that he was born in you
And so was born for us.
    Humbly
I pray you: Be my guide
And bring me guidance
So I may go without fail
Where joy never fails;
For in my heart I believe
That anyone who believes in you
Will not die for eternity,
But live again in joy.

3 Queen of heaven, Queen of honor,
Since all those who honor you,
If they are firm and have no doubts,
Will be honored without doubt
    A thousand times
By you; O bountiful spring
In whom God found bounty

In all good things,
I beseech your protection.
May your Son protect me
And pardon my sins, since he pardons
The faithful who cry out to him,
For he is merciful and kind.

4   Virgin, one joy comforts me
Always, with loving comfort,
Since by the virginal portal
God entered your safe port,
    Delivering us
From unending death;
Our life had died
When Adam turned wrong
By wrongly eating the fruit;
But you give me consolation,
Hope that consoles me
That your goodness will take me
To glorious joy.

5   Flower of paradise, honored
By the honored archangels,
Flower lifted up to heaven,
Flower who lift your beloved,
    Flower of peace,
Flower enshrining joy,
Flower enshrined in purity,
Flower not deflowered
By the fruit, but left in flower
When God was born
Of you, Virgin born without peer,
I pray to you, take mercy on me,
Let me go with those who are saved.[1]

6   Just as I have been made welcome
Where virtue is welcome,
In your honored chamber
In Uzeste, where you honor
Many unfit and make them fit,
I pray you, Virgin: against the foolish thing
For which a man is damned,[2]
Please be our protector.
    Amen.

---

[1]   As in sculptures of the Last Judgment on the tympana over cathedral doors, in which the saved go to salvation on the right hand of God while the damned go to hell on his left.

[2]   The "foolish thing / For which a man is damned" is sin.

121

Anonymous

When I see that the rains are past

This anonymous Hebrew religious song for Passover, or *piyut*, uses erotic imagery to express religious feeling, as in the Song of Songs. Believed to come from Provence, it has been dated broadly in the thirteenth to sixteenth century. Since it employs prosodic techniques developed by Hebrew poets in Spain in the eleventh century, it may have been composed relatively early. Our version is adapted from the translation by Carmi in the *Penguin Book of Hebrew Verse*.

The Dove and the Hart

1   *She*
    When I see that the rains are past
    And the fruit of every tree is in blossom;
    When the time of singing birds has come
    And the vines give forth their fragrance;
    When Time stirs the winds of love,
    Which seek me out, and rise all around me—
    Then my heart makes sweet melody,
    Singing to my hart, my chosen one.
    [He is as wise as] Joseph, master of mysteries,[1]
    And as dear as a son.

2   *He*
    O dove, it is you I desire,
    And deep in my heart
    I fan these passionate flames.
    But out of fear, I have concealed my fiery passion,
    Saying: Hush, I must not mention your name,
    My mouth must remain dumb,
    Lest my rival find you out and wag his head.
    He will tell a pack of lies,
    He will make mouths at me
    To undo our love.

3   *She*
    O hart, my heart roars with pain,
    Like a lion, because you are gone.
    It has surrendered itself to desire
    And flies after you on wings of exile.
    This passion pierces my loins
    And cuts deep into my vitals.
    It strung its bow to shoot at me,
    And my blood splashed onto the wall.
    It splintered all my bones,
    Made its arrows drunk [with my blood].

---

[1]   While Joseph was enslaved in Egypt, Pharoah gave him a name meaning "he who reveals secrets" (Genesis 41:45).

4 *He*
O dove, listen to the groaning of this prisoner,
Bewailing your absence.
My life has worn away:
My days are like grass, like a vanishing flower.
I pray for death to come,
So fierce are the pangs that passion hurls at me.
Today, I hold death most dear,
And I prize the victims of Desire.
I count the dead more precious
Than the fine gold of Ophir.[2]

5 *He*
Fair dove, I shall celebrate the wine of your fame,
This perfume so expertly blended.
And, moved by desire, I shall raise my voice in song,
In swelling songs of praise.
I shall pay homage to your beauty,
And bow down before it.
For your Lord has shed a bright light
Over your face.
He has made your cheek a moon,
A shining star!

[2] A biblical country from which Solomon brought gold, silver, and other treasures (1 Kings 9:26–8, etc.).

122

Anonymous

Non puesc mudar non plainha ma rancura /
I cannot help but tell you of my woe

This anonymous poem, contained in a manuscript from the first half of the fourteenth century, may have been written at that time or earlier. Although it does not employ a word meaning "leprosy," it seems clear that it was written by a poet afflicted with that disease who had withdrawn to a colony on the island of Les Embiez, on the Mediterranean coast near Toulon. The poem may be compared to the French *congés* (leave-takings) of Arras, written in the thirteenth century by Jean Bodel and Baude Fastoul, who were both victims of the same disease.[1]

1   I cannot help but tell you of my woe,
      Lord Austorc,[2] since you are from my home,
      For all my joy and luck have gone.
      . . .[3]
      I have lost the pleasure of society,
      I have lost the man I used to love,[4]
      And I have lost your company.
      Death, will you not take me? Indeed, you do me wrong.

2   Austorc, my friend, it is hard and cruel,
      Strange and sad to go on.
      Now that I live on Les Embiez,
      I wonder why not be buried alive
      Or go too far away
      Ever to be seen again?
      But since there is no escape,
      I must endure this illness till I die.

3   Once I was friendly with ladies
      And clerks and educated men;
      Now, since I find no other way, I have joined
      Another person parted from the world.
      I used to take pleasure with him,
      Dressed in armor winter and summer;
      Now my pleasures are those of a cow,
      And I am caught like a bear on a stake.[5]

4   Once I sang to amuse myself
      And my lady, whom I used to love,
      But now when I sing, I weep for my loss,
      For I have caught this dread disease!
      I have lost flesh, but what do I care?

---

[1] See *Les congés d'Arras: Jean Bodel, Baude Fastoul, Adam de la Halle*, ed. Pierre Ruelle (Bruxelles: Presses Universitaires de Bruxelles, 1965).

[2] This individual is otherwise unknown, although the name is attested.

[3] A line is missing in the single manuscript.

[4] *Luy que sueill amar fort*, literally, "him whom I used to love."

[5] The poet refers to bearbaiting, "The sport of setting dogs to attack a bear chained to a stake" (*Oxford English Dictionary*, 2nd ed.).

To Christ I have given my soul;
The repentance I feel, the woes that I bear,
I'm willing to suffer, along with my fear.[6]

---

[6]   Lepers were considered to be suffering Purgatory in this life; their torment was seen as more holy than that of other people.

Raimon de Cornet

A San Marsel d'Albeges, prop de Salas /
At Saint-Marcel d'Albigeois, near Salles

Raimon de Cornet was the only prolific poet among the successors of the troubadours, known as the "School of Toulouse," who wrote in Occitan during the fourteenth and fifteenth centuries. A priest and friar, Raimon was active around 1324–40. He left more than forty Occitan lyrics, two Latin poems, and other works including verse letters, an *ensenhamen* or didactic treatise, a grammar, and several texts on computation.

In this poem Raimon narrates a comic episode in the first person, drawing humorous effect from his identity as a priest. The tale recalls the fabliau of Guilhem IX (Poem 6); it has contemporary parallels in the fourteenth-century Spanish *Book of Good Love* by Juan Ruiz, archpriest of Hita, and later ones in Chaucer's *Miller's Tale*.

Trifle

1   At Saint-Marcel d'Albigeois, near Salles,[1]
     I took a room with a lordly priest;
     But a gorgeous girl made a fool of me,
     Made me so mad I wished she'd been burned
     And I'd been hanged, as I should have been,
     For tripping into so evil a trap.
     I'll tell the whole tale to make you laugh.

2   I loved that girl with all my heart,
     And she loved me, or pretended to;
     We kissed and kissed with love so true.
     But then one day she saw her chance
     To take a fierce revenge—
     I don't know why, but maybe because
     She saw me kissing someone new.

3   The next day, glowing with a joyful look
     She came to call in our secret place
     In the room I'd found close to hers;
     As soon as I saw her, I sent my clerk
     Away, hoping to celebrate Miss,[2]
     But she cried, "No! Don't embarrass
     Me. In faith, don't touch for another day."[3]

4   My hopes had risen but fell with the news,
     So I kissed her and fondled her breasts
     Until I slept, for the hour was late.
     I'll tell you what that crazy witch did:
     With a pair of shears, she snipped and she snapped,

---

[1]   The Albigeois is the region around Albi in the department of Tarn, north-east of Toulouse.
[2]   *Far l'orde de San Macari*, literally "to do the order of Saint Macari," punning on *ma car*, "my flesh."
[3]   Perhaps a reference to menstruation.

And she shaved my head![4] She left me bald
And sneaked away with my hair in her purse.

5   In the morning I woke and thought I'd take
Her, but she had disappeared;
Not yet aware that my hair was gone,
In grief I slapped my cheek
And thanked God no knife was there
To stab myself and damn my soul.[5]
But now, I'll tell you about my pate.

6   Saint Michael's feast came on the morrow,
And I prepared to say the Mass—
But as soon as I put on my cope
My flock laughed and said the Pope
Should offer a pardon to the lady priest[6]
Who shaved my head, and then began the buzz
Over who she was who had trimmed my fuzz.

7   "It's one thing to walk but better to run,"
I thought to myself when I saw my betrayer
Among them, all laughing and having fun;
To be buried alive was my only prayer.

---

[4]   The girlfriend gave him a tonsure, symbolic of the renunciation of worldly desire associated with the monastic orders.

[5]   A disappointed lover threatens to kill himself, for example, in Marie de France's *Lanval*. Suicide was a mortal sin.

[6]   *Preveyressa*, "concubine of a priest" or "priestess." The term is ironic; priests had been required to be celibate since the twelfth century.

124

Raimon de Cornet

Dels soptils trobadors / From the artful troubadours

Raimon de Cornet composed a versified treatise on Occitan grammar and poetics in 1324, and included within it the following *sirventés*, or poem of moral reflection, urging his reader to read the "artful troubadours." Born about 1300, Raimon by this time had become a priest.

1   From the artful troubadours,
    Founders of worth and fame,
    Those who can should learn
    How they speak of praise,
    True love and other things.
    If you want to understand
    Do not reproach them,
    Casting shame upon their poems;
    If you do not want to listen
    Then do as you please,
    For no one can harm
    Another, I think,
    If everyone ignores him.

2   In the fields I hear shepherds,
    Herdsmen and farmhands
    Singing high and low,
    And I hear in the workshop
    People at their labors
    Debating in their songs,
    And I hear minstrels performing,
    Making good money;
    I can serve them all, if they like,
    And give them all some pleasure;
    For he is no more than a peasant
    Who fails to rejoice when he can
    Without offending God.

3   Poetry serves holy Church,
    Which makes verse for its use,
    Rhyming rows of words;
    Dukes and kings do the same,
    And so does many a lord;
    Poetry must be good!
    But greedy self-servers
    And misers despise
    Joy, laughter, songs,
    Satires and verses;
    When they've done all the harm
    They can, they end in villainy
    Or die in poverty.

4   Those who value
     Poetic art
     Are full of courtly grace,
     So they do not sing
     Or tell a tale
     In an unsuitable place;
     Instead, they perform
     With the greatest skill
     In appropriate space
     Where the people are wise;
     But to peasants, roughly dressed,
     With manners unrefined,
     They speak of coarser things.

5   Some evil people
     Try to censure poems
     And poets all day long,
     Because they think poets
     Lose esteem
     By writing verse;
     But their opinion
     Is foolish, I know,
     For poetry has won me worth
     And never made me lose it—
     It has made me seek
     Renown and brought
     Me the company of lords.

6   Not for any complainer
     Shall I give up making stanzas
     When I see the cheerful season
     And my rosebud of May
     In meadows that seem painted—
     Not until I pass away
     Or can do it no longer.

7   *Sirventés*, go and take your road;
     Tell those lying critics
     I don't think they deserve
     To be burned at the stake,
     But I'd like to see them shoved
     So hard they'd never return
     From the land of Syria!

125

Petrarch

Chiare, fresche et dolci acque / Clear, cool, and gentle waters

Francesco Petrarca was born in Arezzo in 1304 and died in Arquà, near Padua, in 1374. The creator of the wave of Petrarchism that swept over Europe, he is said to be the founder of Renaissance Humanism. He has sometimes been called "the first modern man." His monumental poetic achievement in Italian may be seen as the culmination of the art of the troubadours.[1]

Petrarch spent much of his childhood near Avignon, where his father moved in the service of the pope; later he returned to France, living in Avignon and then in Vaucluse (Provence) for half of his adult life. For a sketch of Vaucluse in Petrarch's hand, see Figure 6.

Petrarch wrote the following poem in Vaucluse, during either his first residence there in 1337–41 or his second residence in the summer of 1343.[2] It may be read as a version of the *pastorela* that incorporates the erotic intensity of the *cansó* together with the spiritual ardor of songs in praise of the Virgin. The perspective of the poet near death recalls Guilhem IX of Aquitaine (Poem 8).

1   Clear, cool, and gentle waters[3]
Where she alone who is Lady to me
Bathed her beautiful limbs;
Noble branch, where it pleased her
(Sighing I remember)
To lean her lovely flank;
Grass and flowers that lay beneath
Her graceful gown, her angel's breast;
Sweet breeze, sacred and serene,
Blowing from where, with her ravishing eyes,
Love opened my heart;
Come gather close, all of you,
To hear my sorrowful, dying words.

2   If it is indeed my destiny
And Heaven above agrees
That Love should close my weeping eyes,
Then let some grace bury my body
Wretched here among you, and my soul
Come back naked here to its home.[4]
Death will seem less cruel
In the fearful pass
If I hold high this hope,
For my tired soul
Could not in more peaceful port
Or more tranquil grave
Flee its weary flesh, these bones.

[1] See Paden, "Petrarch, Poet of Provence."
[2] For the first date see Ernest Hatch Wilkins, *The Making of the "Canzoniere" and Other Petrarchan Studies* (Rome: Edizioni di Storia e Letteratura, 1951), p. 350. For the second, *Francesco Petrarca: Canzoniere*, ed. Marco Santagata, new ed. (Milan: Mondadori, 1996), pp. 580, 590.
[3] The Sorgue river in Vaucluse.
[4] That is, Let me die here, beside the river.

3   Perhaps the time is yet to come
     When the wild and beautiful one
     Will go back to her haunt
     And there where she found me
     On that blessed day
     Turn her eyes, hungry for love,
     Looking for me; and oh, what pity!
     When she sees that I am dust among stones,
     Love will inspire her
     To sigh so sweetly
     She will win mercy for me
     And charm heaven
     When she dries her eyes with her veil.

4   A rain of flowers fell
     (Sweet to remember)
     From the beautiful boughs into her lap,
     And she sat
     Humble in so much glory,
     Soon covered with the cloud of love.
     One flower fell onto her skirt,
     Another on her flaxen braids,
     Burnished gold and pearls
     To look upon that day;
     One dropped to earth, another to water;
     One, tumbling and turning as it fell,
     Seemed to say, "Here reigns Love."

5   How many times did I say,
     Touched by wondrous awe,
     "She must have been born in Paradise!"
     Her heavenly bearing,
     Her face, her words and her dear smile
     Had so filled me with oblivion
     And so driven me
     From her true image
     That I said with a sigh,
     "How did I come here, or when?"
     Thinking I was in heaven, not where I was.
     From that time on, this grass
     Has so pleased me that elsewhere I have no peace.

6   If you, [my song,] had beauty equal to your passion,
     You could boldly leave the woods
     And pass among the people.

258

126

Petrarch

Voi ch'ascoltate in rime sparse il suono / You who hear in scattered rhymes

This sonnet, the first in the *Canzoniere*, was composed late in Petrarch's life. Scholars who have attempted to date it disagree about the details. According to Ernest Hatch Wilkins, the sonnet was written in Provence, during Petrarch's third residence at Vaucluse in 1345–7.[1] Marco Santagata places it a little later, in 1349 or 1350, when the poet was living in Parma.[2] Whenever and wherever Petrarch wrote the poem, he incorporated a tensive relation between the present (his maturity or age) and the past (his youth as a lover). This dynamism between his personal present and personal past suggests a longer view of history, one in which, as he states elsewhere, troubadour songs fed his heart and nourished his poetry.[3]

> You who hear in scattered rhymes
> The sound of sighs that fed my heart
> When I was young and wrong, in part,
> Living in another time—
>
> As you hear how I weep and declaim
> Between vain hope and heart's vain hurt,
> I hope if you know what loving's about
> You will pardon my youth and pity my shame.
>
> Since time long past, now it seems
> I have been the talk of every tongue,
> Which often makes me feel ashamed.
>
> My pride consumes my self-esteem;
> Penance brings wisdom clear and strong—
> To please the world is a fleeting dream.

[1] Ernest Hatch Wilkins, *The Making of the "Canzoniere" and Other Petrarchan Studies* (Rome: Edizioni di Storia e Letteratura, 1951), p. 352.

[2] *Francesco Petrarca: Canzoniere*, ed. Marco Santagata, new ed. (Milan: Mondadori, 1996), pp. 5–6.

[3] *Triumphus Cupidinis* IV, in Petrarch, *Trionfi, rime estravaganti, codice degli abbozzi*, ed. Vinicio Pacca and Laura Paolino (Milano: Mondadori, 1996).

SOURCES FOR THE TEXTS AND LIVES
OF THE TROUBADOURS

The reader who wishes to see the Occitan text of a poem will find here indication of where to look. First we give the edition on which our translation is based, followed by other editions, with preference for editions in English. Hill and Bergin, *Anthology* (2nd edition, 1973), provides the most extensive publication of Occitan texts in an English work, including 181 items with notes and a glossary. (For bibliographical details, see Abbreviations.) For the trobairitz, Bruckner, *Songs*, gives the text with notes and an English translation. We have added reference to major English-language editions of individual troubadours. Major publications in other languages that should be consulted by scholarly readers include Riquer, *Trovadores* (in Spanish), the largest collection of texts yet published in a modern edition, with 371 items, notes, translations, and an introduction on the troubadours and their poetry; Rieger, *Trobairitz* (in German), fundamental for the women troubadours; and Bec, *Chants d'amour* (in French), for the trobairitz and other poems about women.

For the lives of the troubadours we have referred to Riquer, *Trovadores*, and other sources; for the trobairitz, Wilson, *Women in the Middle Ages*.

1 Anonymous, *Tomida femina / A swollen woman*. Paden, "Before the Troubadours," pp. 513–15.

2 Anonymous, *Phebi claro nondum orto iubare / By the bright glow of Phoebus, ready to rise*. Paden, "Before the Troubadours," pp. 517–21.

3 Anonymous, *O Maria, Deu maire / O Mary, mother of God*. Howell D. Chickering and Margaret Louise Switten. *The Medieval Lyric*, 4 vols. (South Hadley, MA: Mount Holyoke College, revised ed. 1988; with compact disks, 2001), vol. 1, pp. 21–9.

4 Anonymous, *Las, qu'i non sun sparvir, astur / Oh, to be a sparrow-hawk, a goshawk!* Paden, "Before the Troubadours," pp. 522–5.

5 Guilhem IX of Aquitaine, *Ab la dolchor del temps novel / With the sweet beauty of the new season*. Paden, *Introduction to Old Occitan*, p. 65. Hill and Bergin, *Anthology*, no. 7; vol. 1, p. 8. Life: Riquer, *Trovadores*, vol. 1, p. 105. See also *The Poetry of William VII, Count of Poitiers, IX Duke of Aquitaine*, ed. Gerald A. Bond (New York: Garland Publishing, 1982).

6 —— *En Alvernhe, part Lemozi / In Auvergne, beyond the Limousin*. Paden, *Introduction to Old Occitan*, p. 74 (based on manuscript C). Hill and Bergin, *Anthology*, no. 4; vol. 1, p. 3 (based on manuscript V, with two more stanzas at the beginning that are now illegible in V and poorly transcribed in N).

7 —— *Farai un vers de dreit nien / I'll make a song about nothing at all*. Hill and Bergin, *Anthology*, no. 3; vol. 1, p. 2.

8 —— *Pos de chantar m'es pres talenz / Since I want to make a song*. Paden, *Introduction to Old Occitan*, p. 83. Hill and Bergin, *Anthology*, no. 8; vol. 1, p. 9.

9 Jaufré Rudel, *Pro ai del chan essenhadors / I have many singing-masters*. Hill and Bergin, *Anthology*, no. 23; vol. 1, p. 32. Life: Riquer, *Trovadores*, vol. 1, p. 148. See also *The Songs of Jaufré Rudel*, ed. Rupert T. Pickens (Toronto: Pontifical Institute of Mediaeval Studies, 1978); *The Poetry of Cercamon and Jaufre Rudel*, ed. Roy Wolf and Roy Rosenstein (New York: Garland Publishing, 1983).

10 —— *Lanqan li jorn son lonc en mai / When days grow long in May.* Paden, *Introduction to Old Occitan*, p. 136. The order of stanzas differs in Hill and Bergin, *Anthology*, no. 24; vol. 1, p. 34.

11 —— *Qan lo rius de la fontana / When the brook that flows from the spring.* Hill and Bergin, *Anthology*, no. 22; vol. 1, p. 31.

12 Marcabru, *Dire vos vuelh ses duptansa / I wish to speak firmly.* Paden, *Introduction to Old Occitan*, p. 125. Hill and Bergin, *Anthology*, no. 12; vol. 1, p. 15. Life: Riquer, *Trovadores*, vol. 1, p. 170. See also *Marcabru: A Critical Edition*, ed. Simon Gaunt, Ruth Harvey, and Linda Paterson (Cambridge, UK: Brewer, 2000).

13 —— *L'autrier jost'una sebissa / The other day I found a shepherdess.* Paden, *Introduction to Old Occitan*, p. 116. Hill and Bergin, *Anthology*, no. 15; vol. 1, p. 20.

14 —— *Pax in nomine Domini! / Peace in the name of the Lord!* Paden, *Introduction to Old Occitan*, p.106. Hill and Bergin, *Anthology*, no. 11; vol. 1, p. 13. *Marcabru: A Critical Edition*, ed. Gaunt, Harvey, and Paterson, no. 35, adopts a different manuscript as base, thus changing certain details in the text, and dates the poem in 1147.

15 —— *A la fontana del vergier / Near the stream in the garden.* Hill and Bergin, *Anthology*, no. 14; vol. 1, p. 18.

16 Cercamon, *Lo plaing comenz iradamen / In grief I begin this lament.* Hill and Bergin, *Anthology*, no. 20; vol. 1, p. 29. Life: Riquer, *Trovadores*, vol. 1, p. 220. See also *The Poetry of Cercamon and Jaufre Rudel*, ed. Roy Wolf and Roy Rosenstein (New York: Garland Publishing, 1983).

17 —— *Puois nostre temps comens'a brunezir / Since our season is turning dark.* *The Poetry of Cercamon and Jaufre Rudel*, ed. Wolf and Rosenstein, no. 8, p. 58.

18 Bernart Martí, *Bel m'es lai latz la fontana / I like it near the fountain.* Riquer, *Trovadores*, no. 30; vol. 1, p. 248. Life: Riquer, *Trovadores*, vol. 1, p. 245.

19 Peire d'Alvernhe, *Rossinhol, el seu repaire / Nightingale, please go see.* Hill and Bergin, *Anthology*, no. 52; vol. 1, p. 78. Life: Riquer, *Trovadores*, vol. 1, p. 311.

20 —— *Ben ha tengut dreg viatge / The bird went straight.* Hill and Bergin, *Anthology*, no. 53; vol. 1, p. 79.

21 Rigaut de Berbezilh, *Atressi con l'orifanz / Like an elephant that falls.* Hill and Bergin, *Anthology*, no. 62; vol. 1, p. 92. Life: Riquer, *Trovadores*, vol. 1, p. 281.

22 Rögnvald, Earl of Orkney, *Víst's, at frá berr flestum / For certain, wise girl.* *Orkneyinga Saga: The History of the Earls of Orkney*, trans. Hermann Pálsson and Paul Edwards (Harmondsworth: Penguin Books, 1978), chapters 86 and 87; for the Old Norse text of the stanza, Roberta Frank, *Old Norse Court Poetry: The Dróttkvætt Stanza* (Ithaca, NY: Cornell University Press, 1978), no. 49; for discussion of this episode, William D. Paden, "Un comte des Orcades à la cour de Narbonne: Ermengarde la jeune et le scalde Rögnvald," *Actes du Huitième Congrès International de l'Association Internationale d'Etudes Occitanes, Bordeaux, 12–17 septembre 2005*, ed. Guy Latry (Bordeaux: Presses Universitaires de Bordeaux, to appear 2007). On Ermengard's life see F. L. Cheyette, *Ermengard of Narbonne and the World of the Troubadours* (Ithaca, NY: Cornell University Press, 2001).

23 Raimbaut d'Aurenga, *Ar resplan la flors enversa / Now shines the flower inverted.* Hill and Bergin, *Anthology*, no. 43; vol. 1, p. 64. Life: Riquer, *Trovadores*, vol. 1, p. 418. See also *The Life and Works of the Troubadour Raimbaut d'Orange*, ed. Walter T. Pattison (Minneapolis: University of Minnesota Press, 1952).

24 —— *Escotatz, mas no say que s'es / Listen! I don't know what it is.* Hill and Bergin, *Anthology*, no. 41; vol. 1, p. 60.

25 Raimbaut d'Aurenga and Giraut de Bornelh, *Era.m platz, Giraut de Bornelh / Now I'd be pleased, Giraut de Bornelh.* Hill and Bergin, *Anthology*, no. 49; vol. 1, p. 72.

26 Anonymous Trobairitz (perhaps Azalais de Porcairagues) and Raimbaut d'Aurenga, *Amics, en gran cossirier / My friend, I'm in anguish.* Riquer, *Trovadores*, no. 77; vol. 1, p. 452. Bruckner, *Songs*, no. 25, p. 88.

27 Azalais de Porcairagues, *Ar em al freg temps vengut / Now we've come to the cold time.* William D. Paden, "The System of Genres in Troubadour Lyric," *Medieval Lyric: Genres in Historical Context*, ed. William D. Paden (Urbana: University of Illinois Press, 2000), pp. 1–67 (p. 44). Riquer, *Trovadores*, no. 79; vol. 1, p. 460. Bruckner, *Songs*, no. 11, p. 34. Life of Azalais de Porcairagues: Riquer, *Trovadores*, vol. 1, p. 459; Wilson, *Women in the Middle Ages*, vol. 1, p. 53.

28 Bernart de Ventadorn, *Chantars no pot gaire valer / Singing can hardly be strong.* Paden, *Introduction to Old Occitan*, p. 143. Hill and Bergin, *Anthology*, no. 28; vol. 1, p. 40. Life: Riquer, *Trovadores*, vol. 1, pp. 342–52. See also *The Songs of Bernart de Ventadorn*, ed. Stephen G. Nichols, Jr., John A. Galm, A. Bartlett Giamatti, Roger J. Porter, Seth L. Wolitz, and Claudette M. Charbonneau (Chapel Hill: University of North Carolina Press, 1962).

29 —— *Can la frej'aura venta / When the cold breeze blows.* Hill and Bergin, *Anthology*, no. 35; vol. 1, p. 50.

30 —— *Qan vei la lauzeta mover / When I see the lark beat his wings.* Paden, *Introduction to Old Occitan*, p. 159. Hill and Bergin, *Anthology*, no. 37; vol. 1, p. 53.

31 —— *Non es meravelha s'eu chan / It is no wonder if I sing.* Hill and Bergin, *Anthology*, no. 27; vol. 1, p. 38.

32 Peire and Bernart de Ventadorn, *Amics Bernartz de Ventadorn / My friend Bernart de Ventadorn.* Paden, *Introduction to Old Occitan*, p. 152. Hill and Bergin, *Anthology*, no. 36; vol. 1, p. 52.

33 Alfonso II of Aragon, *Per mantas guizas m'es datz / In many ways I am given.* Riquer, *Trovadores*, no. 104; vol. 1, p. 568. Life: Riquer, *Trovadores*, vol. 1, p. 566.

34 Guilhem de Berguedà, *Cansoneta leu e plana / I'll make a ditty, short and pretty.* Riquer, *Trovadores*, no. 93; vol. 1, p. 529. Life: Riquer, *Trovadores*, vol. 1, p. 519.

35 —— *Arondeta, de ton chantar m'azir / Swallow, your singing unnerves me.* Riquer, *Trovadores*, no. 97; vol. 1, p. 541. See also Ruth Verity Sharman, *The Cansos and Sirventes of the Troubadour Giraut de Borneil: A Critical Edition* (Cambridge: Cambridge University Press, 1989).

36 —— *Mais volgra chantar a plazer / I'd like to sing more pleasingly. Guillem de Berguedà: edición crítica, traducción, notas y glosario*, ed. Martín de Riquer, 2 vols. (Poblet: Abadía de Santa María, 1971), no. 27; vol. 2, p. 232.

37 Giraut de Bornelh, *Reis glorios, verais lums e clardatz / Glorious King, true light and brilliance.* Hill and Bergin, *Anthology*, no. 47; vol. 1, p. 69. Life: Riquer, *Trovadores*, vol. 1, pp. 463–74.

38 —— *Per solatz reveillar / To arouse rejoicing.* Hill and Bergin, *Anthology*, no. 50; vol. 1, p. 74.

39 Giraut de Bornelh and Alamanda, *S'ie.us quier cosselh, bel' ami' Alamanda / If I ask you for advice, my fair friend Alamanda.* Paden, *Introduction to Old Occitan*, p. 172. Hill and Bergin, *Anthology*, no. 48; vol. 1, p. 70. Bruckner, *Songs*, no. 13, p. 42. Life of Alamanda: Wilson, *Women in the Middle Ages*, vol. 1, p. 15.

40 Bertran de Born, *Un sirventes on motz non faill / A sirventés where no word misses the target. The Poems of the Troubadour Bertran de Born*, ed. William D. Paden, Tilde Sankovitch, and Patricia H. Stäblein (Berkeley: University of California Press, 1986), no. 3, p. 120. Hill and Bergin, *Anthology*, no. 73; vol. 1, p. 106. Life: Riquer, *Trovadores*, vol. 2, p. 679.

41 —— *Mon chan fenis ab dol et ab maltraire / For now and forever, I close my song in grief. The Poems of the Troubadour Bertran de Born*, ed. Paden, Sankovitch, and Stäblein, no. 15, p. 215. Paden, *Introduction to Old Occitan*, p. 199.

42 —— *Ges de far sirventes no.m tartz / Sirventés come to me so fast. The Poems of the Troubadour Bertran de Born*, ed. Paden, Sankovitch, and Stäblein, no. 19, p. 248. Paden, *Introduction to Old Occitan*, p. 209.

43 —— *Belh m'es quan vey camjar lo senhoratge / I like to see power changing hands. The Poems of the Troubadour Bertran de Born*, ed. Paden, Sankovitch, and Stäblein, no. 24, p. 294. Hill and Bergin, *Anthology*, no. 79; vol. 1, p. 113.

44 —— *Miez sirventes vueilh far dels reis amdos / Half a sirventés I'll make about two kings.*
The Poems of the Troubadour Bertran de Born, ed. Paden, Sankovitch, and Stäblein, no. 38,
p. 396. Hill and Bergin, *Anthology,* no. 77; vol. 1, p. 111.

45 La Comtessa de Dia, *A chantar m'er de so qu'eu non volria / I'll sing of him since I am his*
love. Hill and Bergin, *Anthology,* no. 64; vol. 1, p. 95. Bruckner, *Songs,* no. 2, p. 6. Life:
Riquer, *Trovadores,* vol. 2, p. 791; Wilson, *Women in the Middle Ages,* vol. 1, p. 207.

46 —— *Ab joi et ab joven m'apais / From joy and youth I take my fill.* Paden, *Introduction to Old*
Occitan, p. 51. Bruckner, *Songs,* no. 1, p. 2.

47 —— *Estat ai en greu cossirier / I have been in heavy grief.* Paden, *Introduction to Old Occitan,*
p. 58. Hill and Bergin, *Anthology,* no. 65; vol. 1, p. 96. Bruckner, *Songs,* no. 3, p. 10.

48 —— *Fin joi me don'alegransa / True joy gives me gladness.* Bruckner, *Songs,* no. 4, p. 12.

49 Raimon Jordan (?), *No puesc mudar no digua mon vejaire / I cannot keep silent; I must say*
what I think. Riquer, *Trovadores,* no. 106; vol. 1, p. 576. Bruckner, *Songs,* no. 28, p. 98. Life:
Riquer, *Trovadores,* vol. 1, p. 574.

50 Arnaut Daniel, *L'aur'amara / The bitter breeze.* Hill and Bergin, *Anthology,* no. 67; vol. 1,
p. 98. Life: Riquer, *Trovadores,* vol. 2, pp. 605–16. See also *The Poetry of Arnaut Daniel,* ed.
James J. Wilhelm (New York: Garland Publishing, 1981).

51 —— *En cest sonet coind' e leri / In this little song, playful and pretty.* Hill and Bergin,
Anthology, no. 68; vol. 1, p. 101.

52 —— *Lo ferm voler qu'el cor m'intra / The firm intent that into my soul enters.* Hill and Bergin,
Anthology, no. 70; vol. 1, p. 103.

53 —— *Sols sui qui sai lo sobrafan que.m sortz / Alone, I know the supergrief that surges.* Hill
and Bergin, *Anthology,* no. 69; vol. 1, p. 102.

54 Gaucelm Faidit (?), *Us cavaliers si jazia / Once a knight was lying.* Paden, *Introduction*
to Old Occitan, p. 37. Hill and Bergin, *Anthology,* no. 94; vol. 1, p. 131. Attributed to Bertran d'Alamanon by Riquer, *Trovadores,* no. 294; vol. 3, p. 1414. Life of Gaucelm Faidit:
Riquer, *Trovadores,* vol. 2, p. 755.

55 Gaucelm Faidit, *Del gran golfe de mar / From the great gulf of the sea.* Hill and Bergin,
Anthology, no. 92; vol. 1, p. 128.

56 —— *Fortz chausa es que tot lo major dan / It's a terrible thing that the greatest pain.* Hill and
Bergin, *Anthology,* no. 93; vol. 1, p. 130.

57 Maria de Ventadorn and Gui d'Ussel, *Gui d'Ussel, be.m pesa de vos / Gui d'Ussel, I am*
concerned. Bruckner, *Songs,* no. 12, p. 38. Life of Maria de Ventadorn: Wilson, *Women in*
the Middle Ages, vol. 2, pp. 593–5. Life of Gui d'Ussel: Riquer, *Trovadores,* vol. 2, p. 1009.

58 Peire Vidal, *A per pauc de chantar no.m lais / I'm about ready to give up on singing.* Hill and
Bergin, *Anthology,* no. 89; vol. 1, p. 125. Life: Riquer, *Trovadores,* vol. 2, pp. 858–69.

59 —— *Ab l'alen tir vas me l'aire / I breathe in the air.* Paden, *Introduction to Old Occitan,*
p. 25. Hill and Bergin, *Anthology,* no. 87; vol. 1, p. 123.

60 —— *Drogoman senher, s'agues bon destrier / My lord Dragomán, if I had a good steed.* Hill
and Bergin, *Anthology,* no. 86; vol. 1, p. 122.

61 Raimbaut de Vaqueiras, *Eras quan vei verdeyar / Now when I see the meadows turning*
green. Hill and Bergin, *Anthology,* no. 108; vol. 1, p. 153. Life: Riquer, *Trovadores,* vol. 2,
p. 811. See also *The Poems of the Troubadour Raimbaut de Vaqueiras,* ed. Joseph Linskill
(The Hague: Mouton, 1964).

62 —— *Altas undas que venez suz la mar / O high waves bounding across the sea.* Hill and
Bergin, *Anthology,* no. 113; vol. 1, p. 164.

63 —— *Gaita be, gaiteta del chastel / Keep good watch, Guardsman of the castle.* Hill and Bergin, *Anthology,* no. 114; vol. 1, p. 165.

64 —— *Kalenda maya / When May Day comes.* Hill and Bergin, *Anthology,* no. 107; vol. 1,
p. 151. *The Poems of the Troubadour Raimbaut de Vaqueiras,* ed. Linskill, no. 15, p. 185, gives
persuasive reasons to add stanza 5.

65 —— *Ges, si tot ma don' et amors / Although my lady and Love.* Hill and Bergin, *Anthology,*
no. 106; vol. 1, p. 150.

66 The Monk of Montaudon, *L'autrier fuy en paradis / The other day I went to Paradise*. Hill and Bergin, *Anthology*, no. 99; vol. 1, p. 138. Life: Riquer, *Trovadores*, vol. 2, pp. 1024–7.

67 Anonymous, *Dieus sal la terra e.l palai / God save the land and the great hall*. Bec, *Chants d'amour*, no. 13, p. 114. Bruckner, *Songs*, no. 35, p. 136.

68 Anonymous, *Aissi m'ave cum a l'enfant petit / What happened to me recalls a little child*. Riquer, *Trovadores*, no. 368; vol. 3, p. 1705.

69 Alais, Iselda, and Carenza, *Na Carenza al bel cors avinenz / Lovely Lady Carenza*. Attributed to Alaisina Yselda by Bruckner, *Songs*, no. 27, p. 96. Discussion of authorship in Paden, *Voice*, p. 227; Wilson, *Women in the Middle Ages*, vol. 1, p. 13.

70 Raimon de Miraval and Aesmar, *Miraval, tenzon grazida / Miraval, I think we should make*. *Les poésies du troubadour Raimon de Miraval*, ed. L.T. Topsfield (Paris: Nizet, 1971), p. 345. Life of Raimon de Miraval: Riquer, *Trovadores*, vol. 2, p. 983.

71 Isabella and Elias Cairel, *N'Elyas Cairel, de l'amor / Sir Elias Cairel, I want you to tell*. Bruckner, *Songs*, no. 18, p. 60. Life of Isabella: Wilson, *Women in the Middle Ages*, vol. 2, p. 964. Life of Elias Cairel: Riquer, *Trovadores*, vol. 2, p. 1144.

72 Castelloza, *Mout aurez fag lonc estage / You've been away so long*. "The Poems of the *Trobairitz* Na Castelloza," ed. William D. Paden with Julia C. Hayes, Georgina M. Mahoney, Barbara J. O'Neill, Edward J. Samuelson, Jeri L. Snyder, Edwina Spodark, Julie A. Storme, and Scott D. Westrem, *Romance Philology* 35 (1981): 158–82 (p. 177). Bruckner, *Songs*, no. 7, p. 22. Life: Riquer, *Trovadores*, vol. 3, p. 1325; Wilson, *Women in the Middle Ages*, vol. 1, p. 139.

73 —— *Ja de chantar non degr'aver talan / I should never want to sing*. "The Poems of the *Trobairitz* Na Castelloza," ed. Paden *et al.*, p. 173. Riquer, *Trovadores*, no. 268; vol. 3, p. 1328. Bruckner, *Songs*, no. 5, p. 14.

74 —— *Amics, s'ie.us trobes avinen / My friend, if I found you charming*. Paden, *Introduction to Old Occitan*, p. 221. "The Poems of the *Trobairitz* Na Castelloza," ed. Paden *et al.*, p. 170. Bruckner, *Songs*, no. 6, p. 18.

75 Castelloza (?), *Per joi que d'amor m'avegna / Whatever delight I get from love*. "The Poems of the *Trobairitz* Na Castelloza," ed. Paden *et al.*, p. 179. Bruckner, *Songs*, no. 8, p. 26.

76 Bernart Arnaut and Lombarda, *Lombards volg'eu esser per Na Lombarda / I'd like to be a Lombard for the love of Lady Lombarda*. Bruckner, *Songs*, no. 21, p. 70. Life of Lombarda: Wilson, *Women in the Middle Ages*, vol. 2, p. 561.

77 Falquet de Romans (?), *Vers Dieus, el vostre nom e de sancta Maria / True God, in your name and the name of holy Mary*. Attributed to Falquet de Romans by Riquer, *Trovadores*, no. 245; vol. 3, p. 1221, and in *L'oeuvre poétique de Falquet de Romans, troubadour*, ed. Raymond Arveiller and Gérard Gouiran (Aix-en-Provence: CUERMA, 1987), no. 13, pp. 143–54. Attributed to Folquet de Marseilla by Hill and Bergin, *Anthology*, no. 97; vol. 1, p. 135. Life of Falquet de Romans: Riquer, *Trovadores*, vol. 3, p. 1215.

78 Anonymous, *Ab lo cor trist environat d'esmay / With saddened heart wrapped in grief*. Bec, *Chants d'amour*, no. 14, p. 117. Bruckner, *Songs*, no. 31, p. 120. Wilson, *Women in the Middle Ages*, vol. 1, p. 140.

79 Tibors, *Bels dous amics, ben vos puosc en ver dir / My fair sweet friend, I can truly say*. Bruckner, *Songs*, no. 36, p. 138. Life: Wilson, *Women in the Middle Ages*, vol. 2, p. 896.

80 Peire Cardenal, *Ab votz d'angel, lengu'esperta, non blesza / With the voice of an angel, with a tongue that never stammers*. Paden, *Introduction to Old Occitan*, p. 267. Hill and Bergin, *Anthology*, no. 138; vol. 1, p. 197. Life: Riquer, *Trovadores*, vol. 3, p. 1478.

81 —— *Clergue si fan pastor / The clergy pretend to be shepherds*. Hill and Bergin, *Anthology*, no. 140; vol. 1, p. 200.

82 —— *Un sirventes novel voill comensar / I want to begin a novel sirventés*. Paden, *Introduction to Old Occitan*, p. 277. Hill and Bergin, *Anthology*, no. 144; vol. 1, p. 205.

83 —— *Las amairitz, qui encolpar las vol / These amorous ladies, if someone reproves them*. Hill and Bergin, *Anthology*, no. 139; vol. 1, p. 199.

84 —— *Una ciutatz fo, no sai cals / Once was a city, I can't say its name.* Hill and Bergin, *Anthology*, no. 145; vol. 1, p. 207.

85 Domna H. and Rofin, *Rofin, digatz m'ades de quors / Rofin, you're an expert in these matters.* Bruckner, *Songs*, no. 23, p. 78. Life of Domna H.: Wilson, *Women in the Middle Ages*, vol. 1, p. 401.

86 Anonymous, *Vida* of Jaufré Rudel. Paden, *Introduction to Old Occitan*, p. 16. Boutière, *Biographies*, p. 16.

87 Uc de Saint Circ (?), *Vida* of Bernart de Ventadorn. Paden, *Introduction to Old Occitan*, p. 43. Boutière, *Biographies*, p. 20.

88 Anonymous, *Vida* of Guilhem de Cabestanh. Paden, *Introduction to Old Occitan*, p. 31. Boutière, *Biographies*, p. 530.

89 Arnaldo and Alfonso X of Castile, *Senher, adars ie.us venh querer / My lord, I come now to ask.* Bec, *Burlesque*, no. 33, pp. 157–60. Mercedes Brea, *Lírica profana galego-portuguesa: corpus completo das cantigas medievais*, 2 vols. (Santiago de Compostela: Centro de Investigacións Lingüísticas e Literárias Ramón Piñeiro, 1996), no. 21,1; vol. 1, p. 162.

90 Sordel, *Planher vuelh en Blacatz en aquest leugier so / I shall grieve for Sir Blacatz to this sprightly tune.* Hill and Bergin, *Anthology*, no. 154; vol. 1, p. 222. Life: Riquer, *Trovadores*, vol. 3, p. 1455.

91 Anonymous, *Coindeta sui, si cum n'ai greu cossire / I am pretty, but my heart is aching.* Bruckner, *Songs*, no. 33, p. 130.

92 Lanfranc Cigala and Guilhelma de Rosers, *Na Guilielma, maint cavalier arratge / Lady Guillelma, a group of wandering knights.* Bruckner, *Songs*, no. 22, p. 74. Life of Lanfranc Cigala: Riquer, *Trovadores*, vol. 3, pp. 1359–60. Life of Guillelma de Rosers: Wilson, *Women in the Middle Ages*, vol. 1, p. 390.

93 Anonymous, *A l'entrade del tens clar—eya / On the opening day of spring, Tra la.* Hill and Bergin, *Anthology*, no. 177; vol. 1, p. 258.

94 Anonymous, *Lassa, mais m'agra valgut / Unhappy me! It would have been better.* Bec, *Chants d'amour*, no. 34, p. 231.

95 Anonymous, *Quan vei los pratz verdesir / When I see the meadows turning green.* Bec, *Chants d'amour*, no. 26, p. 197.

96 Guilhem de Montanhagol, *Ar ab lo coinde pascor / Now in harmonious spring.* Hill and Bergin, *Anthology*, no. 162; vol. 1, p. 231. Life: Riquer, *Trovadores*, vol. 3, p. 1429.

97 Guiraut Riquier, *Ad un fin aman fon datz / A true lover once awaited.* Hill and Bergin, *Anthology*, no. 173; vol. 1, p. 250. Life: Riquer, *Trovadores*, vol. 3, p. 1609.

98 —— *L'autre jorn m'anava / The other day I was walking.* Paden, *Medieval Pastourelle*, no. 134; vol. 2, p. 342. Hill and Bergin, *Anthology*, no. 172; vol. 1, p. 248.

99 —— *L'autrier trobei la bergeira d'antan, / The other day I saw again a shepherdess I'd seen before.* Paden, *Medieval Pastourelle*, no. 135; vol. 2, p. 346.

100 —— *Gaya pastorelha / A merry shepherdess.* Paden, *Medieval Pastourelle*, no. 136; vol. 2, p. 348.

101 —— *L'autrier trobei la bergeira / The other day I found the shepherdess.* Paden, *Medieval Pastourelle*, no. 137; vol. 2, p. 352.

102 —— *D'Astarac venia / From Astarac I was going.* Paden, *Medieval Pastourelle*, no. 138; vol. 2, p. 356.

103 —— *A Sant Pos de Tomeiras / To Saint-Pons-de-Thomières.* Paden, *Medieval Pastourelle*, no. 139; vol. 2, p. 360. Hill and Bergin, *Anthology*, no. 174; vol. 1, p. 251.

104 —— *Be.m degra de chantar tener / I should really cease to sing.* Paden, *Introduction to Old Occitan*, p. 303.

105 Guiraut Riquier and Bonfilh, *Auzit ay dir, Bofil, que saps trobar / I hear tell, Bonfilh, that you know how to compose.* René Nelli, *Ecrivains anticonformistes du moyen-âge occitan: I. La femme et l'amour* (Paris: Phébus, 1977), p. 294.

106 Cerverí de Girona, *Al fals gelos don Deus mala ventura / God give bad luck to that lying, jealous man.* *Obras completas del trovador Cerverí de Girona*, ed. Martín de Riquer (Barcelona:

Instituto Español de Estudios Mediterráneos, 1947), no. 8, p. 16. Life: Riquer, *Trovadores*, vol. 3, p. 1556.

107 —— *No.l prenatz lo fals marit / Don't marry that liar.* Hill and Bergin, *Anthology*, no. 175; vol. 1, p. 255.

108 Daspols (Guilhem d'Autpol?), *Fortz tristors es e salvaj' a retraire / It is a terrible sadness and cruel to explain.* "The Poems of the Troubadours Guilhem d'Autpol and 'Daspol,'" ed. William D. Paden with Linda H. Armitage, Olivia Holmes, Theodore Kendris, Audrey Lumsden-Kouvel, and Terence O'Connell, *Romance Philology* 46 (1993): 407–52, no. 4, p. 442.

109 Guido Cavalcanti, *Una giovane donna di Tolosa / A young lady from Toulouse.* *The Poetry of Guido Cavalcanti*, ed. Lowry Nelson, Jr. (New York: Garland Publishing, 1986), no. 29, p. 42.

110 —— *Era in penser d'amor quand' i' trovai / I was thinking of love when I came upon.* *The Poetry of Guido Cavalcanti*, ed. Nelson, no. 30, p. 44.

111 David Hakohen, *Bow down, my soul, and kneel before my rock of refuge.* Carmi, *Penguin Book of Hebrew Verse*, pp. 115, 396.

112 Anonymous, *En un vergier sotz fuelha d'albespi / In an orchard under hawthorn blooms.* Hill and Bergin, *Anthology*, no. 178; vol. 1, p. 259. Bruckner, *Songs*, no. 34, p. 134.

113 Anonymous, *Quan lo rossinhols escria / While the nightingale makes his cries.* Riquer, *Trovadores*, no. 365; vol. 3, p. 1697.

114 Isaac Gorni, *From its very first day, the city of Arles was known as a city of strength.* Carmi, *Penguin Book of Hebrew Verse*, pp. 116, 399. Life: Susan Einbinder, "Isaac b. Abraham haGorni: The Myth, the Man, and the Manuscript," International Medieval Congress, Western Michigan University, Kalamazoo, Michigan, May 2005.

115 —— *I shall now lament my desires.* Carmi, *Penguin Book of Hebrew Verse*, pp. 116, 397.

116 Tribolet (?), *Us fotaires qe no fo amoros / A fucker who was not in love.* Francesco Carapezza, *Il canzoniere occitano G (Ambrosiano R 71 sup.)* (Napoli: Liguori, 2004), pp. 254–6. Bec, *Burlesque*, p. 167.

117 Bietris de Romans, *Na Maria, pretz e fina valors / Lady Maria, your virtue and pure worth.* Bruckner, *Songs*, no. 10, p. 32. Life: Wilson, *Women in the Middle Ages*, vol. 1, p. 95.

118 Rostanh Berenguier, *Tot en aisi con es del balasicz / Just as the look of the basilisk.* Meyer, *Derniers troubadours*, p. 90. Life of Rostanh Berenguier: Meyer, *Derniers troubadours*, p. 73; Bec, *Burlesque*, p. 118.

119 Dante, *The Divine Comedy: Purgatorio*, canto 26, lines 115–23, 133–48. *Dante Alighieri: The Divine Comedy*, ed. Charles S. Singleton, 3 vols. in 6 (Princeton: Princeton University Press, 1970–5), *Purgatorio*, part 1, p. 286.

120 Arnaut Vidal, *Mayres de Dieu, verges pura / Mother of God, Virgin pure.* Alfred Jeanroy, *Les joies du gai savoir* (Toulouse: Privat, 1914), no. 1, p. 1. Life: *Dictionnaire des lettres françaises: le Moyen Age*, 2nd ed., revised by Geneviève Hasenohr and Michel Zink (Paris: Fayard, 1992), p. 91.

121 Anonymous, *When I see that the rains are past.* Carmi, *Penguin Book of Hebrew Verse*, pp. 122, 446.

122 Anonymous, *Non puesc mudar non plainha ma rancura / I cannot help but tell you of my woe.* Meyer, *Derniers troubadours*, p. 118.

123 Raimon de Cornet, *A San Marsel d'Albeges, prop de Salas / At Saint-Marcel d'Albigeois, near Salles.* Paden, *Introduction to Old Occitan*, p. 332. Life: Noulet and Chabaneau, *Deux manuscrits*, p. xxix.

124 —— *Dels soptils trobadors / From the artful troubadours.* Noulet and Chabaneau, *Deux manuscrits*, p. 212.

125 Petrarch, *Chiare, fresche et dolci acque / Clear, cool, and gentle waters.* *Petrarch's Lyric Poems*, ed. Durling, no. 126, p. 244.

126 —— *Voi ch'ascoltate in rime sparse il suono / You who hear in scattered rhymes.* *Petrarch's Lyric Poems*, ed. Durling, no. 1, p. 36.

MUSIC

For the following poems, editions of the musical scores may be found in Rosenberg, *Songs of the Troubadours*, or Paden, *Introduction to Old Occitan*. Recorded performances may be found as noted on the compact disks that accompany Rosenberg and Paden.

8 Guilhem IX of Aquitaine, *Pos de chantar m'es pres talenz / Since I want to make a song*. Paden, p. 560.

10 Jaufré Rudel, *Lanqan li jorn son lonc en mai / When days grow long in May*. Rosenberg, p. 56. Paden, p. 567 and CD.

11 —— *Qan lo rius de la fontana / When the brook that flows from the spring*. Rosenberg, p. 57.

12 Marcabru, *Dire vos vuelh ses duptansa / I wish to speak firmly*. Rosenberg, p. 47. Paden, p. 565.

13 —— *L'autrier jost' una sebissa / The other day I found a shepherdess*. Rosenberg, p. 49. Paden, p. 563 and CD.

14 —— *Pax in nomine Domini! / Peace in the name of the Lord!* Rosenberg, p. 51 and CD. Paden, p. 560.

30 Bernart de Ventadorn, *Qan vei la lauzeta mover / When I see the lark beat his wings*. Rosenberg, p. 68. Paden, p. 570 and CD.

31 —— *Non es meravelha s'eu chan / It is no wonder if I sing*. Rosenberg, p. 64 and CD.

32 Peire and Bernart de Ventadorn, *Amics Bernartz de Ventadorn / My friend Bernart de Ventadorn*. Rosenberg, p. 61. Paden, p. 569.

37 Giraut de Bornelh, *Reis glorios, verais lums e clardatz / Glorious King, true light and brilliance*. Rosenberg, p. 83.

39 Giraut de Bornelh and Alamanda, *S'ie.us quier cosselh, bel' ami' Alamanda / If I ask you for advice, my fair friend Alamanda*. Rosenberg, p. 84. Paden, p. 572 and CD.

45 La Comtessa de Dia, *A chantar m'er de so qu'eu non volria / I'll sing of him since I am his love*. Rosenberg, p. 98.

52 Arnaut Daniel, *Lo ferm voler qu'el cor m'intra / The firm intent that into my soul enters*. Rosenberg, p. 93.

56 Gaucelm Faidit, *Fortz chausa es que tot lo major dan / It's a terrible thing that the greatest pain*. Rosenberg, p. 128.

64 Raimbaut de Vaqueiras, *Kalenda maya / When May Day comes*. Rosenberg, p. 156.

82 Peire Cardenal, *Un sirventes novel voill comensar / I want to begin a novel sirventés*. Paden, p. 575.

WORKS CITED

Arnaut Daniel. *The Poetry of Arnaut Daniel*. Ed. James J. Wilhelm. New York: Garland Publishing, 1981.

Bec, Pierre. *Burlesque et obscénité chez les troubadours: pour une approche du contre-texte médiéval*. Paris: Stock, 1984.

——. *Chants d'amour des femmes-troubadours*. Paris: Stock, 1995.

——. *La lyrique française au moyen âge (XIIe–XIIIe siècles)*. 2 vols. Paris: Picard, 1977–8.

——. "Prétroubadouresque ou paratroubadouresque? Un antécédent médiéval d'un motif de chanson folklorique *Si j'étais une hirondelle . . .*" *Cahiers de civilisation médiévale* 47 (2004): 153–62.

Beech, George T. "L'attribution des poèmes du Comte de Poitiers à Guillaume IX d'Aquitaine." *Cahiers de civilisation médiévale* 31 (1988): 3–16.

——. "The Eleanor of Aquitaine Vase, William IX of Aquitaine, and Muslim Spain." *Gesta* 32 (1993): 3–10.

——. "Troubadour Contact with Muslim Spain and Knowledge of Arabic: New Evidence Concerning William IX of Aquitaine." *Romania* 113 (1992–5): 14–42.

Bernart de Ventadorn. *The Songs of Bernart de Ventadorn*. Ed. Stephen G. Nichols, Jr., John A. Galm, A. Bartlett Giamatti, Roger J. Porter, Seth L. Wolitz, and Claudette M. Charbonneau. Chapel Hill: University of North Carolina Press, 1962.

Bertran de Born. *The Poems of the Troubadour Bertran de Born*. Ed. William D. Paden, Tilde Sankovitch, and Patricia H. Stäblein. Berkeley: University of California Press, 1986.

Boutière, J., and A.-H. Schutz, with I.-M. Cluzel. *Biographies des troubadours: textes provençaux des XIIIe et XIVe siècles*. 2nd ed. Paris: Nizet, 1973.

Brea, Mercedes. *Lírica profana galego-portuguesa: corpus completo das cantigas medievais*. 2 vols. Santiago de Compostela: Centro de Investigacións Lingüísticas e Literárias Ramón Piñeiro, 1996.

Brittain, Frederick. *The Penguin Book of Latin Verse*. Baltimore: Penguin, 1962.

Bruckner, Matilda Tomaryn; Laurie Shepard; and Sarah White. *Songs of the Women Troubadours*. New York: Garland Publishing, 1995.

Burckhardt, Jacob. *Die Cultur der Renaissance in Italien: Ein Versuch*. Basel: Schweighauser, 1860. Translated by S. G. C. Middlemore as *The Civilization of the Renaissance in Italy*. London: Penguin, 1990.

Bynum, Caroline Walker. *Jesus as Mother: Studies in the Spirituality of the High Middle Ages*. Berkeley: University of California Press, 1982.

Carmi, T. *The Penguin Book of Hebrew Verse*. New York: Viking Press, 1981.

Castelloza. "The Poems of the *Trobairitz* Na Castelloza." Ed. William D. Paden with Julia C. Hayes, Georgina M. Mahoney, Barbara J. O'Neill, Edward J. Samuelson, Jeri L. Snyder, Edwina Spodark, Julie A. Storme, and Scott D. Westrem. *Romance Philology* 35 (1981): 158–82.

Cercamon. *The Poetry of Cercamon and Jaufre Rudel*. Ed. Roy Wolf and Roy Rosenstein. New York: Garland Publishing, 1983.

Cerverí de Girona. *Obras completas del trovador Cerverí de Girona*. Ed. Martín de Riquer. Barcelona: Instituto Español de Estudios Mediterráneos, 1947.

Cheyette, F. L. *Ermengard of Narbonne and the World of the Troubadours*. Ithaca, NY: Cornell University Press, 2001.

Chickering, Howell D., and Margaret Louise Switten. *The Medieval Lyric*. 4 vols. South

Hadley, MA: Mount Holyoke College. Revised 1988. With compact disks, 2001.

Dante Alighieri. *De Vulgari Eloquentia*. Ed. and trans. Steven Botterill. Cambridge: Cambridge University Press, 1996.

Dante Alighieri: The Divine Comedy. Ed. Charles S. Singleton. 3 vols. in 6. Princeton: Princeton University Press, 1970–5.

Daspols. "The Poems of the Troubadours Guilhem d'Autpol and 'Daspol.'" Ed. William D. Paden with Linda H. Armitage, Olivia Holmes, Theodore Kendris, Audrey Lumsden-Kouvel, and Terence O'Connell. *Romance Philology* 46 (1993): 407–52.

Dictionnaire des lettres françaises: le Moyen Age. 2nd ed., revised by Geneviève Hasenohr and Michel Zink. Paris: Fayard, 1992.

Egan, Margarita, trans. *The Vidas of the Troubadours*. New York: Garland Publishing, 1984.

Einbinder, Susan. "Isaac b. Abraham haGorni: The Myth, the Man, and the Manuscript." International Medieval Congress, Western Michigan University, Kalamazoo, Michigan, May 2005.

Ellenblum, Ronnie. "Were There Borders and Borderlines in the Middle Ages? The Example of the Latin Kingdom of Jerusalem." *Medieval Frontiers: Concepts and Practices*. Ed. David Abulafia and Nora Berend. Aldershot: Ashgate, 2002. Pp. 105–19.

Elliot, Dyan. *Spiritual Marriage: Sexual Abstinence in Medieval Wedlock*. Princeton: Princeton University Press, 1993.

Falquet de Romans. *L'oeuvre poétique de Falquet de Romans, troubadour*. Ed. Raymond Arveiller and Gérard Gouiran. Aix-en-Provence: CUERMA, 1987.

Forster, Leonard. *The Penguin Book of German Verse*. Harmondsworth: Penguin, 1957.

France, John. *Western Warfare in the Age of the Crusades, 1000–1300*. Ithaca, NY: Cornell University Press, 1999.

Frank, István. *Trouvères et Minnesänger: Recueil de textes pour servir à l'étude des rapports entre la poésie lyrique romane et le Minnesang au XIIᵉ siècle*. Saarbrücken: West-Ost-Verlag, 1952.

Frank, Roberta. *Old Norse Court Poetry: The Dróttkvætt Stanza*. Ithaca, NY: Cornell University Press, 1978.

Frederick II Hohenstaufen. *The Art of Falconry, Being the De arte venandi cum avibus*. Trans. Casey A. Wood and F. Marjorie Fyfe. Stanford: Stanford University Press, 1943.

Gaucelm Faidit. *Les poèmes de Gaucelm Faidit, troubadour du XIIᵉ siècle*. Ed. Jean Mouzat. Paris: Nizet, 1965.

Guido Cavalcanti. *The Poetry of Guido Cavalcanti*. Ed. Lowry Nelson, Jr. New York: Garland Publishing, 1986.

Guilhem IX of Aquitaine. *The Poetry of William VII, Count of Poitiers, IX Duke of Aquitaine*. Ed. Gerald A. Bond. New York: Garland Publishing, 1982.

Guilhem de Berguedà. *Guillem de Berguedà: edición crítica, traducción, notas y glosario*. Ed. Martín de Riquer. 2 vols. Poblet: Abadía de Santa María, 1971.

Hale, J. R. *Renaissance Europe: Individual and Society, 1480–1520*. Berkeley: University of California Press, 1977 (original 1971).

Harthan, John. *The Book of Hours*. New York: Crowell, 1977.

Hatto, Arthur T., ed. *Eos: An Enquiry into the Theme of Lovers' Meetings and Partings at Dawn in Poetry*. The Hague: Mouton, 1965.

Hill, R. T., and T. G. Bergin. *Anthology of the Provençal Troubadours*. 2nd ed., with the collaboration of Susan Olson, William D. Paden, Jr., and Nathaniel Smith. 2 vols. New Haven: Yale University Press, 1973.

Jaufré Rudel. *The Poetry of Cercamon and Jaufre Rudel*. Ed. Roy Wolf and Roy Rosenstein. New York: Garland Publishing, 1983.

——. *The Songs of Jaufré Rudel*. Ed. Rupert T. Pickens. Toronto: Pontifical Institute of Mediaeval Studies, 1978.

Jean Bodel *et al. Les congés d'Arras: Jean Bodel, Baude Fastoul, Adam de la Halle*. Ed. Pierre Ruelle. Bruxelles: Presses universitaires de Bruxelles, 1965.

Jeanroy, Alfred. *Les joies du gai savoir*. Toulouse: Privat, 1914.

Karras, Ruth Mazo. *Sexuality in Medieval Europe: Doing Unto Others*. New York: Routledge, 2005.

Klingebiel, Kathryn. "Lost Literature of the Troubadours: A Proposed Catalogue." *Tenso* 13.1 (1997): 1–23.

MacKay, Angus, and David Ditchburn, eds. *Atlas of Medieval Europe*. London: Routledge, 1997.

Marcabru: A Critical Edition. Ed. Simon Gaunt, Ruth Harvey, and Linda Paterson. Cambridge, UK: Brewer, 2000.

Martin, John Jeffries. *Myths of Renaissance Individualism*. New York: Palgrave Macmillan, 2004.

Méjean-Thiolier, Suzanne, and Marie-Françoise Notz-Grob. *Nouvelles courtoises occitanes et françaises*. Paris: Livre de Poche, 1997.

Meyer, Paul. *Les derniers troubadours de la Provence*. Paris, 1871; reprint Geneva: Slatkine, 1973.

Moran i Ocerinjauregui, Josèp. "Inicio y desarrollo del Catalán escrito." *Medioevo Romanzo* 27 (2003): 311–19.

Morris, Colin. *The Discovery of the Individual, 1050–1200*. New York: Harper & Row, 1972.

Nelli, René. *Ecrivains anticonformistes du moyen-âge occitan: I. La femme et l'amour*. Paris: Phébus, 1977.

Nolhac, Pierre de. *Pétrarque et l'humanisme*. Paris: Champion, 1907.

Noulet, J.-B., and Camille Chabaneau. *Deux manuscrits provençaux du XIVe siècle*. Paris: Leclerc, 1888.

Orkneyinga Saga: The History of the Earls of Orkney. Trans. Hermann Pálsson and Paul Edwards. Harmondsworth: Penguin Books, 1978.

Pächt, Otto, C. R. Dodwell, and Francis Wormald. *The St. Albans Psalter (Albani Psalter)*. London: The Warburg Institute, 1960.

Paden, William D. "Before the Troubadours: The Archaic Occitan Texts and the Shape of Literary History." *"De sens rassis": Essays in Honor of Rupert T. Pickens*. Ed. Keith Busby, Bernard Guidot, Logan E. Whalen. Amsterdam: Rodopi, 2005. Pp. 509–28.

——. "Bernart de Ventadour le troubadour devint-il abbé de Tulle?" *Mélanges de langue et de littérature occitanes en hommage à Pierre Bec*. Poitiers: Centre d'études supérieures de civilisation médiévale, 1991. Pp. 401–13.

——. "Christine de Pizan and the Transformation of Late Medieval Lyrical Genres." *Christine de Pizan and Medieval French Lyric*. Ed. Earl Jeffrey Richards. Gainesville: University of Florida Press, 1998. Pp. 27–49.

——. "De l'identité historique de Bertran de Born." *Romania* 101 (1980): 192–224.

——. *An Introduction to Old Occitan*. New York: The Modern Language Association of America, 1998.

——. *The Medieval Pastourelle*. 2 vols. New York: Garland Publishing, 1987.

——. "Petrarch as a Poet of Provence." *Annali d'italianistica* 22 (2004): 19–44.

——. "The System of Genres in Troubadour Lyric." *Medieval Lyric: Genres in Historical Context*. Ed. William D. Paden. Urbana: University of Illinois Press, 2000. Pp. 1–67.

——. "Troubadours and Jews." *Études de langue et de littérature médiévales offertes à Peter T. Ricketts*. Ed. Dominique Billy and Ann Buckley. Turnhout: Brepols, 2005. Pp. 471–84.

——. "Un comte des Orcades à la cour de Narbonne: Ermengarde la jeune et le scalde Rögnvald." *Actes du Huitième Congrès International de l'Association Internationale d'Etudes Occitanes, Bordeaux, 12–17 septembre 2005*. Ed. Guy Latry. Bordeaux: Presses Universitaires de Bordeaux. To appear 2007.

——, ed. *The Voice of the Trobairitz: Perspectives on the Women Troubadours*. Philadelphia: University of Pennsylvania Press, 1989.

Peire Cardenal. *Poésies complètes du troubadour Peire Cardenal (1180–1278)*. Ed. René Lavaud. Toulouse: Privat, 1957.

Peirol, Troubadour of Auvergne. Ed. S. C. Aston. Cambridge, UK: At the University Press, 1953.

Petrarch. *Francesco Petrarca: Canzoniere.* Ed. Marco Santagata. New ed. Milan: Mondadori, 1996.

——. *Petrarch's Lyric Poems.* Ed. Robert M. Durling. Cambridge, MA: Harvard University Press, 1976.

——. *Trionfi, rime estravaganti, codice degli abbozzi.* Ed. Vinicio Pacca and Laura Paolino. Milano: Mondadori, 1996.

Pillet, Alfred, and Henry Carstens. *Bibliographie der Troubadours.* Halle: Niemeyer, 1933.

Poe, Elizabeth Wilson. *From Poetry to Prose in Old Provençal: The Emergence of the* Vidas, *the* Razos, *and the* Razos de trobar. Birmingham, AL: Summa, 1984.

Raimbaut de Vaqueiras. *The Poems of the Troubadour Raimbaut de Vaqueiras.* Ed. Joseph Linskill. The Hague: Mouton, 1964.

Raimbaut d'Aurenga. *The Life and Works of the Troubadour Raimbaut d'Orange.* Ed. Walter T. Pattison. Minneapolis: University of Minnesota Press, 1952.

Raimon de Miraval. *Les poésies du troubadour Raimon de Miraval.* Ed. L. T. Topsfield. Paris: Nizet, 1971.

Ricketts, Peter T. *Concordance de l'occitan médiéval: COM 2, Les troubadours, les textes narratifs en vers.* Turnhout: Brepols, 2005.

——. "L'influence de la culture arabe sur le lexique de l'ancien occitan, en particulier dans le domaine musical." *L'espace lyrique méditerranéen au Moyen Age: nouvelles approches.* Toulouse: Presses Universitaires du Mirail, 2006. Pp. 291–301.

Rieger, Angelica. *Trobairitz: Der Beitrag der Frau in der altokzitanischen höfischen Lyrik. Edition des Gesamtkorpus.* Beihefte zur Zeitschrift für romanische Philologie 233. Tübingen: Niemeyer, 1991.

Riquer, Martín de. *Los trovadores: historia literaria y textos.* 3 vols. Barcelona: Planeta, 1975.

Rosenberg, Samuel N., Margaret Switten, and Gérard Le Vot. *Songs of the Troubadours and Trouvères: An Anthology of Poems and Melodies.* New York: Garland Publishing, 1998.

Saenger, Paul. *Space between Words: The Origins of Silent Reading.* Stanford: Stanford University Press, 1997.

Schippers, Arie. "La poésie de la nature en Al-Andalus." *La France latine,* n.s. 140 (2005): 115–28.

Sharman, Ruth Verity. *The Cansos and Sirventes of the Troubadour Giraut de Borneil: A Critical Edition.* Cambridge: Cambridge University Press, 1989.

Spaggiari, Barbara. "Il tema 'west-östlicher' dell'aura." *Studi medievali,* 3rd ser., 26 (1985): 185–290.

van der Werf, Hendrik. *The Chansons of the Troubadours and Trouvères: A Study of the Melodies and Their Relation to the Poems.* Utrecht: Oosthoek, 1972.

Wilkins, Ernest Hatch. *The Making of the "Canzoniere" and Other Petrarchan Studies.* Rome: Edizioni di Storia e Letteratura, 1951.

Wilson, Katharina M., and Nadia Margolis. *Women in the Middle Ages: An Encyclopedia.* 2 vols. Westport: Greenwood Press, 2004.

SUGGESTIONS FOR FURTHER READING

Occitan Language

Abley, Mark. *Spoken Here: Travels among Threatened Languages*. Boston: Houghton Mifflin, 2003. Chapter 8, "The Lion's Tongue: Provençal," pp. 128–55, on the precarious situation of the Occitan language at the beginning of the twenty-first century.

Grandgent, C. H. *An Outline of the Phonology and Morphology of Old Provençal*. Revised ed. Boston: D. C. Heath & Co., 1905; reprint New York: AMS, 1973. Concise treatment of the medieval language as derived from Latin.

Levy, Emil. *Petit dictionnaire provençal-français*. Heidelberg: Carl Winter Universitätsverlag, 1909. Often reprinted. The standard one-volume dictionary of medieval Occitan.

Paden, William D. *An Introduction to Old Occitan*. New York: The Modern Language Association of America, 1998. Grammar of the medieval language with readings from the troubadours, notes, and glossary; one chapter on modern Occitan.

Troubadours and Medieval Lyric Poetry

Akehurst, F. R. P., and Judith M. Davis, eds. *A Handbook of the Troubadours*. Berkeley: University of California Press, 1995. Contributions on major aspects of the subject, including non-lyric texts; *vidas* and *razos*; the spread of lyric forms to Northern France, Germany, Spain, and Italy; manuscripts; translation, and so on.

Aubrey, Elizabeth. *The Music of the Troubadours*. Bloomington: Indiana University Press, 1996. An able synthesis.

Chambers, Frank M. *An Introduction to Old Provençal Versification*. Philadelphia: American Philosophical Society, 1985. Chronological treatment of verse forms.

Dronke, Peter. *The Medieval Lyric*. 3rd ed. Cambridge, UK: D. S. Brewer, 1996. Broad survey of medieval poetry in Latin and the emerging vernacular languages.

Gaunt, Simon, and Sarah Kay, eds. *The Troubadours: An Introduction*. Cambridge, UK: Cambridge University Press, 1999. Chapters on major facets, including courtly culture; early, middle, and late troubadours; rhetoric; intertextuality; desire; orality; the troubadour manuscripts as books, and so on.

Marks, Claude. *Pilgrims, Heretics, and Lovers: A Medieval Journey*. New York: Macmillan, 1975. Popularizing narrative of the troubadour age, interweaving history and poetry. Illustrated.

Menocal, María Rosa. *Shards of Love: Exile and the Origins of the Lyric*. Durham: Duke University Press, 1994. Argument that associates medieval culture with the lyric and postmodernism, in contrast to the Renaissance, narrative, and the modern. "Let us . . . take pleasure from fragments and the riotous pluralities and often-chaotic poetics that made much of the medieval world so resistant to that smooth narrative" (p. 10).

Menocal, María Rosa. *The Arabic Role in Medieval Literary History: A Forgotten Heritage*. Philadelphia: University of Pennsylvania Press, 1987. Claims that the importance of Arabic culture in medieval Europe has been suppressed for colonialist, nationalistic, or xenophobic reasons.

Merwin, W. S. *The Mays of Ventadorn*. Washington, D.C.: National Geographic, 2002. The castle of Ventadour, troubadour poetry, the history of the region, and the life of the author, woven together by a major poet in his own right.

Paden, William D., ed. *Medieval Lyric: Genres in Historical Context*. Urbana: University of Illinois Press, 2000. Essays that analyze and challenge the traditional idea of genre in medieval lyric poetry.

Wilhelm, James J. *Seven Troubadours: The Creators of Modern Verse*. University Park, Pennsylvania State University Press [1970]. Well-informed introductions to major figures.

History and Culture

Bouchard, Constance Brittain. *Strong of Body, Brave and Noble: Chivalry and Society in Medieval France*. Ithaca: Cornell University Press, 1998. Synthesis of major revisions in historians' views of medieval society since about 1950; focuses on northern France, but includes Occitania.

Camille, Michael. *The Medieval Art of Love: Objects and Subjects of Desire*. New York: Harry N. Abrams, 1998. Study of art objects representing the medieval experience of love. Many images in color.

Le Roy Ladurie, Emmanuel. *Montaillou: The Promised Land of Error*. Translated by Barbara Bray. New York: Vintage, 1978. Probing analysis of the culture of an Occitan village in the fourteenth century, drawing upon records of the inquisitor charged with eliminating the Albigensian heresy.

Paterson, Linda M. *The World of the Troubadours: Medieval Occitan Society, c. 1100–c. 1300*. Cambridge, UK: Cambridge University Press, 1993. Invaluable synthesis of the troubadours' social context, drawn primarily from literary sources.

O'Shea, Stephen. *The Perfect Heresy: The Revolutionary Life and Death of the Medieval Cathars*. New York: Walker, 2000. A "telling of the Cathar drama, intended for nonspecialists," well informed and well written.

Troubadour Poetry in Poetic Translations

Apter, Ronnie. *A Bilingual Edition of the Love Songs of Bernart de Ventadorn in Occitan and English: Sugar and Salt*. Lewiston: Edwin Mellen Press, 1999. The Occitan texts with translations in both free-verse and singable form.

Blackburn, Paul, trans. *Proensa: An Anthology of Troubadour Poetry*. Berkeley: University of California Press, 1978.

Bonner, Anthony, ed. and trans. *Songs of the Troubadours*. New York: Schocken Books, [1972].

Kehew, Robert, ed. *Lark in the Morning: The Verses of the Troubadours*. Chicago: University of Chicago Press, 2005. Fifty-seven translations by Ezra Pound, W. D. Snodgrass, and Robert Kehew, with the Occitan texts.

Lindsay, Jack. *The Troubadours and Their World of the Twelfth and Thirteenth Centuries*. London: F. Muller, 1976. Versions matching the rhyme schemes and verse forms of the originals, set within a narrative account of the troubadours from Guilhem IX to Peire Cardenal; a chapter on Arabic influences.

Pound, Ezra. *Forked Branches: Translations of Medieval Poems*. Ed. Charlotte Ward. Iowa City: Windhover Press, 1985. Pound's translations from the troubadours and other medieval poetry.

INDEX OF FIRST LINES

References in the indexes are to poem by number, except as indicated..

INDEX OF AUTHORS

INDEX OF TERMS

Key: hn = headnote, n = footnote, p. = page

Printed and bound by CPI Group (UK) Ltd, Croydon, CR0 4YY

13/04/2025

14656515-0003